Family Counseling for All Counselors

David M. Kaplan & Associates

ISBN 1–56109-097-2

This publication is funded in part by the U.S. Department of Education, Office of Educational Research and Improvement, Contract No. ED-99-CO-0014. Opinions expressed in this publication do not necessarily reflect the positions of the U.S. Department of Education, OERI, or ERIC/CASS.

Creative Designer
    Kaye Davis

Professional Editing
    Kirsteen Anderson

EPD Monitor
    Lynn Spencer

ERIC
Educational Resources Information Center

Table of Contents

Preface

There are many things to like about this publication! First of all, it targets broad and growing areas of the importance of family counseling in all counseling specialties. In one way or another, almost all areas of counseling must contend with matters relating to families. Marital concerns, student school performance, sibling relationships, reconstituted families, and career choice and planning are just some of the topics where family relationships and interactions are important foci for counseling.

Counselors whose specialty is marriage and family counseling develop a theoretical and research base and acquire countless hours experience on which to drive their interventions. Most counselors and other helping professionals whose specialty is in another area do as well as they can lacking specific theoretical concepts and experience from which to operate. Many counselors have expressed their own uncertainty, even trepidation, when the focus of their counseling moves into family concerns (which it invariably does).

It is for those counselors who are accomplished in a specialty other than marriage and family who desire to improve their ability to manage family issues that this book is primarily intended. Using some of the concepts and interventions developed by family counseling specialists can significantly enhance their overall counseling by avoiding a downturn or misdirection in their counseling when family dynamics become a central issue.

Because of the quality of the writing, it also is likely that even experienced counselors may find useful ideas in this monograph. If nothing else, it will surely improve the quality of the communication among counseling specialties and in the situations where a referral to a family counseling specialist is desirable.

I want to express my appreciation first of all to David Kaplan for his courage and resolve to assume the writing challenge to oversee this publication at a time when, as the President of the American Counseling Association, he was experiencing numerous demands on his time and energy. I also want to thank the authors of the various chapters who excelled in translating their family counseling skills into usable interventions for counselors and other helping specialists who are not family counseling specialists. Great appreciation is due. In my view, they earned A+'s for their contributions to this unique and compelling endeavor.

This monograph is the product of an evolving collaboration between the American Counseling Association Foundation and the ERIC Counseling and Student Services Clearinghouse. The goal of this collaboration is to strengthen the path between knowledge generators and knowledge users so as to make available to practitioners, researchers, and developers new ideas and resources as quickly as possible! We were also pleased to have the International Association of Marriage & Family Counselors as a sponsor of the monograph as well.

This monograph represents one component of this collaboration – a means for an ACA president to more effectively communicate his theme to the membership. Other components will follow, but the intent will remain the same; to enhance and extend the flow of ideas and resources to those who can use and act upon them.

Garry R. Walz, PhD
Co-Director, ERIC Counseling and Student Services Clearinghouse
Professor Emeritus, University of Michigan

Prologue

In talking with professional counselors across the spectrum of specialties and modalities, I have found that many would like to incorporate family counseling into their work. Counselors working in school or college counseling, career development, rehabilitation sites, the addiction field, and other specialties do not want to become marriage and family counselors per se, but they would like to work with families in particular situations where doing so might be helpful to their clients. However, many of these counselors were not exposed to family counseling in their graduate programs and do not know where to start. That is where this book comes in.

Family Counseling for All Counselors provides a framework for involving the family in counseling when you feel this is in your client's best interest. It focuses on the question, "Now that I've got the family in my office, what do I do?" Although reading this book will not make you an expert in couples and family counseling (experience, further reading, workshops, conferences, and supervision will do that), it will get you off to a good start.

So read on for ideas on how to establish good relationships with families, assess family issues, set goals for family progress, select interventions for families, assess the effectiveness of family interventions, and reach closure with families. I also hope you enjoy the chapters on diversity issues and using technology.

About This Book

Family Counseling for All Counselors grew from a suggestion by Dr. Judy Lewis to write a book focusing on my presidential theme for the international Association of Marriage and Family Counselors. While I had written many journal articles, book chapters, and an occasional magazine column response, I had never before taken on the responsibility for an entire book. Knowing that Dr. Lewis had written a number of books and having great faith in her judgement, I solicited her recommendation for a publisher. Without hesitating, she suggested Garry Walz and ERIC/CASS. I am most grateful that she did. Garry expertly guided me through the complex process that turns an idea into three hundred and sixty pages. He respected my approach while making suggestions that improved the manuscript. He also guided me through the process of working with chapter authors. Steven Benish, Gary Bischof, Steven Craig, Dennis Pelsma, Fran Steigerwald, Patricia Stevens, and Richard Watts deserve their own recognition for taking the time and considerable effort to mold their style to an approach that allowed consistency throughout the book.

After the chapters were completed, Dr. Walz catalyzed an innovative publishing collaboration between ERIC/CASS, the American Counseling Association, and the ACA Foundation. I am grateful to Richard Yep, ACA Executive Director, and Dr. Quincy Moore, Chair of the ACA Foundation, for their willingness to make this collaboration happen.

In closing, let me simply state that if you want to write a book, there are no better hands to be in than Garry Walz and ERIC/CASS, Richard Yep and ACA, and Quincy Moore and the ACA Foundation.

David M. Kaplan

Acknowledgments

I would like to acknowledge the assistance of Vickie Kaplan and Melody Cole.

David M. Kaplan

Introduction

A few years ago, when David Kaplan was president of the International Association of Marriage and Family Counselors (IAMFC), he provided a clear and consistent message to members and colleagues. His presidential theme, *"You've Got a Home,"* told counselors that the principles and practices of family counseling were relevant to them, regardless of their work settings or specialties, and that IAMFC could help them develop knowledge and skills in this domain. His message resonated with everyone who heard it. In a very concise way, Kaplan helped us understand that anyone who works with people works with family systems as well.

Now, with this innovative book, David Kaplan broadens and deepens a theme that has always been central to his practice and his scholarship. He reminds us again that counselors—regardless of their settings—frequently find themselves addressing family issues. Every individual's behavior does, after all, take place in context! The challenges that we face as counselors involve being intentional in our work with families and integrating systemic thinking into our day-to-day practices. I believe that, as you read the chapters that follow, you will feel more and more encouraged and optimistic about your ability to meet these challenges.

Kaplan suggests that an effective counseling process includes the steps of establishing a relationship, assessing the problem, setting goals, selecting an intervention, assessing the intervention, and reaching closure. In this book, he and his fellow authors take the reader through each of these steps. At every point along the way, they clarify the connections between individual and family concerns, always emphasizing the fact that basic counseling skills lay the groundwork for all counseling specialties, including work with families. Whether the issue at hand is relationship building, assessment, or application of a particular intervention, the authors describe practical applications that can work with diverse families in varied settings. With these tools in hand, counselors can more effectively meet the needs of the clients and students they see in the context of their own specialty areas.

I feel certain that you will find in this book a wealth of ideas for enhancing your work. You might be so intrigued that you will want to delve more deeply into the family counseling literature. The community of family counselors welcomes you.

Judy Lewis
Past President, American Counseling Association and Professor
Governors State University

Family Counseling
for All Counselors

David M. Kaplan & Associates

Chapter One

Why Incorporate Family Counseling Into Your Practice?

David M. Kaplan

"Counselors recognize that families are usually important in clients' lives and strive to enlist family understanding and involvement as a positive resource, when appropriate."
American Counseling Association Code of Ethics
and Standards of Practice

Family intervention has come full circle. Both couples/marriage and family counseling began as a sideline for physicians, ministers, psychologists, lawyers, social workers, and teachers (Gurman & Kniskern, 1981). Practitioners in each of these professions saw that family problems were intertwined with a variety of legal, religious, medical, psychological, sociological, and educational issues. An interesting example from the mid-1960s comes from pediatricians working with diabetic children at the Children's Hospital of Philadelphia (Baker, Minuchin, Milman, Liebman, & Todd, 1975). When a child was first diagnosed with diabetes, one of the staff pediatricians would sit down with the patient and his or her parents to review nutritional requirements and protocols for taking insulin. Most families were able to follow these instructions and keep the child in good health. Some of the children, however, would show up in the emergency room with episodes of ketoacidosis, a potentially life-threatening condition that occurred when the children stopped taking insulin and their blood sugar skyrocketed. After each emergency, the child's pediatrician would again sit down with the child and parents, point out the seriousness of ketoacidosis, and review the insulin protocols. After this review, most children took their insulin and kept their blood sugar in check. A certain number of diabetic children, however, continued to show up in the emergency room on a regular basis. The pediatricians decided to find out why.

The answer lay in family dynamics. The children with repeated ketoacidosis episodes had one characteristic in common: they came from homes where the mother and father experienced significant conflict. When Mom and Dad would fight, the child would become frightened that the family would break apart, stop taking insulin, and end up in a hospital bed. At that point, the worried parents would act as a team, focusing on the health and well-being of their son or daughter. Unfortunately, the ketoacidosis was only a distraction that did not resolve the ongoing conflicts between Mom and Dad. Therefore, once the child was home and the emergency had passed, the parents resumed fighting. Then the cycle started all over again, as the child would again sabotage his or her insulin regime in order to create an emergency that would distract Mom and Dad from problems that threatened to cause a separation or divorce.

This example illustrates why practitioners from various disciplines discovered that involving relatives of their patients, clients, parishioners, or students could be helpful. The emergence of couples/ marriage counseling and family therapy as related specialties led to the formation of the American Association for Marriage Counselors in 1942. The association changed its name to the American Association of Marriage and Family Counselors in 1970, and became the American Association for Marriage and Family Therapy in 1978. The latter name change marked the point when many practitioners of family work began to view family therapy as a separate discipline distinct from other helping professions. It also marked a time when outcome research came into focus. Enough research has now been generated to allow us to answer questions about the utility of family work.

Is Family Work Supported by Research?

Although not everyone is unanimous that marriage/couples counseling and family therapy (MFT) are efficacious (see Baldwin & Huggins, 1998), research demonstrates that outcomes are as good as or better than in most areas of psychotherapy (Shadish, Ragsdale, Glaser, & Montgomery, 1995). Substantial clinical data support the use of family interventions (Carlson, 1993). Various reviews of the family therapy literature have expressed this theme:

> Judging from our recent meta-analysis . . . it is clear that marital and family therapy works. (Shadish et al., 1995, p. 345)

> The efficacy of marital and family therapy has been well supported by clinical research. (Carlson, 1993, p. 64)

> MFT works . . . [and] is not harmful. MFT does not appear to have negative or destructive effects. In all of the research reviewed, there has not been one replicated and controlled study in which patients and families receiving family or marital therapy had poorer outcomes than patients receiving no therapy. (Pinsof & Wynne, 1995, p. 604)

> Marriage and family therapy outcome research has repeatedly supported the use of family-contextual interventions for a variety of presenting problems, including those traditionally treated with intrapsychic individual psychotherapy. The outcome results indicate success over a broad scope of practice for marriage and

family therapy, especially when used in collaboration with other treatment modalities. (Baldwin & Huggins, 1998, p. 212)

What is the "broad scope of practice" that Baldwin and Huggins refer to in the preceding quotation? It refers to research showing that a treatment plan incorporating family counseling is more effective than one using individual counseling alone in addressing a wide range of problems including childhood disorders, drug and alcohol abuse, mood disorders, eating disorders, psychosis, physical illness, and obesity (Pinsof & Wynne, 1995). Family work has also been found to increase the efficacy of standard treatments for anxiety disorders (Nathan & Gorman, 1998). There is also empirical evidence to support the effectiveness of family involvement in treating psychosomatic illnesses, school problems, dissociative identity disorder, traumatic brain injury and, as would be expected, family conflict and divorce complications (Carlson, 1993).

Childhood and School Problems

A significant body of literature supports the use of family counseling in treating childhood disorders. In a literature review of studies regarding children with a psychiatric diagnosis, Estrada and Pinsof (1995) concluded that children diagnosed with oppositional defiant disorder, conduct disorder, attention deficit disorder, school phobia, and autism improve when family counseling is incorporated into treatment.

Research conducted by Morrison, Olivos, Dominguez, Gomez, and Lena (1993) focused on evaluating a family systems approach in an elementary school setting. Thirty multicultural families (25 Hispanic, 4 Anglo, and 1 African American) participated in a team effort to address such issues as refusal to do homework, fighting, abusive language, truancy, tardiness, stealing, and emotional outbursts. Parents attended from one to seven team meetings. The results indicated that school-related behavior improved in 67% of the students in the program. Impressively, the vast majority of the students who improved (93%) did not relapse over a two-year period.

Campbell and Patterson (1995) reviewed the literature on pediatric obesity and found that family work is a crucial component in helping children maintain long-term weight loss. With regard to studies of childhood physical illness, the same authors concluded that incorporating family counseling into medical treatment had significant physical and psychosocial benefits for children with chronic illnesses such as severe asthma, diabetes, and recurrent abdominal pain. A third area the authors focused on was adolescent eating disorders. Their summary of the literature revealed that adolescents diagnosed with anorexia nervosa gained significantly more weight when family work was a component of their counseling as compared with when they received individual counseling only.

better results w/ + of family

Psychotic Disorders

Adding a family component also appears to increase the effectiveness of therapeutic approaches to psychosis (Goldstein & Miklowitz, 1995). This finding makes intuitive sense, given that "it has been well established that marital and family processes and affective illnesses are significantly and complexly interrelated" (Prince & Jacobson, 1995, p. 395). Falloon, Hole, Mulroy, Norris, and Pembleton (1988) developed a behavioral family therapy model for families of individuals diagnosed with schizophrenia. Their approach incorporates an educational component in which family members learn about the nature of schizophrenia, as well as how to recognize early symptoms of the condition in order to monitor medication compliance. A third family component is training in stress management techniques.

Mood Disorders

Research has indicated that a family therapy component increases the effectiveness of treatments for mood disorders. In their literature review, Baldwin and Huggins (1998) found that incorporating family work into outpatient treatment was particularly useful for clients with depression who felt that their family life contributed to their mood disorder. Frank and Kupfer (1986) reported better compliance with treatment regimes for depression when a family psychoeducational component was included. There are also data to indicate that adding family counseling to a standard regime with patients hospitalized for bipolar disorder increases the efficacy of treatment (Baldwin & Huggins, 1998). This conclusion is in keeping with research indicating that the level of stress in a family is predictive of the prognosis for relapse in bipolar disorder (Nathan & Gorman, 1998). Finally, research by O'Leary and Beach (1990) indicates that behavioral marital therapy is more effective than individual cognitive therapy in treating depression when marital distress is a major contributor to the depression.

Anxiety Disorders

Nathan & Gorman (1998) describe an interesting study from India regarding obsessive-compulsive disorder (OCD; see Mehta, 1990). Thirty unmarried young people who had been diagnosed with OCD unresponsive to pharmacological treatment were selected for the investigation. All participants received 24 sessions of systematic desensitization over a period of 12 weeks. Half were randomly assigned to a group that received family work as part of the treatment. Participants in the family group designated one member of their immediate family to help with homework assignments, supervise relaxation training, aid in response prevention, and provide support when the participant became anxious or depressed. Treatment efficacy was evaluated at the end of the 12-week treatment regime and 6 months later. Results indicated that participants who received systematic desensitization alone reduced their OCD symptoms by 39% at the end of treatment and by 29% after six months. In contrast, the participants who received family assistance in addition to the systematic desensitization showed a 56% reduction in symptoms at the conclusion of treatment and a 61% reduction after six months. It is interesting that the family component resulted in a 17% greater gain immediately post-intervention. But it is even more interesting that the treatment produced an additional 5% reduction in symptoms six months later whereas participants who did not receive the family component reported a 10% *increase* in symptoms over the same time. It appears that the former group may have learned the benefits of including relatives in a treatment regime and continued to utilize family support and assistance on a long-term basis.

Physical Health

There is strong empirical evidence to support a family component in treating physical illnesses and promoting physical health. Campbell and Patterson (1995) reviewed health intervention research in family therapy, family psychoeducation, family information and support programs, and programs that provide direct services to an entire family. They concluded that a family approach (especially one with a psychoeducational component) is more effective than an individual approach in treating physical illnesses such as asthma, diabetes, abdominal pain, chronic illness, and dementia. An interesting study reviewed by Campbell and Patterson found that marriage counseling can reduce hypertension (see Ewart, Taylor, Kraemer, & Agras, 1984). Twenty patients with chronic high blood pressure were provided couples communication skills training. Following training, these patients had less marital hostility, fewer displays of hostility, and significantly lower blood pressure than did the control group.

Campbell and Patterson (1995) also reviewed family-based health studies on nutrition. The largest of these studies (Family Heart Study Group, 1994) was conducted in Britain and included 1,200 couples recruited from more than 25 general practices. Each couple received family counseling focused on developing a healthy lifestyle. At a one-year follow-up, the couples had significantly reduced their smoking, blood pressure, and cholesterol levels, lowering their cardiac risk scores by an average of 16%. The authors predicted that this reduction would likely result in an 8% decrease in heart attacks and cardiac fatalities. Campbell and Patterson conclude from this and other studies that "a number of intervention studies have demonstrated that a family intervention to improve nutrition is effective and results in better outcomes than no intervention" (p. 573).

Dissociative Disorders

I was unable to find any empirical studies on the use of family work with dissociative disorders. However, numerous experts in the field have posited that a family component is a critical part of treating dissociative identity disorder (DID), previously known as multiple personality disorder (Nathan & Gorman, 1998). Nathan and Gorman state that for people with DID, the focus of family work should be the current family rather than the family of origin. This recommendation makes sense because the family of origin is associated with significant and multiple traumas, and contact would promote painful abreactions and encourage splitting. Colin Ross, a leader in the field of dissociation, supports Nathan and Gorman's view in his pioneering book, *Multiple Personality Disorder* (1989). Ross states, "Spouses may participate intensively in therapy or may take an informed and supportive but less involved stance. Either can be satisfactory. The spouse needs to know the diagnosis and to be educated as to etiology, treatment, and prognosis" (p. 294).

Substance-Related Disorders

Various literature reviews have come to the same conclusion about utilizing family work for alcohol and drug abuse: It is an important part of the treatment plan for both adolescents and adults (see Edwards & Steinglass, 1995; Liddle & Dakof, 1995; Pinsof & Wynne, 1995). One of the most beneficial aspects of family involvement is that it greatly increases the likelihood of a substance abuser entering treatment. Edwards and Steinglass (1995) reviewed four studies investigating the role of family members in the assessment of alcoholism. They found in various studies that admission rates ranged from 0% to 31% in the absence of family involvement. Including family members in the assessment of alcoholism led to significantly increased admission rates, ranging from 57% to 86%. Such a significant increase led Edwards and Steinglass to recommend that "the inclusion of nonalcoholic family members in the assessment phase of treatment be built in as a routine component of alcoholism treatment programs" (1995, p. 485).

Liepman, Silvia, and Nirenberg (1989) also found that family involvement increases the likelihood of admission to an alcohol treatment program. They specifically looked at the efficacy of a technique called *intervention*, in which family members gather to confront a substance abuser. The authors trained 24 families of active alcoholics in how to conduct an intervention. Seven of these families subsequently carried out the formal confrontation. Seventeen of the families choose not to follow through on their training. Of the alcoholics in families that did not engage in an intervention, 17% entered treatment. In contrast, 86% of the alcoholics in the families that did engage in the trained confrontation entered treatment. In addition, the alcoholics who were confronted by their families stayed sober without a relapse for an average of 11 months versus less than 3 months for the alcoholics who were not confronted by family members.

There is also evidence that family work is a useful component of substance abuse treatment across cultures. Szapoczink and colleagues (1988) investigated the usefulness of family therapy with Hispanic drug abusers. They found that when treatment was switched from an individual to a family approach, abstinence rates increased dramatically at both six-month and one-year follow-ups. Specifically, the rates increased from 7% to 80%.

Why Is Family Work Effective?

Incorporating family work into counseling is effective because it allows a counselor to address the client's familial and social environment. As Carlson (1993) succinctly puts it, "Regardless of the number of clients being treated, the family counselor conceptualizes problems in terms of the systems perspective" (p. 63).

Systems

Depression provides an illustration. We know that family conflict is correlated with increased risk for depression, impaired recovery, and a greater likelihood for relapse; that depression increases after psychosocial stressors; and that mothers with depression typically have greater amounts of anger and resentment toward their children, as well as greater feelings of inadequacy as a parent, when compared with non-depressed mothers (Prince & Jacobson, 1995). There is also evidence that married individuals who need to be hospitalized for depression have a divorce rate nine times greater than that of the general population (Merikangas, 1984). That is why Prince and Jacobson (1995) conclude, "Close relationships are a potential source of intimacy and social support which can buffer the effects of such events and moderate the relationship between stress and development of symptoms" (p. 379). As such, "failure to address the interpersonal environment of the depressed individual may in part be responsible for the high rates of treatment failure and relapse reported for individual therapies" (p. 383).

Another reason for the efficacy of incorporating family work into counseling is because it adds a psychoeducational component. Family members learn about etiology, prognosis, and treatment options. They are also provided communication training, problem solving skills, and crisis intervention techniques (Pinsof & Wynne, 1995). Psychoeducation works, in part, by increasing the level of support within a family (Prince & Jacobson, 1995). Goldstein and Miklowitz (1995) reviewed six studies comparing a family-based psychoeducational approach with a psychopharmacological/ individual approach to major mental illnesses. They found that the psychoeducational model cut relapse rates by more than 70%.

Finally, incorporating family work into counseling is effective because it allows a counselor to help more than the individual client. Estrada and Pinsof's (1995) literature review indicates that utilizing family counseling with children who have behavioral disorders not only reduces aggression and treatment noncompliance in the children, but also provides direct benefits to parents and relatives. Specifically, a family component in treating conduct disorders and autism allows parents and other family members to learn effective child-management skills that help to minimize symptoms, to gain a knowledge base that increases self-efficacy, and to reframe the problem away from guilt and blame, thus improving family members' outlook. Epstein, Keitner, Bishop, and Miller (1988) examined the effectiveness of adding a family-counseling component to a standard psychotropic antidepressant treatment approach. The researchers attempted to involve as many relatives of the individual with depression as possible and focused on family communication, problem solving skills, emotional involvement, roles, and behavior management. Interestingly, they found that not only did the family counseling component help clients recover more quickly from depressive episodes, but also that overall family functioning improved.

Conclusion

I began this chapter by stating that family work has come full circle. Family involvement started as a useful tool for a variety of professionals, including physicians, ministers, psychologists, lawyers, social workers, and teachers. With the success of family interventions, family therapy emerged. Over the past 25 years, a group of individuals have come to define themselves as marriage and family therapists and their field of practice as a distinct profession. What had been a modality is now typically seen as a specialty. Over the last quarter century, this trend has caused many mental health specialists to shy away from utilizing their clients' families as a resource.

In recent years a broad array of mental health professionals have begun reclaiming family work and incorporating it into their practice. Counselors employed in elementary, middle, and high schools; mental health centers; rehabilitation settings; private practice; college counseling centers; penal institutions; career and employment centers; hospital and wellness clinics; pastoral settings; and a variety of other work sites are finding that, in keeping with the literature reviewed in this chapter, bringing a client's family into the office can be very helpful.

Why does family involvement work? The literature reviewed in this chapter suggests a number of reasons. Family work

- helps to place the presenting problem within the context of the family system
- permits you to see whether family issues are contributing to or exacerbating the presenting problem
- allows you to utilize and build on family strengths
- has the potential to maximize support and minimize guilt and blame
- offers the possibility of helping more than the individual client

The contributors to this book do not advocate family counseling as a replacement for individual, group, or any other type of counseling. Family work supplements and supports the approach that you have developed (or are developing) with your particular clients for their particular issues in your particular setting. We view family work as another modality you may use in counseling when your professional judgment indicates that it is appropriate and will be helpful. This balanced approach is in keeping with the research which indicates that although involving a significant number of family members increases positive outcomes across a spectrum of presenting problems, family work by itself is not effective with many presenting problems (see Baldwin & Huggins, 1998; Carlson, 1993; Pinsof & Wynne, 1995).

References

Baker, L., Minuchin, S., Milman, L., Liebman, R., & Todd, T. (1975). Psychosomatic aspects of juvenile diabetes mellitus: A progress report. *Modern Problems in Pediatrics, 12.*

Baldwin, C., & Huggins, D. (1998). Marital and family therapy research: Outcomes and implications for practice. *The Family Journal: Counseling and Therapy for Couples and Families, 6,* 212–218.

Campbell, T., & Patterson, J. (1995). The effectiveness of family therapy in the treatment of physical illness. *Journal of Marital and Family Therapy, 21,* 545–583.

Carlson, J. (1993). *Marriage and family counseling. Counselor efficacy: Assessing and using counseling outcomes research.* Greensboro, NC: ERIC Counseling and Student Support Services Clearinghouse.

Edwards, M., & Steinglass, P. (1995). Family therapy treatment outcomes for alcoholism. *Journal of Marital and Family Therapy, 21,* 475–510.

Epstein, N. B., Keitner, G. I., Bishop, D. S., & Miller, I. W. (1988). Combined use of pharmacological and family therapy. In J. F. Clarkin, G. L. Haas, & I. D. Glick (Eds.), *Affective disorders and the family: Assessment and treatment* (pp. 153–172). New York: Guilford.

Estrada, A., & Pinsof, W. (1995). The effectiveness of family therapies for selected behavioral disorders of childhood. *Journal of Marital and Family Therapy, 21,* 403–440.

Ewart, C. K., Taylor, C. B., Kraemer, H. C., & Agras, W. S. (1984). Reducing blood pressure reactivity during interpersonal conflict: Effects of marital communication training. *Behavior Therapy, 15,*

473–484.

Falloon, I., Hole, V., Mulroy, L., Norris, L., & Pembleton, T. (1988). Behavioral family therapy. In J. F. Clarkin, G. L. Haas, & I. D. Glick (Eds.), *Affective disorders and the family: Assessment and treatment* (pp. 117–133). New York: Guilford.

Family Heart Study Group. (1994). Randomized controlled trial evaluating cardiovascular screening and intervention in general practice: Principal results of British family heart study. *British Medical Journal, 308,* 313–319.

Frank, E., & Kupfer, D. (1986). Psychotherapeutic approaches to treatment of recurrent unipolar depression: Work in progress. *Psychopharmacology Bulletin, 23,* 558–563.

Goldstein, M., & Miklowitz, D. (1995). The effectiveness of psychoeducational family therapy in the treatment of schizophrenic disorders. *Journal of Marital and Family Therapy, 21,* 301–376.

Gurman, A., & Kniskern, D. (1981). *Handbook of family therapy.* New York: Brunner/Mazel.

Liddle, A., & Dakof, G. (1995). Efficacy of family therapy for drug abuse: Promising but not definitive. *Journal of Marital and Family Therapy, 21*(4), 511–543.

Liepman, M., Silvia, L., & Nirenberg, T. (1989). The use of family behavior loop mapping for substance abuse. *Family Relations, 38,* 282–287.

Mehta, M. (1990). A comparative study of family-based and patient-based behavioral management in obsessive-compulsive disorder. *British Journal of Psychiatry, 157,* 133–135.

Merikangas, K. (1984). Divorce and assortative mating among depressed patients. *American Journal of Psychiatry, 141,* 74–76.

Morrison, J. A., Olivos, K., Dominguez, G., Gomez, D., & Lena, D. (1993). The application of family systems approaches to school behavior problems on a school-level discipline board: An outcome study. *Elementary School Guidance and Counseling, 27,* 258–272.

Nathan, P., & Gorman, J. (1998). *A guide to treatments that work.* New York: Oxford University Press.

O'Leary, K., & Beach, S. (1990). Marital therapy: A viable treatment for depression and marital discord. *American Journal of Psychiatry, 147,* 183–186.

Pinsof, W., & Wynne, L. (1995). The efficacy of marital and family therapy: An empirical overview, conclusions, and recommendations. *Journal of Marital and Family Therapy, 21,* 585–613.

Prince, S., & Jacobson, N. (1995). A review and evaluation of marital and family therapies for affective disorders. *Journal of Marital and Family Therapy, 21,* 377–401.

Ross, C. (1989). *Multiple personality disorder.* New York: John Wiley and Sons.

Shadish, W., Ragsdale, K., Glaser, R., & Montgomery, L. (1995). The efficacy and effectiveness of marital and family therapy: A perspective from meta-analysis. *Journal of Marital and Family Therapy, 21,* 345–358.

Szapoczink, J., Perez-Vidal, A., Brickman, A. L., Foote, F. H., Santisteban, D., Hervis, O., & Kurtines, W. M. (1988). Engaging adolescent drug abusers and their families in treatment: A strategic structural systems approach. *Journal of Consulting and Clinical Psychology, 56,* 552–557.

Chapter Two

Identifying the Need
for Family Involvement

David M. Kaplan

So when do you suggest to clients that they bring family members into your office? When the theoretical framework that best fits a particular counseling situation is family systems theory. Let's review family systems theory and its application.

Family Systems Theory

It has been said that family systems theory is not just another theoretical framework but a major *paradigm shift;* that is, an entirely different way of thinking. Let's look at the International Association of Marriage and Family Counselors (IAMFC) organizational chart as an example. Traditional organizational charts are a linear and hierarchical representation of the chain of command. As Figure 1 shows, the systems theory provides a very different way of viewing the structure of an organization. As stated on the IAMFC web site, "This organizational chart reflects the systemic nature of IAMFC and our belief that all members and leaders play a vital role in our mission of promoting excellence in the practice of couples and family counseling. The collaborative nature of entities is represented by both the bidirectional flow of information and the flow of services from the inner circle out towards the most important circle: the membership" (International Association of Marriage and Family Counselors, n.d.). For practitioners immersed in the world of individual counseling, family systems theory requires this type of paradigm shift and ability to think "outside the box."

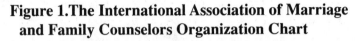

Figure 1.The International Association of Marriage and Family Counselors Organization Chart

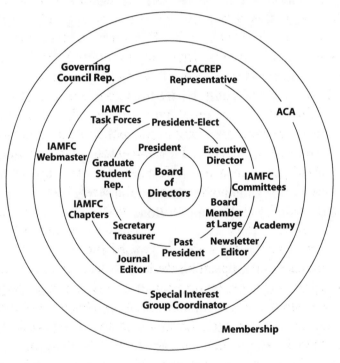

The origination of family systems theory is often credited to Ludwig von Bertalanffy (1968). However, many of us who are at least thirty years old received our first exposure to systems theory in the early 1970s with the advent of Earth Day. At that time the

American public became aware that different parts of our environmental system, or ecosystem, are strongly interrelated. For example, we began to understand that sulfur emissions from industrial smokestacks in the Midwest were acidifying lakes and killing large quantities of fish in New England. We began to see that refrigerant used in automobile air conditioners could be depleting the ozone layer many miles above the earth and increasing the risk of skin cancer.

With this recognition of the interdependence of seemingly unrelated parts of the ecosystem (who would have thought a smokestack in Ohio had anything to do with dead fish in Vermont?), it became natural for many counselors to gravitate toward a theory that viewed families in the same way. Counselors and therapists exposed to systems theory began to see that separate family members are interdependent and have a great effect on each other. They also began to see that, as is true in nature, the family tries to maintain a balance (called *homeostasis*) that allows life to run smoothly. For example, I counseled a family where the father was gone for long stretches of time due to his employment in the Navy. The eldest daughter became her mother's best friend and confidant, helping to meet Mom's need for a partner. This homeostasis worked well for the family: Dad provided Mom with emotional intimacy when he had shore leave, and the daughter provided it when Dad was at sea. Then Dad retired. The family system was not set up for Dad to be around on a constant basis and to be the primary provider of Mom's intimacy. The change in the family caused the daughter to feel neglected and cast aside, upsetting the homeostasis. As a result, she started to express her anger by refusing to do any chores or to spend time with her parents. A previous therapist had diagnosed her with oppositional defiant disorder. I was much less interested in the diagnosis than I was in helping the family to develop a new homeostasis where appropriate parent-child intimacy could replace the mother-daughter adult intimacy that was no longer needed.

It is the family's need for balance that grounds the approach of systems-oriented counseling (Napier & Whitaker, 1978). The remainder of this chapter focuses on four basic components of homeostasis: communication, problem solving, roles, and boundaries.

These components are important to understand because homeostatic problems in any one can contribute significantly to common presenting problems across counseling specialties.

Communication

Virginia Satir is often credited as a pioneer who helped us understand both how important constructive communication is in maintaining balance in a healthy family and also how poor communication leads to myriad presenting problems in counseling (e.g., Satir & Baldwin, 1983). If you are new to systems theory, three aspects of communication that you may wish to focus on with your clients are *frequency of communication, quality of communication,* and *triangulation.*

Frequency of Communication

Stinnett and DeFrain (1985) point out that in order to have good-quality communication, a family must first have a sufficient *quantity* of communication (i.e., if family members don't spend time talking to each other, they are in big trouble). The stereotype of a family that has little communication has been one in which the father is a truck driver, constantly on the road and therefore never around to talk to his wife and children. Especially in this day and age, however, a parent does not need to be physically absent in order for family members to spend little time together. Given both the number of single-parent families where the custodial mother or father has to work and the number of dual-parent households where both partners work, it is easy for many families to spend all their free time catching up on chores and errands. Add to this the number of children who are involved in innumerable extracurricular activities such as work, sports, and theater productions, and you end up with families that just don't have time to see each other (Ventura, 1995). In fact, this problem of lack of shared time has become so common that it has been somewhat facetiously labeled "temporal deficit disorder" (Walchek, 1995).

It is interesting to compare mainstream Anglo culture with that of the Amish. Most of us know that Amish homes do not have modern conveniences such as electricity, television, telephones, or automobiles. What is not as well known is the reason why these tools are rejected. Each Amish district evaluates any new technology on the basis of whether it promotes family and community relationships (Kraybill, 1994). The technology is approved for use only if it enhances these relationships. The Amish feel that without the previously mentioned modern conveniences, neighbors interact more and rely on each other for help. Families spend time interacting together in the evening rather than staring at a television set, working in isolation on a computer, or talking to a non–family member on the telephone. It would seem that temporal deficit disorder is not a systemic problem in the Amish culture.

When a family gets out of balance due to not spending enough time together, one member will often come to a counselor's office (typically for individual therapy) with a presenting problem of loneliness, isolation, and depression. Insufficient contact with other family members may show up in schoolchildren as rebelliousness ("acting out"), oppositional behavior ("looking for attention"), and plummeting grades. As an example, a woman came to my office asking for help in dealing with depression. As we talked, it became clear that she felt isolated and very lonely. She worked as a lounge waitress from six in the evening until two in the morning. As a result, she was on an entirely different schedule than her husband and school-aged children. She described her relationship with her family as "two ships passing in the night." No wonder she was depressed. The family was clearly out of balance in terms of frequency of communication. (Chapter Six discusses interventions to restore balance to communication.)

Quality of Communication

The quality of a family's communication has a significant influence on homeostasis. One aspect of communication quality involves the rules family members use when they talk to each other (Satir &

Baldwin, 1983). Certain rules about how family members express anger and affection to each other can facilitate a healthy balance and good feelings in a family. These rules include no put-downs, no cursing, no yelling and screaming, and limiting fights to 15 minutes or less. Families that break these rules on a regular basis often enter counseling with parents who feel out of control and children who talk back or curse in school and exhibit low self-esteem. With regard to the cursing issue, an interesting question to ask parents of a child who uses foul language in school is: Who else uses those exact words? The parents usually state that it is the child's friends. The child, however, often acknowledges that those words were modeled after one or both parents. Therefore, encouraging the parent or parents who curse at home to discontinue using that vocabulary around the family (sometimes more easily said than done) may greatly help a student discontinue using the same language in school.

Triangulation

Triangulation refers to the recruitment of one family member by another to take sides against a third family member (Bowen, 1971). In counseling situations, we typically see a parent who asks a child, either overtly or covertly, for help against the other parent. A common example occurs in divorce situations, where a parent may tell the children what a terrible person his or her former spouse is, using such statements as, "Your father is a no-good womanizer" or "Your mother ruined the family by running up charge cards." Left unchecked, this triangulation can escalate into a game called "cut down," where each parent attempts to get the children to blame the divorce and marriage problems on the other (Bridgeman & Willis, 1976).

Cut down creates serious problems for the children because it forces them to triangulate and choose sides. Do they believe Mom when she tells them what a rotten husband Dad was and that he never pays the child support on time, or do they believe Dad when he says that Mom is a tramp and sleeps around? I remember one parent attempting to justify venomous comments to the kids about a former spouse by stating that this was simply telling the truth. I tried to explain that this "truth" was forcing the children into the middle of an adult war. Children do not want to have to choose sides in a divorce; they want to be unconditionally loved and accepted by both parents. And, interestingly, cut down usually backfires because the children typically side against the parent who is making the nasty remarks. I have had a number of children of divorce say to me, "If Dad is saying those bad things about Mom when she is not around, he is probably saying bad things about me when I am not around." Being forced into triangulation through the cut down game may lead children to enter individual counseling with such presenting issues as extreme anxiety, dysthymia, depression, nightmares, school problems, and even suicidal ideation (because death is seen as an escape).

One approach to this situation involves working to help the parents understand that the divorce was between the two adults. Encourage the parents to tell the children on a regular basis that their mother will always be their mother, their father will always be their father, and that they do not need to choose between them. You can also help parents practice dealing directly with each other about sources of anger, rather than talking to the children about the former spouse (Bridgeman & Willis, 1976).

Although I have focused on facilitating communication within families, counselors who work as business consultants or career development specialists may want to note that these issues also pertain to maintaining a healthy balance in the work environment. It is important for coworkers to talk to each other on a regular basis, to implement healthy rules about how ideas are communicated, and to refrain from triangulation (for example, where two or more employees team up against another employee or the boss). Disruption of healthy communication in the work site may cause a client to present with similar problems as when family communication is disrupted: anxiety, isolation, depression, and in extreme situations, suicidal ideation.

Problem Solving

If you are perceptive, you will find that many clients feel depressed, anxious, or hopeless because important family problems are never solved and keep coming up over and over. In their 1978 book, *The Family Crucible,* Augustus Napier and Carl Whitaker point out that the same or similar difficulties often can be traced through several generations of a family. For example, parents who come to counseling because their children refuse to take school seriously may have a family history of grandparents and great-grandparents who felt the same way about school. Another family may have a history of alcohol abuse that has caused disruption for many decades. Therefore, teaching effective problem-solving skills may be an essential component in allowing families to resolve conflicts effectively— sometimes for the first time in generations. Three problem-solving skills that promote healthy homeostasis in families are *the art of compromise, developing healthy family rules,* and *becoming comfortable with change.*

The Art of Compromise

One of the reasons families may fall into an unhealthy cycle of recurring fights and arguments over a period of months, years, or generations is that they learn to put themselves in a win-lose situation. In other words, these families fight as if they were embroiled in an adversarial legal system where somebody has to win and somebody has to lose. In such a situation, the combatants dig their heels in, becoming bound and determined to get their way and not to lose face. Given that other family members are equally determined to get their way, the problem is never resolved.

As an example, I counseled one couple who fought over how much money should be saved toward retirement. One partner felt that at least 20% of their gross income should be put in savings, while the other partner wanted to live for today and spend everything. This couple had recurrent fights because they could not agree either to save 20% or to save nothing. Another example involved a family where the parents were having bitter arguments with their teenage children. Mom and Dad were determined that their kids would go to college, a scheme the children wanted no part of. The fighting could not be resolved because the family could not agree which side won.

An approach to these situations is to help the family understand that they have put themselves in a win-lose situation. You can then propose an alternative course of action that sets up a cooperative win-win situation where everyone can feel successful. To do this, you can teach the art of compromise by helping the family brainstorm a new solution different from any of those proposed by individual members. In the previous example, where the couple was fighting over how much money to save toward retirement, I asked each partner to come up with a third possibility that was not exactly what either partner wanted but was close enough for both to feel comfortable. I explained that it was important for the final solution to be different than either of the original positions because that allowed both husband and wife to save face. The partners were willing to enter into negotiations and subsequently agreed to save 10% of their family income.

In the example of the family fighting over the children attending college, we brainstormed alternatives to full-time enrollment and explored options for returning to school in the future if the children decided to pursue full-time employment immediately after high school. The family finally settled on a compromise that all could live with. The children agreed to get full-time jobs upon graduation but to enroll in college and take at least one course as part-time students for the first two semesters after high school.

Developing Healthy Family Rules

Unresolved problems may be passed on from generation to generation because the family has developed unhealthy rules around these problems (Napier & Whitaker, 1978). As an extreme example, fathers who commit sexual abuse may come to a counselor (often because of a court order) stating that incest is a proud tradition in their family and is taught to sons by their fathers. As one father stated to me during a counseling session, "Who better to break in my daughter than her own father?" Obviously, it can be very useful to help the family identify such an unhealthy rule and understand why they need to change it.

Family rules that were developed in previous generations also may cause problems when they have outlived their usefulness but continue to be followed. I remember a particular career counseling client, a high school senior who steadfastly refused to consider any type of postsecondary training after high school. This obviously limited the options we could explore. I became curious as to why he refused to consider postsecondary education, given that he reported liking most of his high school classes. I found the answer while exploring the rules his family had about work. It turned out that he came from a long line of farmers. The family had established a rule long ago that one earns one's keep in society by hard, physical work. This rule was quite useful 100 years ago because many important jobs required manual labor. My role was to help the student understand that in modern times, this rule could have serious negative consequences because our society has become one where service and technical jobs are prevalent.

Getting Used to Change

Haley (1982) points out that a third important reason why families may have trouble solving problems is because change in a family's homeostasis is often difficult and uncomfortable. For example, a single parent may be fully aware that working an evening shift and leaving the children alone when they get home from school is problematic. Changing this situation may be very difficult, however, if no first shift positions are available or the pay differential is needed to support the family. A mistake that counselors often make in this type of situation is to expect too much from individuals and families by demanding that they implement healthy changes at the snap of a finger. (For example, stating to the parent in this situation, "There are no excuses; you have to find a day job.") When a counselor makes too many suggestions and expects changes to occur too quickly, families and individuals will often respond by dropping out of counseling.

Haley proposed that an alternative to expecting families to move immediately from unhealthy to healthy positions is to encourage families to get used to the process of change in ways that feel safe, even if this initially means moving from one unhealthy pattern to another. Using paradoxical techniques may be useful in these situations (Haley, 1982). As an example, a mother and father came for counseling because their adolescent daughter refused to come home at night. The parents were insisting that their daughter be home by 7:30 on school nights, but the child was insisting that she should be able to stay out as late as she wished. After many attempts to introduce effective problem solving (changing from a win-lose to a win-win situation as discussed previously), the family was not better off. Therefore, I decided to follow Haley's suggestion and help the family become comfortable with change by moving from one dysfunctional system to a different dysfunctional system.

I suggested an experiment where the girl had to stay out until at least 2:00 a.m. every night for two weeks. She could not under any circumstance set foot in the house before that time. (Provisions were made to ensure the daughter's physical safety, and the International Association of Marriage and Family Counselors 1993 ethical guidelines for intrusive interventions were followed.) The daughter immediately agreed to this experiment with a gleam in her eye. The parents were hesitant, but they had developed a relationship of trust with me and therefore decided to give it a try. All parties understood that they could phone me at any time in an emergency.

Four days into the experiment, the young woman called and asked for an immediate session. When the family came to my office, the daughter stated that she wanted to stop the exercise because she was bored to death. She had been staying out late at night, and all her friends had gone home around 10:00 or 11:00 p.m. Consequently, the girl reported that she ended up sitting on her doorstep for three hours every night, waiting to be let into the house. I then asked both parents and daughter what they felt would be a reasonable solution to this problem. The response on both sides was a willingness to negotiate a curfew that, although somewhat later than what the parents wanted and earlier than what the daughter wanted, was reasonable.

Roles

So far, I have mentioned three pioneers of family systems theory: Virginia Satir, Carl Whitaker, and Jay Haley. A fourth, Salvador Minuchin, is often credited with helping us understand how important family roles are in maintaining a healthy balance in life.

When we focus on roles in a family, we are not speaking of gender stereotyping; for example, that men take out the garbage and women do the vacuuming. Rather, two important roles that family systems theory focuses on are those of parent and child (Gladding, 1995). To maintain a healthy family balance, it is important for parents to take on the responsibilities that come with that role and to allow children to be children (Minuchin & Fishman, 1981). When families get out of balance, these roles sometimes will be reversed: parents become the children and the children are asked to assume a parental role. One situation where this reversal may happen is when a father dies. The mother and extended family may ask the oldest son to become "the man of the family." This puts a great deal of pressure on the child to assume adult responsibilities before he is ready to do so and may result in depression, low self-esteem, and feelings of inadequacy and failure. These symptoms are a direct result of the son thinking that he must be a terrible person because he can't help his mother by successfully replacing his father as the man of the family.

A second example is seen in an estranged marriage and typically involves a daughter. It is not unusual for mothers in emotionally distant marriages to ask a daughter to take on the role of confidant to help her deal with loneliness. This places the daughter in the difficult position of listening to personal disclosures about such issues as sexuality and personal finances that really should be discussed with another adult.

Many parents in unhappy marriages who "stay together for the sake of the children" wait until the last child has left home to separate and file for divorce. As a result, counselors working in college counseling centers (or with young adults) need to be attuned to role reversals. I remember one freshman who had made a quick decision in the middle of the fall semester to pack up and go home immediately. Her father had just moved out of the family house and into the apartment of a woman 20 years younger than he. Tears flowed freely as the student explained that she loved college and hated to leave, but she needed to take care of her devastated mother. I asked the student if we could conduct a conference call with Mom. During the call, I asked the mother if she wished her daughter to leave college to take care of her (a role reversal). Mom stated emphatically that she did not want that to happen and that she would rely on the support of other family members, friends, and her therapist to get through the trauma. A look of relief came over my client's face as she realized she was off the hook. She waited until the semester ended to go home and successfully completed her college career without interruption.

There are other situations where sons and daughters commonly are asked to become adults, and identifying and helping children return to their proper role in these instances can be an important counseling goal. Children of single parents may be asked to take on greater responsibility than they can handle because of the absence of a second parent in the household. Children of mentally ill adults may be placed in the position of taking care of their parent because of the incapacitating nature of mental illness. In both of these situations, children may be expected to do adult chores such as bill paying and managing the household, or to take care of themselves or younger siblings without supervision for long stretches of time.

A final role-related problem occurs when parents decide to become best friends with their children. There is absolutely nothing wrong with wanting to be close to a son or daughter. However, crossing the line of becoming a child's best friend typically establishes a family homeostasis that disrupts both the parents' and the child's lives. As an example, I have worked with parents who, in an attempt to be buddies, regularly smoke pot with their child. I have also worked with parents who are so wrapped up in their relationship with their child that they become jealous and angry when their son or daughter spends time with peers. Finally, I suspect most of us know more than one parent who became clinically depressed upon their child growing up and leaving home because of the void created by a lack of quality adult relationships. Given the frequency of these types of situations, I and many other family counselors have the philosophy that family roles are best kept in a healthy balance when parents have another adult as their best friend and children have another child as their best friend.

Boundaries

Boundaries refer to the amount of emotional distance we have from the people we care about (Minuchin, 1974). Family systems pioneer Murray Bowen (1978) helped us to understand that maintaining a healthy balance in relationships with the people one cares about is important for one's mental health. Neither being too distant (which we now refer to as *disengagement*) nor being too closely involved (which we now refer to as *enmeshment*) with one's family members is healthy.

Disengagement

As I discussed in the communication section, many families in this day and age simply do not spend enough time with each other. The result may be disengagement that leaves family members feeling isolated and terribly alone. Clients in such a situation may come to counseling not only with feelings of isolation and aloneness, but also with symptoms such as depression, alcohol abuse (an attempt to cover up the pain), or rebellious behavior (an attempt to get attention from other family members). With regard to rebellious behavior, it is often useful to investigate whether children labeled with conduct disorder or oppositional defiant disorder (American Psychiatric Association, 1994) are acting out in an attempt to become less disengaged from their parents.

I will never forget one client who crystallized the concept of disengagement. She was a woman in her early twenties who wanted help with bulimia. I asked her when the problem started, and she told me the following story:

> My parents had been drifting apart for many years. By the
> time I was in high school, they were sleeping in separate
> bedrooms, cooking separate meals, living separate lives
> and virtually never speaking to each other. When I was a
> junior, they decided to separate. My mother assumed that
> my father would stay in the house and took off for
> California. My dad assumed that my mom would stay in
> the house and moved to Michigan. My younger sister and
> I were abandoned until one of my parents called two weeks
> later and realized what had happened. That was when I
> started to purge.

In subsequent family counseling sessions, the father confirmed the
veracity of this story of extreme disengagement.

Enmeshment

Enmeshment describes families who have "too much of a good thing":
they are too close to each other (Minuchin, 1974). Members of an
enmeshed family tend to lose their individual characteristics and
autonomy, causing a feeling of loss of control.

When I was a college counselor, I often liked to walk around
campus on the first day of school to meet and greet the students and
their families and make sure that everything was going smoothly.
Periodically, I ran into parents who said, "*We* are going to college."
These parents identified themselves too closely with their children
and felt as if the whole family were attending the institution. I then
diplomatically responded to the parents that their *child* was going to
college and that *they* were going home.

The loss of individual identity to family identity may result in a
lack of privacy in the home of an enmeshed family. Family members
may not close the bathroom door when using the facilities, and parents
often do not allow their children to shut their bedroom door. One 22-

year-old client who still lived at home and felt the need for more privacy put a lock on her bedroom door. The father promptly took the door off its hinges.

Problems resulting from enmeshment often present themselves in counseling as issues of control, of clients who feel that they are not in charge of their lives. A classic example is anorexia. Women with anorexia often come from enmeshed families and typically are very up front about the fact that their eating disorder is a way to gain some of the control over their lives that they feel their parents have taken away (Minuchin, 1984). It is not unusual to hear clients with anorexia say, "If I can't control my life and my parents insist on telling me everything that I have to do, at least I can control my own weight." Therefore, when enmeshment may be an issue in a family, any intervention that helps individuals regain appropriate control of their lives can be very useful. For example, having the client write an essay entitled, "Who I Am" is one way to begin the process of exploring how the client is unique and has different characteristics, goals, and rules than parents and siblings.

Enmeshment may also put pressure on a family member to be perfect and constantly strive for the highest level of achievement. This pressure occurs because the individuals do not merely represent themselves; they represent the family. Therefore, a failure means that the family has failed. As such, enmeshed families often present themselves to the world as the perfect family whose motto is "Everything is fine." The unwillingness to acknowledge, discuss, or problem-solve conflict may create a great deal of stress (especially in children). Working with enmeshed families can be a real challenge because they often sit in your office telling you how great everything is. A number of times I have had to look parents in the eye and say, "If everything is fine, why did your child attempt suicide?"

The perfectionist aspect of enmeshment may also lead to the family rule that family members' accomplishments are never good enough. Children who make the honor role may be quizzed as to why they didn't make the high honor role. Parents may feel pressured to achieve constantly at work. Young adults who graduate from college may be expected to pursue a graduate degree whether they want to or not. All of these examples reflect the enmeshed family's unwillingness to allow members to pat themselves on the back for a job well done and to take a rest. As would be expected, the result is a great deal of tension, and clients in this situation often state that they want help in reducing anxiety or coping with stress.

Interdependence

Interdependence is the name given to the healthy balance between disengagement and enmeshment. It is the best of both worlds because whereas disengagement is problematic due to the resulting sense of isolation, it has the advantage of allowing each family member to develop an individual identity. Enmeshment, on the other hand, produces problematic issues with control but is advantageous in that it produces intimacy. Interdependence is a healthy balance in which family members are close enough to develop intimacy, yet separate enough to develop individual identities. This balance is achieved in counseling by helping family members learn to allow for individual differences and yet remain close and intimate. Methods for helping clients achieve interdependence will be discussed in chapter 6.

Conclusion

Family systems theory is a paradigm shift that views problems in an entirely different way than do approaches that focus on the individual. Systems theory helps us to recognize that many presenting problems in counseling have nothing to do with intrapsychic issues. Rather, they are a reflection of problems in the homeostasis of a client's family. Helping your client to develop healthy ways of communicating, problem solving, establishing roles, and delineating boundaries may make all the difference in the world when presenting problems are due to, or exacerbated by, imbalances in the family system.

This chapter is a beginning, and I encourage you to explore family systems theory in greater depth. The following annotated list of classic texts can get you started. They are listed in order of suggested reading sequence:

✗ Napier, A., & Whitaker, C. (1978). *The family crucible.* New York: Harper & Row.
The Family Crucible is one of my favorite books. If you don't get excited about systems theory after reading this book, you might want to check your pulse. *The Family Crucible* includes a thorough list of suggested readings.

Satir, V. (1964). *Conjoint family therapy.* Palo Alto, CA: Science & Behavior Books.

Any book by Satir is useful in understanding the importance of communication in families and how to change dysfunctional patterns to functional ones.

Minuchin, S., Rosman, B. L., & Baker, L. (1978).*Psychosomatic families: Anorexia nervosa in context.* Cambridge, MA: Harvard University Press.

You get two for the price of one with this book. It provides insight into the importance of understanding and changing family roles and boundaries, as well as the family dynamics of eating disorders.

Haley, J. (1982). *Problem solving therapy* (2nd ed.). San Francisco: Jossey-Bass.

This excellent and intriguing book addresses how to use paradoxical interventions to produce a lot of change in a short amount of time. This is probably not the first family systems theory book to read, because paradox is one of the riskiest and most powerful interventions available, and the book might intimidate you if you aren't familiar with alternative approaches.

References

American Psychiatric Association. (1994). *Diagnostic and statistical manual of mental disorders* (4th ed.). Washington, D.C.: Author.

Becvar, D. S., & Becvar, R. J. (1993). Family therapy: A systemic integration (2nd ed.). Needham Heights, MA: Allyn & Bacon.

Bertalanffy, L. von. (1968). *General system theory: Foundation, development, applications.* New York: George Braziller.

Bowen, M. (1971). The use of family therapy in clinical practice. In J. Haley (ed.), *Changing families: A family therapy reader* (pp. 159–192). New York: Grune & Stratton.

Bowen, M. (1978). *Family therapy in clinical practice.* New York: Jason Aronson.

Bridgeman, J. A., & Willis, B. A. (1976). *Pain games II* [Film]. (Available: Johnson County Mental Health Center, Olathe, KS).

Gladding, S. (1995). *Family therapy: History, theory, and practice.* Englewood Cliffs, NJ: Prentice Hall.

Haley, J. (1982). *Problem solving therapy* (2nd ed.). San Francisco: Jossey-Bass.

International Association of Marriage and Family Counselors. (1993). Ethical code for the International Association of Marriage and Family Counselors.

The Family Journal: Counseling and Therapy for Couples and Families, 1, 73–77.

International Association of Marriage and Family Counselors. (n.d.) *Organizational chart.* Retrieved January 2, 2001, from the World Wide Web: www.iamfc.org/leadership.htm.

Kraybill, D. B. (1994). War against progress: Coping with social change. In D. B. Kraybill & M. A. Olshan (eds.). *The Amish struggle with modernity* (pp. 35–50). Hanover, NH: University Press of New England.

Minuchin, S. (1974). *Families and family therapy.* Cambridge, MA: Harvard University Press.

Minuchin, S. (1984). *Family kaleidoscope.* Cambridge, MA: Harvard University Press.

Minuchin, S., & Fishman, H. C. (1981). Family therapy techniques. Cambridge, MA: Harvard University Press.

Napier, A., & Whitaker, C. (1978). *The family crucible.* New York: Harper & Row.

Satir, V., & Baldwin, M. (1983). *Satir step by step.* Palo Alto, CA: Science and Behavior Books.

Stinnett, N., & DeFrain, J. (1985). *Secrets of strong families.* Boston: Little, Brown & Co.

Ventura, M. (1995). The age of interruption. *The Family Therapy Networker, 19*(1), 18–31.

Walchek, A. (1995). Breathless [Letter to the editor]. *The Family Therapy Networker, 19*(3), 9.

Note

This chapter is based on the article, "Systems Theory across the Counseling Spectrum" by D. M. Kaplan and K. A. Collins published in *Journal for the Professional Counselor, 10*(2).

Chapter Three

A Process for Working With Families Across Counseling Specialties

David M. Kaplan

Like many of you reading this book, I had little graduate coursework that focused on counseling families. I did take a parent-counseling class, but the professor essentially told us for 15 weeks to focus on reflecting and restating, just as one would do in individual Rogerian counseling. I plodded along in the world of one-on-one counseling, doing my best and helping a reasonable number of clients, but there were always clients I couldn't help. What especially bothered me was that with many of these clients, I didn't have a clue what was causing the presenting problem.

My turning point came in 1985 during postgraduate supervision for licensure. I had to pay the going rate ($65 at the time) for each hour of supervision. After about three weeks and a couple hundred dollars out of my pocket, my supervisor, Dr. Norm Woerle, stated that I knew as much as he did about individual counseling and he felt bad about wasting my money. Norm then asked if he could earn his fee by teaching me how to work with families. When I agreed, he suggested that I read the classic book *The Family Crucible* (1988) by Augustus Napier and Carl Whitaker. I also began to bring my clients' families into counseling and review their progress in supervision. From that point on, my supervisor earned every penny of his fee. I began to help more clients and to recognize that the etiology of many presenting problems in individual counseling were related to the family dimensions discussed in chapter 2.

I therefore saw the need to develop an approach to counseling that would allow me to incorporate family work into my individual counseling. Two driving forces have shaped this approach. The first is my 14 years in rural private practice. I never knew who would make an appointment or what the presenting problem would be. My clients ran the gamut from adolescent goths flunking out of school to young adults with eating disorders to displaced farmers facing a midlife career change to senior citizens with drinking problems. The second significant factor in developing my counseling approach has been the pragmatic issue that I am not the smartest person in the world. I simply do not have enough space in my brain to have different processes for individual counseling, couples counseling, family counseling, career counseling, substance-abuse counseling, or each type of presenting problem that might appear in my office on any given day. In order to accommodate both of these driving forces, I found it useful to have one counseling process that would accommodate any modality I might be using.

The process I have come to utilize draws upon a broad-based behavior therapy/social learning theory approach. This framework can be summed up in the following paraphrase of what has become known as Paul's Question: How can I take a scientific approach in deciding what works best with this particular client, with this particular problem, with this particular counselor, in this particular setting (Paul, 1967)?

Six-Stage Counseling Process

The following six-stage counseling process allows me to focus on implementing Paul's Question:

1. Establish a relationship ⟶ constant
2. Assess the problem
3. Set goals
4. Select an intervention
5. Assess the intervention
6. Reach closure

Note that this six-stage process is not linear. In other words, these are not discrete steps to be started and stopped at given points; rather, they represent your focus at a particular time. Let me give you an example. I was working with a woman in her mid-thirties who was going through a divorce. Her presenting problem was low self-esteem and feelings of worthlessness precipitated by the separation from her husband. Our goal became to increase her feelings of self-efficacy and empowerment. The first five sessions were productive, and my client was well on her way toward increasing her feelings of competency and self-worth. Then I made a mistake. As part of her empowerment, she had opened her first bank account and proudly showed me the design on the checks she had selected. This particular design looked as if a child had scrawled on the check in crayons. Instead of acknowledging the importance of what she had done, I made a flippant remark about how primitive the design looked. I never saw or talked to her again. (She did not return any of my phone calls.) By ignoring the constant need to work on maintaining a relationship, I lost the opportunity to help a client.

The six-step process serves two very useful purposes. First, it allows you the flexibility to go back and forth between individual and family counseling. Thus, you can work with a client individually and bring family members in and out of counseling as appropriate. Second, this process allows you to utilize and build on skills learned in graduate school. Let's review some of these skills.

Establishing a Relationship

Virtually every current approach to counseling says that the very first thing you want to do with a client is to establish a relationship, and there is good reason for that. In a seminal review of outcome research, Lambert (1992) found that 30% of a client's progress in counseling is due to the counselor-client relationship. This finding is so important that I want to repeat it again: *30% of a client's progress in counseling is due to the counselor-client relationship.*

One of the most important things you can do to establish a positive therapeutic environment before a client ever steps into your office is to have an impeccable reputation as an ethical counselor. Scissions (1993) points out that clients do not automatically trust a counselor; trust must be earned. Consistently acting in an ethical manner earns you a reputation as a safe and trustworthy counselor. To paraphrase Will Rogers, I have never met an ethical code I didn't like. The principles of the American Counseling Association and its divisions (i.e., International Association of Marriage and Family Counselors, American Mental Health Association, American School Counselor Association, National Career Development Association, American Rehabilitation Counseling Association) are substantial and well thought-out. The problem is that over the years so much has been added that it is hard to remember everything contained in these increasingly thick documents. Therefore, for my daily routine, I prefer to utilize a distilled and updated version of the framework provided in the ethical code of the American Psychological Association developed in the early 1980s. This framework is easy to remember because it is parsimonious yet thorough. It guides you to act ethically by focusing on eight factors: responsibility, competence, moral and legal issues, public statements, confidentiality, client welfare, professional relationships, and use of assessment instruments.

Responsibility

You have a responsibility to act in a way that causes no harm to any client. One of the most important aspects of ethical responsibility is informed consent. Clients have the right to know what they are getting into from the very beginning of their counseling experience.

Competence

It is now estimated that 80% of everything we know in counseling becomes obsolete every five years (Kaplan, 1995). If you decide that you paid your dues in graduate school and don't need to learn anything more, your skills become out of date frighteningly fast. Would you go to a physician who is too busy to read any medical journals? Probably not. So it is incumbent upon counselors to stay up to date by maintaining our memberships in professional organizations such as the American Counseling Association and its divisions; attending workshops and conferences; reading books; subscribing to journals and newsletters; and, in general, getting as much information on cutting-edge approaches and techniques as possible. It is not unreasonable to earmark $500 to $1,000 per year for professional development activities; this is the price we pay for having the word *professional* in our titles.

Moral and Legal Issues

You have the responsibility to adhere to the morals and rules of your community and institution and to refrain from suggesting that a client engage in any illegal activity. Doing otherwise traps clients between you and their family, their school, their workplace, or the legal system. As an example, let us say that a rehabilitation counselor sees a family that needs help in adjusting to the father's recent blindness caused by glaucoma. A major problem is that Dad is in great pain because of the abnormally high intraocular pressure that occurs with this disease. The counselor has read some research indicating that smoking marijuana may relieve this pressure. It is unethical to suggest that the family go out on the street and find some pot for Dad to smoke because marijuana use is illegal and your intervention may cause harm by leading to an arrest.

A second example revolves around a high school with a written policy stating that all teachers, staff, and administrators must report any student found smoking in school to the principal. If a school counselor finds a student in the bathroom smoking, that counselor cannot make the decision to look the other way because the student is currently in counseling. The policy must be followed and the incident reported to the principal.

Public Statements

Counselors have a responsibility to refrain from conducting impromptu counseling in public when asked for advice. The rationale for this restriction is that in a few minutes on the radio or during a brief conversation at a party or other gathering, you cannot make a thorough assessment or follow up to evaluate the results of your statements and so your advice may cause harm.

Confidentiality

Confidentiality is often referred to as the "cornerstone ethic," for without it we have nothing. Why would anyone tell us anything remotely personal about himself or herself if we might share this information with others? The American Counseling Association ethical standards highlight the need to keep what clients tell us confidential unless there is clear and imminent danger to an individual or when disclosure is required by law. The words *clear* and *imminent* are coupled with *danger* for a deliberate reason; breaking confidentiality, even when appropriate, may cause irreparable damage to your counseling relationships. My first six years of counseling practice were conducted in college counseling centers, and I sometimes think back to an incident that occurred one October night. I was awakened from a sound sleep after midnight by a telephone call from a client. The client stated, "My roommate has been having a contest with his friends to see how long he can stay high on LSD. He has been tripping for about 36 hours and just freaked out, grabbed a knife, and ran into the woods screaming that he is going to kill himself." Then the student said, " I don't want you to tell anyone about this." Sometimes the decision about whether to break confidentiality is an extremely difficult one, but this was not one of those times. A life clearly needed to be protected, and I immediately called the police and the vice-president of student affairs. A search was conducted, but the police did not find the student until he wandered back home later that day.

Then a funny thing happened. Our counseling center had always had a waiting list for services, with students complaining about the length of time they had to wait for an initial appointment. Suddenly, however, we began to have free slots. Lots of them. Clients were canceling appointments and few students were filling those times. So we did some investigation. Our sources told us the client who had telephoned became very angry that I had called the police because he feared that his stash of drugs would be discovered. Subsequently, my client had started telling every student he knew that the counseling center could not be trusted because the counselors break confidentiality. We had to do a lot of damage control in order to restore our reputation. My point is that if this much damage to the counseling relationship can happen when the responsibility to break confidentiality is so clear-cut, imagine what could happen if we betray a confidence in a more ambiguous situation.

Welfare of the Consumer

We must put our clients' needs before our own. The most frequently raised client welfare issue is the need to refrain from dual relationships. We should avoid being a business partner, teacher, or consultant with any client. Why? There is a risk that the client may become upset at you due to some circumstance in the other relationship (e.g., the person doesn't like the grade you gave, the business decision you made, or the consulting report you submitted). It is unfair to risk souring a counseling relationship because of bad feelings arising from a second relationship with the client.

Due to the potential for extreme damage, a dual relationship that deserves special mention is that of lover. Having sexual relations with a client is a form of selfishness that rivals few others. Clients who have sex with their counselor typically later report that they feel emotionally raped and physically violated. In addition, insurance companies will not cover either lawyers' bills or settlements (which may approach $1,000,000 with damages for pain and suffering) for counselors convicted of sexual contact with a client. The fact that this is typically the only exclusion in a malpractice policy indicates the severity of the damage that counselor-client sex may cause to the client.

During my five-year tenure as chair of the International Association of Marriage and Family Counselors (IAMFC) ethics committee, I was often asked how long a counselor should wait after closure to engage in a romantic relationship with a former client. The IAMFC code (IAMFC, 1993) states that once an individual has become a client, a counselor should never have a romantic relationship with him or her. The rationale for this provision is that in family counseling, clients often may wish to return to the counselor's office (sometimes years later) to address a variety of individual, couples, and family issues. By engaging in a personal relationship, the counselor denies the client the possibility of returning to a counselor that he or she has grown to trust and respect over time. Other ethical codes are more lenient. The American Counseling Association (ACA) code of ethics (ACA, 1997) states that a minimum of two years must pass before a counselor may have a sexual relationship with a former client. In any case, no matter how attractive a client is, his or her right to obtain quality counseling services is clearly more important than the counselor's need for a date.

Professional Relationships

We have the responsibility to refrain from making disparaging remarks to a client about other mental health professions or professionals. Making negative remarks about the professions of psychiatry, psychology, social work, psychiatric nursing, or the creative art therapies, for example, can easily come across as arrogant and self-serving. More important, we may cause a client to avoid beneficial services.

Utilization of Assessment Instruments

Professional counselors are trained experts in the use of objective inventories and tests. These instruments aid in counseling and in diagnosis and decision making. As with any powerful tool, testing materials may cause harm if used improperly. The most common problem I have seen is the use of outdated instruments. Commercial tests and inventories are revised periodically in order to maintain current norms, reliability data, and validity data. Keeping up with these revisions is an irritation, even more so when the revised forms, scoring templates, and manual cost from $50 to more than $200. There is a temptation, therefore, to save the money and time it takes to purchase and master a revised instrument by continuing to use an expired form. Doing so, however, causes harm because you end up comparing your client against a population that no longer exists, and the information you garner from the outdated instrument is not valid. It is better to have no information about a client than to have psychometrically unsound information. So bite the bullet and use only the current forms of tests and inventories.

Assessing the Problem

Conducting a thorough assessment is as important in family work as it is in individual counseling. One way to utilize the assessment skills that you learned in your graduate counseling program is to conduct what I refer to as a *developmental differential diagnosis* (DDD). The concept of differential diagnosis comes from the field of medicine and refers to the physician's ability to determine what specific disorder is causing the patient's illness through the systematic use of diagnostic techniques. A DDD adapts this process to counseling, in that the counselor lists all possible underlying issues that may be causing or encouraging the presenting problem, then does a thorough follow-up assessment to determine which issues are most pertinent. As an example, when I have a new client with the presenting problem of anorexia nervosa, three listings immediately go on my DDD. The first is biology. I need to assess whether biological changes are exacerbating psychological problems or putting the client in physical danger. The definition of anorexia focuses on body weight: the disorder occurs when a client is below 80% of ideal body weight as defined by a standard height and weight chart. There is good reason for this biological definition. When individuals fall below 80% of their ideal body weight, they begin to go through physiological changes that can gravely threaten their health. At this low body weight, clients also go through psychological changes. They are unable to think clearly and develop fuzzy thought patterns. As a result, counseling typically becomes ineffective until the client gains enough weight to think clearly. Therefore, if biological factors are ruled in on my DDD, I attend to those first.

The second issue I routinely add to an eating disorder DDD is culture. I need to know how much the societal emphasis on thinness is contributing to my client's anorexia. If cultural norms are making a significant contribution, I incorporate feminist counseling, psychoeducation, and body image techniques into my work with the client. In contrast, if cultural norms are not a significant contributor to the eating disorder, I will not emphasize these approaches at the beginning of my work with the client.

The final listing on my DDD for anorexia is family enmeshment. Enmeshment occurs when family members are so close that individual identity and the ability to direct one's life are thwarted. Children in enmeshed families often feel a lack of control over their lives. They may use food and body weight as focal points to try and regain this control. As one five-foot-six, 92-pound anorexic young woman told me: "If my parents have control over who I date, the school I attend, and the profession I will enter, at least I can control how much I weigh." When enmeshment is ruled in as an item on my DDD, I make sure that family counseling is an integral component of my work with the anorexic client.

How do you add or delete items on your DDD? One effective procedure is to use a primary assessment approach you probably learned about in your graduate counseling program, Arnold Lazarus' (1989) BASIC ID. With this tool you systematically and thoroughly evaluate the following:

Behavior. What client behaviors contribute to, exacerbate, or alleviate the problem?

Affect. What specific emotions does the client feel? What is the client's level of interoceptive awareness (a fancy term for how much people allow themselves to feel their true emotions)?

Sensation. How is the client experiencing and processing the problem through the five senses of sight, sound, smell, taste, and touch?

Imagery. What images form in the client's mind when he or she focuses on the problem?

Cognitions. What specific thoughts go through the client's head when he or she focuses on the problem?

Interpersonal relationships. What are the quantity and quality of the client's relationships with friends, peers, and family?

Drugs/biology. What legal and illegal drugs is the client taking? Do they contribute to or exacerbate the problem? Do any biological or medical conditions contribute to or exacerbate the problem?

Going through each component of the BASIC ID with a client may greatly assist you in developing your DDD. Substance-abuse counseling with a heroin addict provides an example. Some addicts use heroin primarily because it provides a chemically induced feeling of euphoria that is impossible to replicate by any other means. This issue can be assessed while reviewing sensations, and placing it on your DDD indicates that you need to devise a method for helping the client grieve and deal with the loss of intensely pleasurable physical feelings. Other addicts use heroin because it distracts them from intrapsychic pain. You can assess the amount, intensity, and etiology of this intrapsychic pain while exploring affect under the BASIC ID. When intrapsychic pain is added to the DDD of a client who would like to kick a heroin addiction, you typically need to incorporate an approach that will allow for the (slow) exploration and remediation of childhood pain and low self-esteem.

You can use a number of additional techniques you learned in graduate school to supplement the BASIC ID when generating a DDD:

Use your knowledge of human development. This is the "developmental" part of a DDD. Because human development is a core part of our professional identity, counselors have a better working knowledge of this field than any other mental health professionals. Ask yourself whether the client's problem is related to a developmental issue or a normal developmental stage. As an example, I would put "empty nest syndrome" as an item to be ruled in or out on my DDD for a 43-year-old female who reports that she started to suffer from depression shortly after her youngest child left for college.

Ask the client. Sometimes we forget to do the obvious and ask what the client thinks is causing the problem. I am amazed how often clients know exactly what their DDD is and what they need to do about it.

Talk to parents, teachers, relatives, and other significant people who have regular contact with your client. These individuals are a rich source of information and often can provide valid hypotheses about the cause and maintenance of the client's problem.

Use inventories and tests. As previously mentioned, instruments are powerful tools that can generate items to add to your DDD. For example, a career counselor may be working with a career indecisive client who has not been able to make an occupational decision despite having enough information about the career decision-making process, different careers, and current opportunities. On administering the *Strong Interest Inventory,* the counselor notices that the client blackened the "indifferent" circle on virtually every work value. Knowing that a large number of blackened "indifferent" circles may indicate a lack of energy, the counselor may add depression to the client's DDD as an item for further assessment.

Review the professional literature and current research. Conducting an ERIC or other database search; using an Internet search engine; and reviewing professional journals, newsletters, and workshop notes are all good ways to find out current thoughts about the etiology of a presenting problem. Take advantage of the vast amount of information available, especially when you are presented with a problem you do not see on a regular basis.

Utilize in-house consultation. Present challenging cases at your agency's professional staff meeting and ask for your colleagues' thoughts on items to be added to the client's DDD. Ask for a consultation with a staff counselor who has experience and a good reputation for treating the particular presenting problem that is challenging you. Of course, in-house confidentiality needs to be observed to safeguard client information from leaving your agency or office.

Conduct direct observation. Field observations may provide vital information about the root cause of a presenting problem. Visiting the client's classroom, workplace, or home may be especially useful when the problem is limited to that particular location. For example, I once worked with a disabled veteran with the presenting problem of depression. The client felt that the depression was caused by his inability to accept the need for a wheelchair. One aspect of the depression was that the client was irritable toward his eldest son. Interestingly, the irritability seemed to occur only during mealtimes. So I asked the client to invite me over to dinner. During my observation of the family mealtime dynamics, I noticed that the son kept trying to talk to his dad about an issue, and that the dad was becoming increasingly annoyed and clearly did not want to engage his son in conversation. In our subsequent session, my client acknowledged that he was diverting the conversation. What was he diverting it from? His son had come to the realization that he was gay and wanted to use mealtimes as an opening to talk to his family about his sexual orientation. The dad was very uncomfortable with the idea of having a homosexual son and wanted no part of the conversation. Because of my dinnertime observation, I was able to narrow down my DDD and determine that my client's irritation was due to issues surrounding his son's sexual orientation rather than his own disability.

Setting Goals

You learned in graduate school that setting goals is an important part of the counseling process for individual counseling. Why? Because as we used to say in the 1960s, "If you don't know where you are going, how are you going to know when you get there?" Goal setting is as important when working with a family as it is in individual counseling. Specific goal-setting issues that arise when a family is in your office will be discussed in chapter 4.

There is debate in the field about the level of specificity necessary when setting goals with clients. Behaviorists gravitate toward specific, concrete, and measurable goals. Counselors with a humanistic perspective may be comfortable with fairly global goals. Focusing on Paul's Question (Paul, 1967) lets us tailor the specificity of goals to the particular client, problem, counselor, and setting. For example, with a smoking-cessation client it may be appropriate to set goals around the number of cigarettes smoked each day. On the other hand, with a client whose goal is self-knowledge, a more general goal of personal growth may be best. In working with families, you will have to make a professional judgment about how specific goal setting should be with each family. There is a balance between making goals concrete enough to ensure a focus on modifying important behaviors yet, as Cavanaugh (1982) states, global enough to generate positive feelings of accomplishment.

Mutuality, a goal-setting skill that you learned in graduate school, will come in quite handy when a family is in your office. Both client and counselor have a right to propose goals. Clients appreciate the autonomy that comes with choosing the direction of counseling. At the same time, counselors use their expert assessment skills to uncover additional goals that may be fruitful for exploration. Neither counselor nor client has the right to dictate goals, however. A client has the right to decline to pursue a goal the counselor suggests, and counselors may reject a client's goal if it is unethical or unhealthy. For example, a married man made an individual appointment to see me. He said that he was having an affair and consequently feeling guilty. The client then stated that his goal in counseling was to deal with the guilt so that he could enjoy the ongoing affair. I politely stated that I could not agree to this goal, as it was hurtful to his spouse. A second example involved a high school student who came to see me with the goal of improving his grades. After a thorough assessment of the BASIC ID, I noted problems in his family relationships and offered him the opportunity to work as well on being more comfortable around Mom and Dad. The client decided to stick to the academic issue and declined to bring his parents into counseling.

Selecting an Intervention

After you have completed the DDD and goal-setting processes, it is time to select an appropriate intervention. From a broad-based behavior therapy/social learning theory point of view, the first step in choosing an intervention is to select a theoretical framework to anchor your approach (see, e.g., Lazarus & Beutler, 1993). Select a theoretical framework bearing in mind Paul's Question: Based on my thorough assessment, what theory will work best with this particular client, with this particular problem, with this particular counselor, in this particular setting? I encourage you to consider family systems theory (as discussed in chapter 2) as your theoretical framework of choice when a family is involved in counseling.

After selecting a theoretical framework, the next step in selecting an intervention is to choose specific techniques. First, you can select techniques from the anchor theory you have chosen for the particular situation (chapter 6 will focus on approaches from family systems theory). You can also choose techniques from additional approaches that complement your anchor theoretical framework. This is another area where counselor training pays off. Your theories of counseling class has provided you with a host of different frameworks to add to your arsenal. Many programs use Gerald Corey's *Theory and Practice of Counseling and Psychotherapy* (2001), a text I highly recommend for a review of techniques from the most commonly used theories in counseling. Let us review some of these approaches and some basic ideas about how they can be tied to family work:

Psychodynamic Theory

The psychodynamic approach focuses on developing insight. As such, you may want to use a psychodynamic interpretation when it is therapeutic to link behaviors with needs and motivations. I once worked with an adult child of an alcoholic who had severe fights with her husband. She did not know why she argued with her husband, because otherwise they had a very good marriage. In exploring the timing of these fights, it became clear that they occurred any time the spouse consumed an alcoholic beverage. Even though my client acknowledged that her husband did not have a problem with alcohol, she became afraid and angry because of a hidden fear that he would become abusive just as her dad had done when he drank. Linking the fights with the fear that her husband would act like her father after a drink helped the client to begin the process of understanding that her husband was a different man than her father and would not become violent after having a glass of wine.

Adlerian Theory

Alfred Adler is considered by many to be the father of family counseling. His focus on developing a congruent lifestyle has utility for families that have gotten into a rut where they are behaving in ways that do not promote family unity. For example, when you find that a parent is spending 80 hours each week at the office, you may want to engage him or her in discussions about the impact of this schedule on the family and whether the workaholism is promoting a healthy lifestyle. Adler also promoted social interest as an important component of mental health. Asking clients to focus on the health of the family rather than individual needs may be useful when selfishness is predominant.

Existential Theory

Existential counseling focuses on helping clients develop a philosophy of life. Existential discussions can be used to help parents cope with the anxieties of child rearing and the fear of death (of self, spouse, and offspring) that comes with the birth of children. Children often reflect the fears of their parents, so it is useful to assess whether a child's problem is a mirror of the anxieties of Mom or Dad. If so, helping the parent work out his or her existential issues will help the child. For example, I was working with a rebellious adolescent who was failing classes. It turned out that her father was a worrier who watched his daughter like a hawk to make sure nothing happened to her. The daughter was feeling suffocated, and her poor school performance was a reaction to this feeling. I spent a number of sessions with the father discussing the existential dilemma of not being able constantly to protect those we love most: our children. Over time, he came to terms with the idea that a parent's role is not to prevent pain but to provide support for his children when the inevitable happens. As he began to change, so did his daughter. As her reason for rebelling was removed, she started doing her schoolwork.

Person-Centered Theory

Rogerian concepts are useful on two fronts. First, they facilitate a conducive counseling relationship. Focusing on unconditional positive regard and the qualities of genuineness, warmth, respect, and empathy may soften the more confrontational family-counseling techniques presented in chapter 6. A thorough and practical detailing of person-centered facilitative approaches can be found in *Intentional Interviewing and Counseling* (1999) by Allen and Mary Ivey.

Second, a person-centered approach works well when you have assessed that a particular client knows the answer to his or her problem. As a general rule of thumb, when both you and the client know the solution to a situation, it is better for the answer to come from the client. Reflection, restatement, active listening, and projecting the qualities listed previously provide a safe counseling environment that allows clients to think through their issues.

Gestalt Theory

In assessing affect under the BASIC ID, you may find that family members have low interoceptive awareness and push down feelings. Gestalt techniques may be useful in such a situation because they focus on bringing emotions into the here and now. When a family is reluctant to acknowledge their feelings in a counseling session, you might use the empty chair; "making the rounds"; the reversal technique; rehearsal and exaggeration exercises; "staying with the feeling"; or focusing on nonverbal messages to bring feelings to the surface (see Corey, 2001, pp. 192–227).

Choice Theory

You might choose to incorporate William Glasser's approach into your work when a family needs a structured approach to healthy decision making. Choice theory is also useful in helping family members assume responsibility for their actions. It has been said that one definition of insanity is doing something that doesn't work over and over again. Choice theory helps family members to sort through what they really want, what they are doing now to fulfill those wants, whether those actions are working, and what different behaviors would be more effective. As an example, I worked with a couple in which the husband was chronically indecisive about whether to pursue a medical degree or a Ph.D. in a social science. His inability to make a decision had caused paralysis to the point where the man had neither held a steady job nor taken any classes for more than 18 months.

Although his wife loved him very much, the resulting stress was causing her to consider divorce. Using choice theory the husband developed two different plans of action. The first was a plan for success involving a step-by-step approach for exploring his academic options and making a decision. The second was a plan for failure listing discrete steps for staying stuck and sabotaging progress. When the husband looked at the two plans side by side, he realized that he had to take responsibility for choosing success or failure. It took him a little while, but he chose the plan for success. He applied to graduate school, was accepted, moved his family 400 miles, and has now almost completed his Ph.D. His family is doing fine and his wife is no longer contemplating divorce.

Behavioral Theories

Behavioral techniques fit into systems theory nicely when a family will benefit from changing specific behaviors. Relaxation exercises, assertiveness training, modeling methods, and operant conditioning may all help shape behaviors that promote a healthy family. I often hear parents complain that their children watch endless hours of television and won't interact with Mom and Dad. I then ask the parents what they do to relax after a hard day's work. Inevitably, the answer is "I watch television." I then suggest that Mom and Dad model the behavior they would like to see in their children by leaving the television turned off in the evening and finding alternate forms of relaxation, preferably ones that allow parent-child interaction. Many parents are willing to follow through on this suggestion, but interestingly a substantial number refuse to do so. Although the need to interact with their children is great, apparently the desire to watch TV is greater.

Cognitive Behavior Theory

Pioneers such as Albert Ellis and Aaron Beck have helped us understand that thoughts greatly influence our moods and actions. The techniques of identifying and correcting irrational beliefs,

providing negative examples at well

catastrophizations, overgeneralizations, and black-and-white thinking may be useful in family work. For example, a mother requested that I work with her tenth grade daughter who showed little respect to her parents. The daughter freely acknowledged talking back to her parents. She explained that she was furious because they expected a correct answer on every question on every test and exam. The girl had brought home a report card with a 97% average that placed her on the honor role. The parents' reaction was to berate her for not having received 100%. In a subsequent session, Mom and Dad acknowledged that they were thoroughly disappointed with the report card. I then asked them what specific thoughts were occurring when they felt this disappointment. Their answer was, "My child must get into an Ivy League college in order to be successful. In order to do so, she has to have perfect grades." I tried to help the parents view these statements as irrational beliefs and black-and-white thinking and to understand the intense stress and anger these thoughts caused in their daughter, which was leading to disrespectful behavior. Unfortunately, the parents were threatened by my cognitive-behavioral approach and withdrew their daughter from counseling until they could find a counselor who, as the mother said, "would fix my daughter instead of jeopardizing her academic success and future happiness." Although I did not have a positive outcome in this situation, it does point out the need to assess the family system instead of assuming that all problems lie within a client.

Assessing the Intervention

An important part of the counseling process is to check out whether your intervention was effective. You might use a number of the techniques discussed in the "Assessing the Problem" section to assess whether your and the client's goals are being met:

Ask the client. As in the assessment stage, we sometimes forget that the client is a useful source of information. I like to ask the following questions on a regular basis:

     1. Is our approach working?

2. <u>How</u> can you tell?
3. <u>What have we done</u> that has been <u>helpful</u> in producing change?
4. What have we done that has <u>not been helpful</u>?
5. Are we where you <u>expected</u> to be at this point?

Sometimes I receive an unexpected answer to these questions. I worked with a junior art major who was referred to counseling by the faculty because of signs of depression. After a few sessions I asked whether the counseling was working. The client stated no. I then asked her how she could tell that counseling was not meeting her needs. She replied that she felt less depressed. Confused, I asked her to tell me more. She said, "I thought I wanted to be less depressed. But now that I am, I don't get the dark, creative ideas that drove my work. Give me back my depression so that I can be an artist."

Talk to parents, teachers, relatives, and other significant people who have regular contact with your client. Clients sometimes become frustrated at the slow <u>pace of change</u>, leading to a lack of motivation to continue. Getting regular <u>positive feedback</u> about the changes that are occurring from important people in their life can be a powerful motivating force to continue in counseling. Clients appreciate the pat on the back that comes when family, friends, or colleagues observe that the hard work is paying off. I remember one father who beamed when his wife told him in my office that she noticed and appreciated the fact that he no longer read the newspaper at the table. When I mentioned that I had praised him for his growth but had received a less enthusiastic response, he replied, "I figured that you're a counselor and are supposed to be saying those nice things. This is the first compliment I have received from my wife in ages!"

Use inventories and tests. As mentioned in the "Assessing the Problem" section, <u>objective instruments</u> can be powerful tools for generating a DDD. Another reason to administer an inventory at the beginning of counseling is to provide a <u>baseline</u> of feelings, attitudes, and behaviors related to the presenting problem. This baseline can be compared with data collected from a second administration of the inventory following intervention. As an example, I worked with a family in which a daughter had chronic low self-esteem. After the first session, the girl completed *the Piers-Harris Children's Self-Concept Scale* (Piers & Harris, 1984). The instrument provided evidence that her issues were focused on her physical appearance and lack of popularity. Both were related to the girl's feeling that she needed to look like a model in order to feel good about herself or for anyone to want to hang out with her. After a number of sessions, once she had started giving herself permission to look like an average girl, I readministered the Piers-Harris CSCS. The results indicated that she now felt just fine about the quantity and quality of her friendships. The physical appearance scale scores had improved, but still indicated that the girl was feeling bad enough about her looks to promote low self-esteem. In exploring her answers to the questions, we found out that the girl was focusing on her crooked teeth. So the parents agreed to get her braces. After her teeth were straightened, the girl reported that she now felt satisfied with her appearance. I administered the Piers-Harris CSCS a third time, and the scores supported the girl's report of positive self-esteem.

Reaching Closure

Counselors used to refer to this final stage of counseling as termination. Then Arnold Schwarzenegger and his *Terminator* movies came along. At that point, it seemed appropriate to change the name to closure.

Closure is easy to overlook because your work on the presenting problem has been completed. Like a metaphorical salesclerk, it is easy to ring the bell and move on to the next customer in line. If you do so, you run the risk that clients and families will feel that they were treated as a problem instead of as people and that you cared only as long as they had a diagnosis. In contrast, spending time and energy on closure gives the message that you are not abandoning the client or family and, in my experience, makes them more likely to seek out counseling services in the future if needed. I have had clients come back to my office more than four years after closure to work on new concerns. I firmly believe that my attention to the ending of our first counseling relationship significantly influenced their willingness to make a new appointment years down the road. Chapter 8 will focus on specific approaches for successful closure with families.

Conclusion

The process of establishing a relationship, assessing the problem, setting goals, selecting an intervention, assessing the intervention, and reaching closure provides a framework for working with families across counseling specialties. The remainder of this book is devoted to specific ideas and strategies for implementing this process when more than one family member is in your office. It is comforting to note that the skills, theories, and approaches you learned in graduate school provide a firm foundation for implementing the systems-specific ideas presented in upcoming chapters. As such, family counseling need not be a professional area separate from your current specialty. Instead, it is an extension of the professional counseling skills you already possess.

References

ACA [American Counseling Association]. (1997). *Code of ethics and standards of practice.* Alexandria, VA: Author.

Cavanaugh, M. (1982). *The counseling experience: A theoretical and practical approach.* Prospect Heights, IL: Waveland Press.

Corey, G. (2001). *Theory and practice of counseling and psychotherapy* (6th ed.). Belmont, CA: Wadsworth/Thomson Learning.

International Association of Marriage and Family Counselors. (1993). Ethical code for the IAMFC [International Association of Marriage and Family Counselors]. *The Family Journal: Counseling and Therapy for Couples and Families, 1,* 73–77.

Ivey, A., & M. Ivey. (1999). *Intentional interviewing and counseling: Facilitating client development in a multicultural society* (3rd ed.). Pacific Grove, CA: Brooks/Cole.

Kaplan, D. (1995). Message from the NYCA president: "The 80/5 dilemma." *Journal for the Professional Counselor, 11,* 2.

Lambert, M. (1992). Implications of outcome research for psychotherapy integration. In J. C. Norcross & M. R. Goldfind (Eds.), *Handbook of psychotherapy integration* (pp. 94–129). New York: Basic Books.

Lazarus, A. (1989). *Multimodal therapy.* In R. J. Corsini & D. Wedding (Eds.), *Current psychotherapies* (4th ed., pp. 503–544). Itasca, IL: Peacock.

Lazarus, A., & Beutler, L. (1993). On technical eclecticism. *Journal of Counseling & Development, 71,* 381–385.

Napier, A., & Whitaker, C. (1988). *The family crucible: The intense experience of family therapy.* New York: Harper & Row.

Paul, G. (1967). Insight versus desensitization in psychotherapy two years after termination. *Journal of Consulting Psychology, 31,* 333–348.

Piers, E., & Harris, D. (1984). *Piers-Harris children's self-concept scale: The way I feel about myself.* Los Angeles: Western Psychological Services.

Scissions, E. J. (1993). *Counseling for results: Principles and practices of helping.* Pacific Grove, CA: Brooks/Cole.

Chapter Four

Establishing a
Relationship With Families

David M. Kaplan

In chapter 3 I pointed out that the counseling relationship accounts for 30% of client progress (Lambert, 1992). My hunch is that this figure is even higher when a client's family enters your office. Why? Because clients who come for one-on-one counseling (at least those who come voluntarily) tend to respect your office as your space and power zone. You receive the ascribed power that comes with your advanced degree and training. Although individual clients may be resistant to change (aren't we all!), they will generally respect your position and authority. Families are very different in that they are more likely to be wary of you. Many challenge your authority and power initially, and it is your responsibility to establish a relationship under these circumstances. A family that remains distrustful of you does not allow progress.

In my experience, families maintain their distance when they first meet you for two reasons. First, people tend to be much more protective of their families than they are of themselves. One client was very clear about this when she said, "I can handle it if you screw me up, but don't you dare mess up my family." Second, many parents are embarrassed by family counseling. Look at the experience from their perspective. They have tried as hard as they can for a long time to fix the problem. All of a sudden, some counselor who knows little if anything about their family claims that he or she can make everything okay. Parents may feel embarrassed and ashamed that they have to ask an outsider to do something they see as their responsibility. In order to overcome this natural defensiveness, embarrassment, and shame, which interferes with forming a relationship with a family, you may want to attend to the following ideas and strategies. They are designed to promote family trust and confidence in you.

Getting the Family Into Your Office

To state the obvious, you can't establish a relationship with a family that won't come for counseling in the first place. It is therefore useful to develop a strategy for encouraging a client's family to come to your office. The first part of the strategy involves identifying the family member who has the greatest power and enlisting his or her aid in getting the entire family to come to the first session. Typically, this person is the mother because in our culture, families tend to be socialized to place Mom in charge of emotional issues affecting the family. Sometimes the person is the father or a grandparent. Your client should be able to tell you the best person to approach. If the client cannot or is too young to discuss this issue, try the mother first.

The next step is to ask whether your client would like to approach the family contact person (FCP) or would prefer that you make a phone call. It really doesn't matter whether you or the client approach the family; the decision is mostly a matter of client comfort. Some clients are more comfortable talking to the FCP first and others are relieved when you volunteer to call and request that the family come for a session.

The final step is to contact the FCP. Regardless of who makes the request, a positive focus increases the odds of the FCP agreeing. I have found that the best way to get a family in for the first session is to say four little words: "We need your help." You might explain that the client is dealing with important and complicated issues, and that family members' input is crucial because they know the client better than anyone else, including yourself. The message you are trying to convey is that the family is an invaluable resource and that you respect each member's problem-solving abilities.

In my experience, mothers typically respond well to such a message and agree to come with their children for the first session. Dads are sometimes holdouts because our culture tends to socialize men to be uncomfortable talking about their feelings. Fathers know that this is exactly what will happen if they go to a family counseling session and so sometimes refuse to attend. When a mother calls me back and says that everyone except the father has agreed to come, I ask her to relay a message: "Tell him that he doesn't have to say anything during the session. He only has to come and observe and be there to support his family." I have found that this approach usually does the trick, and I end up with everyone attending the first family session.

The inherent message in this discussion is that it is important for as many family members as possible to be involved in the counseling. It is especially important to have all nuclear members (as defined by the particular household) present at the first session. Having the entire family present ensures that everyone is on the same wavelength about goals and intervention approaches, as well as sending the message that everyone is important. Conversely, if you allow an individual to be absent, you may give the message that he or she is an unimportant member of the family. People who are let off the hook and allowed to skip out on the first family session are likely to sabotage the counseling because you have not had a chance to allay their fears and concerns or to establish a relationship. These problems inherent in beginning family counseling without the entire household present have led to the saying, "It is better to fail to start than to start and fail." If a client shows up at the first family session stating that someone can't make it ("My wife got held up at work, so she will have to come next time" or "My son has a soccer game and can't be here"), you may want to very pleasantly reschedule the session for a time when all family members can be present.

Attire

Counselors typically dress informally. Two media models come to mind. The first is from the movie *Ordinary People,* in which Dr. Berger (Judd Hirsch) wears khakis, a button-down shirt, loafers, and a cardigan. The second example is from the television show *The Sopranos,* in which Dr. Melfi (Lorraine Bracco) wears a pantsuit or skirt, blouse, and sweater. Individual clients see this informal approach as a nice balance between the sloppiness of casual dress (e.g., jeans and sneakers) and the formality of business attire (e.g., suits and coordinated ensembles).

You may want to consider dressing more formally when you have a family appointment, however. This advice applies even when you have been wearing informal attire during a client's individual appointments. The concept of establishing a relationship with family members by wearing business attire may seem counterintuitive, as we were taught in graduate school not to put barriers between our clients and ourselves, and a suit may be perceived as such a barrier. In addition, if we are honest, many of us simply do not like to dress up.

Formal dress serves two purposes when you first meet the family members of a client, however. First, it is a sign of respect. It signals that you honor the family enough to go to the effort of dressing up. This nonverbal message can go a long way in establishing trust with a family. Second, dressing formally gives the message that you are an expert. This message may also seem counterintuitive, as the person-centered influence in counseling often makes us uncomfortable with an implication that we are an expert "above" the client. On the other hand, keep in mind that a family wants exactly that: an expert. They do not want to waste their time or, worse, to have family members and relationships hurt by a counselor who does not know what he or she is doing. That is why, in my experience, one of the worst things you can do when you first meet a family is to give the Rogerian message that the family knows as much about how to approach the problem as you do. You run the danger of having the family decide that they do not want to establish a relationship with a counselor who can't do any better then they have done.

Credentials

The prominent display of credentials also helps establish your expertise and build trust with family members. While waiting for a session to begin, family members should be able to view your graduate diploma(s), license, and any professional certifications. Kent (1994) also suggests placing in your waiting room a one-page resume stating your qualifications and strengths and listing your credentials, experience, professional affiliations, publications, and presentations.

These suggestions apply to all counselors, not just those in private practice. Counselors in schools, agencies, and other employment settings tend to be modest, and sometimes are reluctant to openly display their accomplishments. However, research has shown that the disclosure clients most frequently request at the beginning of the counseling relationship revolves around the counselor's experience and credentials (Braaten, Otto, & Handelsman, 1993). Providing this information in the waiting room allows you to begin establishing credibility (and therefore trust) with family members even before they enter your office for the first time.

An issue related to the display of credentials in establishing a solid relationship with family members regards those counselors who have earned a doctorate. If you have a Ph.D., Psy.D., or Ed.D., consider introducing yourself as "doctor." When I first meet a client in individual counseling, I introduce myself as "David Kaplan," due to the ubiquitous person-centered influence in counseling that encourages a warm and genuine counselor-client relationship. When I first meet a family, however, I introduce myself as "Dr. Kaplan." I want to communicate the level of expertise that our culture grants to this degree so the family can feel that they are in good hands.

Seating

It is quite useful to have flexible seating in your office for times when you will be conducting family work. Movable chairs interspersed around a loveseat allow family members to adjust personal space to their comfort. Movable seating also allows you to assess nonverbal messages, alliances, and roles (more on that later in the section on the first session). Limiting your seating to couches or fixed chairs provides less flexibility, and two family members who are at odds may be forced to sit a lot closer to each other than they would like. Under these conditions, the family is likely to be irritable and grouchy before you even start the session. The worst-case scenario is forcing two recently divorced parents to sit next to each other on a loveseat. If you do this, I can almost guarantee that you will never see either of them again.

Try to set up your office in a way that is comfortable for individual counseling yet also can accommodate a family of five. Doing so will take care of most of your seating needs. Having some folding chairs stored in an easily accessible location is useful for those times when you see a large family or invite grandparents or other extended family members into your office. Don't settle for basic metal folding chairs. Comfortable and attractive padded folding chairs are available through furniture stores and office furniture catalogs. Periodically, you may want to invite more than seven or eight relatives into your office. In that case, you can go into your group-counseling seating mode and set up circled chairs in a bigger group counseling room.

Informed Consent

Informed consent involves the provision of information about your practice to a family so that they can make a knowledgeable decision about whether to enter into a counseling relationship (Kaplan & Culkin, 1995). Informed consent has been a recent focus in the field of family counseling ethics, and that aspect will be addressed in chapter 11. In this chapter, my focus is on using informed consent to help establish and enhance your relationship with a family.

Focusing on informed consent during your first contact with a family helps establish a relationship because it establishes trust. Family members who know what they are getting into are more likely to take the risk of investing themselves in a partnership with you (Borden, 1975). How do you obtain informed consent? Kaplan (2000) provides a seven-step process for gaining informed consent in a way that enhances trust and a relationship with a family:

1. Construct a Thorough Informed Consent Brochure

A purely verbal approach to informed consent with a family is never adequate, regardless of your setting or counseling specialty. Why? Because, contrary to our often lofty opinion about the pearls of wisdom that flow from our lips, clients do not hang on to our every word and may disregard or misinterpret oral statements we make about our practice. When a family member utters the dreaded phrase, "but you never told me that," your goal is to be able to reply immediately, "Let's review the section in my informed consent brochure that speaks directly to what would happen if this issue came up."[1]

As an example, I was working with a family that seemed to like me as both a counselor and a person. After a number of weeks of counseling, they invited me to a big extended-family barbecue that they were having in their backyard. Of course, I had to say no in order to avoid dual-relationship and confidentiality issues. However, I did not want them to take my declining the invitation as rejection. I was able to avoid this by stating, "Let's take another look at page 6 of my informed consent brochure. The second paragraph says that the ethical guidelines of my profession demand that I relate to you strictly in my professional role and that I cannot see you socially. So I apologize, but my hands are tied and I hope you understand that I must decline your generous invitation." Because the family had been informed from the very beginning of counseling that I was not able to engage in social interactions with them, they did not take my response as a personal rejection.

What sections should be in your informed consent brochure? It should contain headings on confidentiality, your theoretical framework and treatment approach, your educational background and training, information on how to make and break appointments, session (and other) charges and fees, any additional points pertinent to your practice, and an acknowledgment page (Zuckerman & Guyett, 1992). Although putting together a brochure does take some time, almost all these sections are fairly easy to write. The exception is the theoretical framework and treatment section. Even (especially?) if you have been practicing for years, sitting down to try to write a mini-essay on your approach to counseling can be a humbling experience. However, doing so is critical. Would you trust a surgeon who could not tell you how he or she performs a specific operation? Probably not. In the same way, parents and children will not trust a counselor who is unable to describe how he or she helps families.

As an example, I have a section in my informed consent brochure titled, *Psychological Treatment*. This section states, in part:

> My treatment approach is called rational eclecticism. It involves selecting an approach that research has indicated works well with your problem. Some of the available approaches involve exploring the past, while others do not. Some interventions make use of homework assignments; some focus on feelings; some on thoughts; some on behaviors. Some approaches work best when family members are involved, while some work best if we work individually. Again, the approach selected will depend upon what research has indicated works best in your situation. If you have a particular approach that you think will work well with you, or would like an explanation of the approach I have chosen for you, please let me know. If at any time you are uncomfortable with the approach we are using, please tell me so that we can figure out a way for you to be more comfortable.

I mentioned the inclusion of additional points in your informed consent brochure. One additional point you may wish to consider addressing in your brochure when doing family work is the issue of testifying in custody battles. Sometimes parents initiate divorce proceedings while you are providing counseling to the family. It is not all that unusual for one parent to ask you to testify that he or she is the better parent and should have custody because, as one dad told me, "you know the kids and have seen how much they love me and how well we get along." Given that agreeing to testify for one of the parents would stop the family work immediately (the other parent would be a fool to continue working with you), you must decline to do any kind of custody evaluation or agree to make statements about who is the better parent once you have begun working with a family. Doing otherwise would destroy the relationship you have with the entire family. In order to nip this issue in the bud, I have the following statement in the "additional points" section of my informed consent brochure:

> It is possible that, if you are married or have children, you may become involved in a divorce or custody dispute. If this occurs, I want you to understand that I will not be available to provide expert testimony in court, and that you should engage a court-appointed child custody evaluator. This decision is based on two factors: (1) my evaluations will be seen as biased in your favor because we have a therapeutic alliance, and (2) because the testimony might negatively affect our therapeutic relationship, I must put your interests first.

2. Ask the Family to Read Your Informed Consent Brochure Before the First Session

Having the family read the brochure in advance helps establish a relationship before you even see them, because it demonstrates that you are open and want to provide helpful information. When a family makes their first appointment, simply request that they come 30 minutes early in order to review your materials. It is useful to have multiple copies available for larger families. If you do not have a secretary, explain that you will be in session when the family arrives and that copies of the brochure will be placed in the waiting room for them.

3. Ask the Family for Feedback on Your Informed Consent Brochure

At the beginning of the first session, as soon as everyone is seated, ask whether anyone has any questions or whether any portion of the brochure was unclear. Parents typically use this time to double-check session or testing fees and inquire about future appointment times to make sure they can see you without interfering with their kids' extracurricular activities. Someone may also ask whether you will see family members individually. Before you agree to this request, review your rules about confidentiality. Asking the family their questions and thoughts on the guidelines of your practice helps establish a relationship because it shows that you are considerate, kind, caring, and respectful (Haas, 1991).

4. Take Time to Review Your Guidelines About Confidentiality

Because confidentiality is the cornerstone ethic, you will want to review this topic with the entire family. The more explicit you are about both what is kept confidential and when you must break confidentiality, the more trustworthy you will appear and the more willing a family will be to enter into a relationship with you (Heppner & Dixon, 1986).

A messy confidentiality issue that often occurs in family work involves individual members who ask to speak to you alone "in confidence." This situation may arise when a parent phones you wanting to share information, when a family member hangs back after a session and asks for a few minutes to speak to you alone, or when one family member requests an individual appointment. Typically, the family member opens with, "I didn't want to mention this in front of [fill in the blank with a family member's name], but I thought you should know that. . . ." The individual who utters these words firmly expects that his or her statements will neither be shared with other family members nor mentioned during a family session.

Agreeing to keep confidential statements made by individual family members is fraught with peril and threatens any relationship you have established with a family. It encourages the keeping of family secrets and ties your hands in discussing potentially important issues with the family. I once worked with a family with an adult daughter who was suicidal. Between sessions the mother called and wanted to tell me about the father's history of suicide attempts, which he had refused to bring up during sessions. However, she wanted to share this for informational purposes only and did not want me to bring it up during sessions. If I had agreed to her request, then I would have been in the bind of having vital information that I could not use.

My most vivid experience of what can go wrong by agreeing to keep a family secret occurred with an individual client who related a devastating couples counseling experience she had had with another counselor. Soon after beginning the couples counseling, her husband called the counselor and asked for an individual session. He used that session to inform the counselor that he was having sex on a regular basis with a good friend of his wife's. After getting this bombshell off his chest, the husband then instructed the counselor to keep the affair confidential and not to bring it up in front of his wife. Because the ethical code of the International Association of Marriage and Family Counselors (1993) states in section III, part E, "Unless alternate arrangements have been agreed upon by all participants, statements made by a family member to the counselor during an individual counseling or consultation contact are to be treated as confidential and are not disclosed to other family members without the individual's permission" (p. 75), the counselor kept this family secret. After three months of counseling, the husband initiated a divorce and subsequently told his wife about the affair. At that point, she initiated individual counseling with me. I will never forget the painful mix of anger and betrayal in the client's voice when she said to me, "That SOB marriage counselor knew all along my husband was having sex with my best friend while pretending to work on the marriage. Why didn't the counselor say something instead of letting me act like a damn fool and think that we were working things out?"

So how do you avoid the trap of having to keep information confidential when an individual family member calls you on the telephone or hangs back after a session? The key is the first 10 words of section III, part E of the IAMFC ethical code described in the previous paragraph: "Unless alternate arrangements have been agreed to by all participants. . . ." You can use your informed consent protocol to address these alternate arrangements. I find it useful to frame this issue during my discussion of informed consent as a question of "who is the client?" I explain to the family that we all need to be on the same wavelength about identifying who the client is. Is it the person who has the problem that initiated counseling? Is it a parent who is worried sick? Is it the siblings who have had to make major accommodations? Is it the infant in the family, who is fussy because of the tension in the household? Is it the family pets who are not getting enough attention because the family is distracted? (I realize the last is a somewhat flippant question, but it does get across the point that everyone in the household is important.)

I then propose viewing the family as the client. In that way, I can address the needs and stresses of all family members, not just the person with the presenting problem. I often joke that if they agree to view the family as the client, they will be getting more for their money, as I do not charge by the number of people in the room.

With an agreement to view the family as the client, I can then discuss what happens if a family member speaks to me individually. I explain that if someone speaks to me alone, I reserve the right to bring up the information in a family session if I make a professional judgment that it is in the best interest of the family (my client) to do so. I very directly state to the family that if they want to make sure a particular piece of information is not shared, they should keep it to themselves. Does this mean that useful information may be kept from me? Certainly. But it also means that I will not be burdened with keeping family secrets. I would much rather not know useful information than be put in the position of knowing the information but being unable to do anything with it.

What if the family declines to view the family as the client? Some families insist on viewing the identified patient (the person with the presenting problem) as the client and want family members (especially the identified patient) to be able to talk confidentially during individual sessions. In my experience, this situation typically arises when the identified patient is an adolescent with school, relationship, or drug issues. The parents may feel that their child will speak more freely in confidential individual sessions. The IAMFC code of ethics (1993) speaks to the egalitarian nature of family counseling and, on a practical level, I don't want to hurt my relationship with the family, so I usually will agree to the family's request. I explain that in accordance with the statements in my informed consent brochure on professional ethics, if I make a professional judgment that any individual is in clear danger of harm, I will break confidentiality in order to protect life. I make it clear, however, that beyond issues of clear danger I may keep information confidential that family members would want shared. Although this is not my preferred approach, it allows me to deal effectively with family secrets and keep a positive relationship with the family.

5. Have All Family Members Sign the Acknowledgement Sheet

Obtaining a signature from each family member provides written confirmation that everyone has had a chance to review the guidelines of your practice. This indication that you value a thoroughly informed family enhances trust. In my view, it is important that every family member of toddler age and above (i.e., everyone old enough to be aware of what is happening in my office) sign the acknowledgement sheet because this is yet another indication that every member of the family is important. Young children can make an "X." Although a child's "X" or signature obviously has no legal standing, the message of inclusiveness is what I am after.

6. Give the Informed Consent Brochure to the Family to Take Home

After you have removed the demographic form(s) and the signed acknowledgement sheet, give the family your brochure so they can refer to your practice guidelines at any time. Doing so is another way to build trust and enhance the counselor-family relationship. Interestingly, it also allows you to have greater trust in the family, because providing a copy of your informed consent brochure reduces the chance of a malpractice lawsuit (Bennett, Bryant, VandenBos, & Greenwood, 1990).

7. Ask Again About the Informed Consent Brochure

At the beginning of the second family session, I typically ask, "Now that everyone has had a chance for a more leisurely review of my informed consent brochure, are there any additional questions about what I do or the guidelines of my practice?" Doing this shows a continuing desire to earn the trust of the family.

The First Session

When I started working with families, I found the first session particularly anxiety provoking. I found myself thinking, "Now that I have them all in here, what the heck do I do?" I also experienced what I refer to as "the Atlantic City undertow." When I was a child I went on a field trip to Atlantic City. It was one of my first visits to the ocean, and I eagerly anticipated swimming in the surf. When I waded out to test the water, a big wave washed over me and the undertow began dragging me along the bottom. I remember the feeling of being pressed down against the ocean floor and the thought, "It is going to be up to the sea whether I live or die. If it decides to let go of me I will live. If it decides to hold on to me I will die." Fortunately, the undertow ceased after the wave passed and I was able to swim back to shore.

Working with a family is in some ways like that undertow. When you welcome a family to your office, you may begin to feel sucked down to the bottom. The family seems to be in total control. Somehow working with people related to each other by blood or love makes the dynamics different. You begin to realize that you are no longer in the land of individual counseling. These statements are meant not to scare you away from doing family work, but to convey the message that you need to be prepared.

Therefore, with the goal of reducing anxiety and providing structure, I present my approach to the first session. Please understand that this is just one approach; you will develop your own style and make modifications as you become more experienced in family work. Keep in mind as well that the downside of offering a structured approach is that it implies that you do exactly the same thing in the same order with every family. Kottler (1986) points out the importance of varying your approach to counseling in order to avoid burnout. So with that caveat, here is my approach to the first session.[2]

Entering the Room

I prefer to let the family enter my office in front of me and seat themselves. The manner in which family members arrange themselves may send some nonverbal messages or help me generate hypotheses about roles and alliances. Please note that the key word is *hypotheses.* I interpret initial nonverbal messages tenuously and tentatively until I have checked them out and either confirmed or disproved them.

The most common nonverbal seating message I have noticed in the first family session reflects emotional distance or conflict. Family members who are comfortable with each other tend to sit close together. Conversely, family members who are either angry or emotionally distant tend to sit farther away from each other. In order to focus on this aspect, I try to keep two related questions in mind at the beginning of the first session. The first is, "Are family members who should be sitting together sitting farther apart than I would expect?" As an example, I worked with a woman in her mid-twenties who was anorexic. Let's call her Debbie. Debbie told me that one problem was that Mom and Dad kept insisting that everything was fine in the family, that there were no conflicts, and that the only real family issue was that their child weighed less than she should. Debbie felt as if she had been born into a Stepford family and was very frustrated that her parents refused to acknowledge any sort of family conflict. (This family motto, "Everything Is Fine!," is quite common in enmeshed families—a common precursor of anorexia—and I recommend Salvador Minuchin and colleagues' classic book *Psychosomatic Families: Anorexia Nervosa in Context* (1978) for anyone wanting to understand and provide therapy for this issue.) When Debbie's parents came to the first family session, I noted that Mom and Dad were sitting as far away from each other as they could get while still being in the same room. Late in the session, I diplomatically asked them why they chose to sit so far apart. Mom answered that she was irritated with her husband. That remark led to a productive discussion of family tensions. Debbie was amazed, as it was the first time that she had ever heard her parents acknowledge that they were not the perfect family.

The second question about family seating is, "Are any family members sitting too close to each other?" This is where having a couch or loveseat in your arrangement comes in handy. I worked with an adult male who had a history of serious drug abuse and suicide attempts. He reported feeling smothered by his parents because they were constantly watching over him. We invited his family in for a session to utilize them as a source of strength. When the family came in, the mother told the son to sit next to her on the loveseat and promptly encircled his body with her arms. The pose was a stark snapshot of a mother scared to death that her son would die and determined to do everything she could not to let that happen. I verbalized the message Mom was giving, upon which she started to weep and express her fear. This was the beginning of my client coming to understand that his family was acting out of love and the fear of his death rather than a desire to control him.

The way family members seat themselves may also give a clue about the roles they play. A role that may become obvious as soon as the family has arranged their seating is that of the family scapegoat. Families with problems will sometimes choose a member to blame as the source of all or most family disturbances. This person becomes the identified patient (Gladding, 1998). You can often tell when your client is the family scapegoat because other family members will cluster around each other and leave your client alone and metaphorically naked in a different part of the room. You can almost imagine them pointing and saying, "It is all _____'s fault. This family would be fine if he/she wouldn't keep screwing up." When you note that a family has isolated your client, you may want to pose the following questions to the family: "If we could wave a magic wand and everything was okay with _____, would everything be all right with the family? Or would there still be problems?" This is another example of how having the entire family in your office pays off. Whereas adults are usually very good at keeping family secrets, preadolescent children usually tell the truth. "John," a college student, was referred to me by his parents because he was flunking out of school. John told me that he was interested in school but was distracted because he was afraid his parents were going to get a divorce. So we invited the entire family in for a session. The mother and father insisted that any squabbles they might have were minimal and that the real problem was that John was lazy. I then turned to their eight-year-old daughter and asked her if everything would be okay in the family if John started getting good grades. She blurted out, "Mom and Dad would still be leaving us," then quickly covered up her mouth in the realization that she had let out a family secret. John's parents were quite shaken by their daughter's statement. They simply had not realized the impact their marital problems had been having upon their children. Thus began a three-session discussion of how the family could keep Mom and Dad's fighting from interfering with their children's lives. A significant outcome was that the parents initiated marriage counseling. As they began resolving their differences and fighting less, John started doing better and better in his classes. Unfortunately, this story does not have a happy ending for John's parents. Although their marriage did improve for a while, they eventually decided that their differences were too basic to stay married and subsequently got a divorce. John did not let his grades suffer, however. He stated that the key was the open parent-child communication that the family counseling had initiated. He told me that he did not like the fact that his parents were divorcing, but he could study as long as he knew what was going on. Not knowing what was happening had been the factor that had distracted him from his work.

A second role you want to look out for in the first session is that of gatekeeper (see Napier & Whitaker, 1978). The gatekeeper guards the safety of the family in your office. You often can detect the gatekeeper before anyone says a word in the first session because that person typically seats himself or herself (at least partially) between you and the family. The nonverbal message is, "In order to get to this family you are going to have to go through me. You are going to need my approval." Not every family has the need for a gatekeeper. But when a family does have one, it is crucial to recognize this dynamic and determine who the gatekeeper is. Why? Because the gatekeeper is going to be the one who determines whether your office is a safe environment for the family. The gatekeeper will control whether family members speak openly and also will be the one who decides whether the family will return for future sessions. Ultimately, the gatekeeper decides if you have permission to establish a relationship with the family.

Therefore, one of your most important tasks in a first family session may be to assess for a gatekeeper and, when one is present, to establish a positive relationship with this crucial family member before the family leaves your office. How do you figure out whether a family has a gatekeeper? First, notice when a family member has placed himself or herself between you and the family. In a functional, healthy family, we would expect either the mother or father to be the gatekeeper because it is a parental responsibility to protect one's children. Sometimes when you have three generations in your office you will find that a grandparent is the gatekeeper because the family defers to her or him as the matriarch or patriarch. However, you need to be prepared for role reversals in some families where the kids end up acting as the parents. You will see this role reversal when parents are unable to fulfill their proper role due to such issues as physical or mental illness, alcohol or other substance abuse, or long periods of absence from the household due to employment. In these cases children, often quite young ones, may become the gatekeeper; after all, someone has to run the family. One of the first families I worked with had a 10-year-old gatekeeper. It was positively frightening to see the power this young child had over who spoke, what that person spoke about, and what the family was willing to work on.

Another way to assess for a gatekeeper is to see whether everyone looks at a specific member before speaking. An example of this occurred with a single mother and two preteen daughters in New York. The mother had asked me to facilitate a discussion about the need for the three of them to move to the West Coast because she had a new job. I noticed that whenever I asked either of the daughters a question, she would subtly glance at her mother. Just as subtly, Mom would shake her head either yes or no to indicate whether the girl had permission to answer the question. Factual questions (e.g., "How do you spend your time when you get home from school?") tended to be met with approval. However, questions that asked for an emotional response (e.g., "How do you feel about moving?") were met with a negative shake of the head, and the girls would just stare at me. It became clear to me that I would need to focus on making Mom feel comfortable in my office so she would allow the kids to take the risk of expressing their feelings. I was able to do this, and the girls received permission to open up when they returned for the second session.

So how do you deal with a gatekeeper when you find one? First, let me tell you what not to do. When I was getting started in family work, my macho side would tend to come out in dealing with gatekeepers. I viewed their protectiveness as a challenge and gave the indirect message that I was better at getting their family to open up than they were at keeping members from talking about important issues. And I found that I did an awful lot of one-contact family work. It was only when I began to respect the role of the gatekeeper that I was consistently able to establish relationships with families. The best way I know to show respect for gatekeepers is to make them your co-therapist. Frequently ask their opinion. Follow their lead. Request their permission to speak to family members. Let's return to the family where Mom wanted help in talking to her two daughters about the upcoming cross-country move. When I realized that Mom was the family gatekeeper, I asked her opinion as to the most important and beneficial questions I should be asking her daughters. She responded that the girls needed to think about making friends in their new home. So that is what I focused on, and Mom gave the girls nonverbal permission to talk about their feelings connected with this issue. When I wanted to change topics, I asked the mother if it was okay to ask the girls how they were adjusting to the idea of having to leave their current friends. Mom thought about this a bit, said yes, and we had a good family discussion about saying goodbye. The mother relaxed more and more as she saw that I was respecting her gatekeeping function. I later asked Mom if we could discuss the girls' father and visitation issues. Mom initially said no, telling me that this topic was too emotionally charged for the girls to handle in the first session. So I stayed away from it. Interestingly, at the beginning of the second session, Mom said, "We have been talking about the visitation issue you brought up last time. I think it would be good if we got into that." I had apparently passed the trust test and the gatekeeper was giving me entry into the family. If I had fought the mother for control during the first session and insisted that we talk about Dad, I doubt very much that I would ever have seen that family again.

Opening the Session

Once the family is seated in my office and I have made a quick perusal for nonverbal messages, I explain who I am and why we are all together, and obtain informed consent. Explaining who you are is important because different family members may have had varying levels of contact with you. Those who have worked with you individually may know all about you. Others may be meeting you for the first time and have no clue who you are or what you do. I worked once with a guardian who wanted help with parenting skills. I suggested she bring the children in for a session so I could get to know the family. Instead of telling the kids about the appointment, she pretended that they were all going for ice cream, loaded the kids in the car, and came to my office. I had two very confused children wondering why they were at some doctor's office instead of Dairy Queen.

Making a statement about why you and the family are all meeting allows you to set the tone for a positive, strength-based approach. I simply state that we are together because I need the family's help to deal with a problem. I also tell the family that they have resources, background information, and ideas that will make the counseling much more efficient and effective than it would be if I worked exclusively with the person who has the problem. You will often see family members visibly relax when they begin to realize that you are not seeking to blame them for the presenting problem.

Gaining informed consent before you delve into family problems is an ethical obligation. You have a responsibility to make sure that every person in your office knows the rules of counseling. In order to fulfill this ethics requirement while using informed consent procedures to help establish a relationship with a family, you may want to utilize the framework for gaining informed consent that I discussed earlier in this chapter.

Getting to Know the Family

I spend the next 20 minutes or so getting to know the family. My usual segue to this topic is, "Now that you know something about who I am, I'd like to get to know who you are." The important point is to spend time talking to every family member, even the youngest child. The message you want to convey is that each individual in the family is important. It is also wise to respect the power hierarchy in the family, so start with Mom or Dad (whichever one you think wields the most power). Then continue with the other parent, the grandparents (if present), the oldest child, and so on down to the youngest child.

Defining the Issue

After getting to know a little bit about each person in the room, I find it productive to ask how each family member perceives the problem.

My typical statement is, "Now that I've had a chance to meet the family, I'd like to ask each of you what the issue is. Mr. Smith, what do you feel brings us together and what would you like to work on?" Again, I respect the power structure of the family by going down the hierarchy. You may have noticed that I started with the father in this example and may wonder how that squares with my previous statement that in a traditional two-parent household, the mother tends to be in charge of affective issues. The answer is a cultural one: families know that Mom is in charge but many pretend that Dad is at the top of the hierarchy so as not to embarrass him in his role as "head of the family." In such an instance, you would want to buy into the family's worldview and speak to Dad first. Otherwise, you will be showing disrespect for the family system, which is not conducive to establishing a relationship. You can (and should) work on cultural stereotyping and gender issues later in the counseling process after you have established trust. Lois Braverman's book, *A Guide to Feminist Family Therapy* (1988) is recommended as resource in this area.

Asking all family members' opinions about why they came to your office and what they would like to accomplish does a number of things. First, it supports the message that everyone's ideas are important. Second, it may give you insight into family conflicts that potentially underlie the presenting problem. Third, it gives you a clue as to what issue will hook each individual family member into coming back for subsequent sessions. Speaking to the last issue, I worked with a single father who brought his two children in because he wanted more help around the house. Understandably, the kids were quite disinterested in talking about this issue; there was nothing in it for them. I then asked them what they would like to work on, and they said that their bedtime was too early. So I proposed a deal to the family: if the kids were willing to talk about the issue of household chores, Dad would talk about curfews. All agreed. The kids perked up when they realized that they might get something out of the counseling, and we had almost a dozen productive sessions that led to the resolution of both issues.

Identify an Issue to Begin Addressing

Next, I ask the family to choose which issue to start with. Usually they choose the presenting problem. As we talk, I use the skills I first learned in my group counseling class to make sure that all individuals contribute to the discussion and that no one monopolizes the time. This is also the point where I try to sit back a bit and assess whether gatekeeping, scapegoating, or any other interesting dynamics are occurring.

Identify Family Problems and Secrets

If time permits, I like to ask the question discussed in the scapegoat section: "If the problem we have been discussing were solved, would everything be okay in the family, or would there still be problems?" This question can go a long way toward disclosing family problems and secrets that are exacerbating the presenting problem.

Closing

I like to end an initial family meeting with a summary, a solicitation of feelings and thoughts about the worth of the session, and a discussion about where we go from here. If you have succeeded in earning trust and establishing a relationship, the family will willingly schedule a follow-up appointment.

References

Bennett, B. E., Bryant, B. K., VandenBos, G. R., & Greenwood, A. (1990).

Professional liability and risk management. Washington, DC: American Psychological Association.

Borden, E. S. (1975). The generalizability of the psychoanalytic concept of the working alliance. *Psychotherapy: Theory, Research and Practice, 16,* 252–260.

Braaten, E. B., Otto, S., & Handelsman, M. M. (1993). What do people want to know about psychotherapy? *Psychotherapy, 30,* 565–570.

Braverman, L. (Ed.). (1988). *A guide to feminist family therapy.* New York: Harrington Park Press.

Gladding, S. T. (1998). *Family therapy: History, theory, and practice* (2nd ed.). Upper Saddle River, NJ: Prentice Hall.

Haas, L. J. (1991). Hide and seek or show and tell? Emerging issues of informed consent. *Ethics and Behavior, 1,* 175–189.

Heppner, P. P., & Dixon, D. N. (1986). A review of the interpersonal influence process in counseling. In W. P. Anderson (Ed.), *Innovative counseling: A handbook of readings* (pp. 8–16). Alexandria, VA: American Association for Counseling and Development.

International Association of Marriage and Family Counselors. (1993). Ethical code for the International Association of Marriage and Family Counselors. *The Family Journal: Counseling and Therapy for Couples and Families, 1,* 73–77.

Kaplan, D. M. (1999). Models of ethical decision making in marriage and family counseling. In P. Stevens (Ed.), *Ethical casebook for the practice of marriage and family counseling* (pp. 3–16). Alexandria, VA: American Counseling Association.

Kaplan, D. M. (2000). Using an informed consent brochure to help establish a solid therapeutic relationship. In R. E. Watts (Ed.), *Techniques in marriage and family counseling* (Vol. 1, pp. 3–10). Alexandria, VA: American Counseling Association.

Kaplan, D. M., & Culkin, M. (1995). Family ethics: Lessons learned. *The Family Journal: Counseling and Therapy for Couples and Families, 3*, 335–338.

Kent, D. (1994). Creating a waiting room resume: Six questions people ask when choosing a therapist. *What's Working in Psychotherapy Practice Building, 15*, 1, 7.

Kottler, J. A. (1986). *On being a therapist.* San Francisco: Jossey-Bass.

Lambert, M. (1992). Implications of outcome research for psychotherapy integration. In J. C. Norcross & M. R. Goldfind (Eds.), *Handbook of psychotherapy integration* (pp. 94–129). New York: Basic Books.

Minuchin, S., Rosman, B. L., & Baker, L. (1978). *Psychosomatic families: Anorexia nervosa in context.* Cambridge, MA: Harvard University Press.

Napier, A., & Whitaker, C. (1978). *The family crucible.* New York: Harper & Row.

Zuckerman, E. L. (1997). *The paper office: Forms, guidelines and resources* (2nd ed.). New York: Guilford Press.

Zuckerman, E. L., & Guyett, J. P. R. (1992). *The paper office: 1.* Pittsburgh, PA: Clinician's Toolbox.

1. For a copy of my informed consent brochure, send $2.00 (to cover copying and mailing costs) to: David Kaplan, Chair; Department of Counselor Education and Rehabilitation Programs; Emporia State University; 1200 Commercial St.; Emporia, KS 66801–5087.

2. When possible, I like the first session to be at least 90 minutes long so that I can cover all points in my outline. Subsequent sessions can be shorter. If a family is traveling long distances, I try to have them come in over a weekend, with up to three hours each scheduled for Friday, Saturday, and Sunday. You will be amazed at how much can be accomplished in a long weekend when family members live too far away to come in on a periodic basis.

Chapter Five

Assessing Family Issues Related to the Presenting Problem

Dennis Pelsma

My youngest son, who is 15 and a half, began driving this summer. Sitting with him as he practices all the things he's learned in driver's education class reminds me of the similarities between learning to drive a car and learning to counsel clients. You can memorize the rules, techniques, and etiquette with a textbook and a good instructor, but actual driving practice is the only way to master the required skills. That's why I wasn't surprised when he came home after the first day of class saying that he drove for the first time that day. The feel of the steering wheel and the response of the car to it can't be simulated in the classroom.

Like young drivers, counselors learn to work with clients by reading about theories, experimenting with techniques in pre-practicums, practicums, and internships; and receiving support and feedback through supervised experiences both during and after their coursework. Learning to work with individual clients is like driving on a summer day in a quiet subdivision. The rules are, "Stay on the road and don't hit anything!" In contrast, counseling families is more like driving in a busy downtown area. The rules are, "Stay on the road, don't hit anything, be careful not to go the wrong way, stop before the crosswalk, avoid the truck, put on your turn signal. . . ." Your goal is not only to avoid hitting anything, but also to watch 50 things at once. While I sit in the passenger side of the car (holding my breath and crossing my fingers), I watch as my son makes a turn, adjusts his speed, and reacts to the changes around him. He is learning to master the road and become a safe driver for many years to come. Working with families is similar. It's like embarking on a car trip with a potential for multiple endings, including the hoped-for outcome that all make it home in one piece. Just as a driver needs directions to his or her destination, you, as the counselor, require an accurate map to understand the family and guide you in navigating through some of the potential problems. I know that the map is not the territory, only a representation of the ground to be covered. Yet without one, you can quickly become lost, overwhelmed, and ineffective.

The purpose of this chapter is to provide you with a road map that will help you in the assessment phase of the family counseling process. Understanding the influence of the family system is extremely helpful when working with individual clients (especially children and adolescents). Even experienced drivers can benefit from knowledge of construction problems on the roadway that may alter or influence their route. The presenting problem or concern may not be directly related to the family, but the family may unknowingly be encouraging the problem in some direct or indirect way. Without knowledge and understanding of family influences on the presenting problem, your influence and the client's efforts to change often are fruitless.

Functions of Assessment

Family assessment serves several important purposes for you and your clients. For you, assessment is an opportunity (1) to collect data about the family firsthand; (2) to determine if you and the setting are appropriate matches with the family; (3) to determine levels of satisfaction, quality, or adjustment in relationships and to pinpoint specific problems; (4) to make decisions about possible referral for other types of treatment; (5) to evaluate the ongoing counseling process at various points throughout counseling; and (6) to determine if and when further counseling is needed (Sporakowski, 1995). Assessment may also serve as an intervention. As you ask specific questions or involve the family in some task or activity, you are overtly or covertly identifying specific issues or areas of importance. For instance, through asking a couple, "What was it like to grow up in your family?" you may learn some important information about the respondent. At the same time, in answering the question, the respondent identifies specific pictures, thoughts, and emotions from the past that may be useful in gaining insight about the present. The question likewise reinforces the idea that their families of origin (i.e., the families they grew up in) have an important influence on the couple today. Understanding and appreciating this significance allows the couple to come to terms with the families' influence. A second example of assessment as an intervention involves the use of a genogram, which will be described later (McGoldrick, Gerson, & Shellenberger, 1999). A genogram provides a way not only to gather important intergenerational information, but also to create a visual graph, or picture, of the family. Having this picture on paper and out in the open is often very enlightening. As one client stated after completing a genogram, "Now I see how far we've come. . . . I feel good about surviving as long as we have." This insight reinforces the concept that assessment, as a process, *is* an intervention. With this in mind, be cautious when asking questions, as each question serves as a new experience that tends to stimulate other components of the individual system, which in turn may affect the family system.

In assessing the family, it is important to consider both the individual and the family as systems. Each system contains certain variables and characteristics that help to maintain the status quo (homeostasis) and allow for alterations and changes (homeogenesis) so the system can survive and grow. Using Lazarus' BASIC ID model described in chapter 3, these variables can be identified and connected in a way that makes sense logically, if not empirically. This modified BASIC ID model also allows you to compare the components of the individual as a system to similar components in the family system. The assumption is that reading one map is easier than trying to read several.

Conceptualizing the Individual as a System

Family systems theory assumes that all individuals are connected to various human systems (i.e., formal and informal groups) and that the family, as one of these groups, exerts a tremendous amount of influence over the individual's behavior, affect, perceptions, cognitions, and physical reactions. To understand how the family influences the individual, it is helpful first to conceptualize the individual as a system. Using part of Lazarus' BASIC ID model, the individual is conceptualized as a system having the connected components of Behavior, Affect, Sensation-Imagery, and Cognition.

Through these four components or modes, a client encounters new information (sensation) and creates mental pictures (imagery) of this information. The individual cognitively processes these perceptions (sensations-images) through self-talk or automatic thinking, which in turn stimulates an emotional reaction (affect). On feeling emotion, the client may (or may not) act or behave in some way to express this reaction (see Figure 1). Various theories of counseling and change involve influencing one or more of the modes or components: the cognitive mode (Ellis, REBT), the affective mode (Rogers, person-centered), or several modes at the same time (Lazarus, BASIC ID). It is assumed that if change takes place in one of these modes, then this change is likely to influence the client's cycle of perceiving, thinking, feeling, and behaving, and a new experience will result. As the client grows and develops within an environment (e.g., the family), each new experience serves to begin or stimulate this cycle. For a child, experience 1 (a gentle touch or soft words from Mother) encourages the perception of self in a safe world flowing from memories of previous similar, positive images. Cognitions of "this is pleasing/I am pleased" follow, producing the emotion of comfort or love. The reaction following such emotion frequently takes the form of a physiological response (lowered heart rate and blood pressure), which may produce a physical display (a smile) and a corresponding action (hugging back). This reaction, experience 2, serves as a link to external systems, in this case Mother.

Figure 1. Interaction of behavior, affect, sensation-imagery, and cognition on behavior according to the Lazurus BASIC ID model.

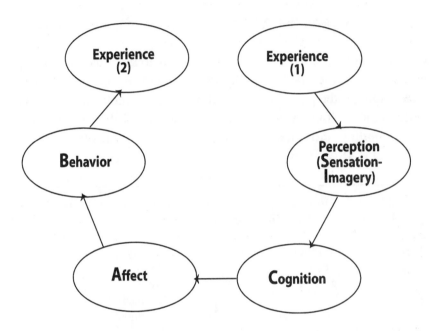

Using as many means of assessment as possible is helpful in understanding the individual as a system; these include talking to the client directly, consulting with others about the problem and individual, using inventories and paper-and-pencil tests, and observing the client directly in the counseling setting. All the information gathered in these ways represents important pieces of the individual system. It is important to compare clients' self-reports of what they see, think, and feel with your observations of their actual behaviors. These observations often reveal a different version of the internal components of which the client may be unaware. Actions and behaviors are windows to other components of the individual system. Although observing clients in their individual environments (e.g., home, playground, or work) is time consuming, you can often gain a more realistic sample of the client's interactions with others in this way. Even if the client is aware of your presence and tries to make a good impression, his or her behavior still provides important data that "speak louder than words."

Conceptualizing the Family as a System

Conceptualizing the family system according to Lazarus' model helps you to identify the systemic components that influence the individual and simplifies the potentially complex and overwhelming process of understanding family process and dynamics. Table 1 represents corresponding individual and family system variables based on the modified BASIC ID model.

Table 1. Corresponding Individual and Family System Variables According to the Modified BASIC ID Model

Individual	Family
Perception	Roles
Cognition	Problem solving
Affect	Boundaries
Behavior	Communication

I present each of the family system components of the modified BASIC ID model to clarify its influence on the family system. Combining these variables with the other two dimensions of a developmental differential diagnosis (i.e., developmental aspects and culture) constitutes a thorough assessment.

Level 1: Developmental Issues

Like individuals, families go through stages of growth and development. Stages are initiated by the changes that occur in families when new members are added (e.g., a new baby is born) and present either an opportunity for the parents to adjust to a new situation or a potential crisis (e.g., first child entering school, last child leaving home for college). As is true of individual development, each stage contains specific tasks that the family must accomplish or overcome in order to cope successfully with the challenges it presents. For example, a family with a child entering high school must cope with the new friends, interests, and activities that the teenager may become involved in, as well as to the peer pressure influencing his or her choices of clothes, hairstyle, and behavior. All these changes require the family to adjust and adapt successfully in order to survive in the present and continue to grow in the future. Questions to consider with regard to stages include the following:

- What stage is the family in?
- What tasks are confronting them?
- How open is the family to change and adaptation?
- Is the family stress caused by a developmental crisis facing the family?

Level 2: Effects of Culture

It is important to appreciate how a family's culture influences their values and traditions. The effects of culture will be discussed in depth in chapter 9. In brief, here are useful questions regarding culture:

- How does the family celebrate holidays and special occasions?
- Who are the extended family members and what importance do they have?
- How has the family adapted to the dominant culture they live in while maintaining the traditions of their culture?
- Do the processes of asking for help and coming to counseling violate the family's norms or traditional expectations about keeping family secrets?

Level 3: Family System Components

As shown in Table 1, the family system components are roles, problem solving, boundaries, and communication.

Family Perception (Roles)

Roles are often assigned by those in charge, and they evolve over time. Individuals perceive their roles based on the responses they get from other members of the family. Birth-order position in the family often designates or reinforces a position or set of responsibilities that is associated with it. Research and empirical evidence have shown that specific expectations are typically attached to particular positions in the family. The eldest or firstborn child, for example, is often given responsibility for overseeing younger siblings. The youngest child typically becomes the baby of the family and receives special attention and service from other family members. An only child, especially one in a single-parent home, is often expected to be the parent's confidant. For example, a mother and teenaged daughter who are used to doing everything together may share information and adult concerns that typically would be shared between the parents in a two-parent family. In most cases, children willingly accept the role that comes with their position in the family. It becomes their opportunity for significance and a place of importance within the family unit. A family's values and expectations sometimes may lead them to groom a child for a position, and in fact the child will supplant or unseat a sibling. For example, in a family with traditional values concerning gender and child care, the eldest child (a boy) may give up his role of being responsible for the siblings to the second born (a girl), who may be expected to care for her siblings (including her brother).

In some families roles are flexible, in others they are fixed. Usually, however, the family members in control establish the roles fairly rigidly. Family members come to expect each individual to think and act in a particular way to fit the family's needs. Two questions aid in understanding a family's role perceptions:

- Are the family members' roles healthy and balanced?
- Are the roles beneficial for each person's personal growth and development?

An example of an unhealthy role is that of scapegoat. Some families, like some groups, need to have a problem child on which to focus their attention. If one member is consistently viewed by others as the one with the problem, that individual has difficulty being successful because everyone expects him or her to fail. With regard to beneficial roles, children should be allowed to be children, not expected to act like adults or to deal with adult problems. Likewise, adults should serve as the protectors and nurturers of children, rather than expecting children to provide these needs for the family.

Family Cognition (Problem Solving)

Problem solving encompasses family members' abilities to make decisions, solve problems, and resolve conflicts. Each family possesses problem-solving capabilities that allow it to work through the problems it encounters. The following questions aid in assessing family problem solving. Hierarchy, control, and the need for order and task accomplishment are all elements to consider in answering these questions.

- How task oriented are the group members?
- Are the members of the system willing and able to compromise and negotiate?
- Who makes the rules and are they negotiable?
- Can rules change over time?
- How organized and efficient is the group?
- Who makes decisions for the group and individual members?
- Who has power and how is that power used?
- How adaptable to change is the group?

Family Affect (Boundaries)

Boundaries involve emotional attachment and the family's ability to keep the system intact and together. They represent the invisible ropes or ties that bind the family together. Without these emotional attachments, a family has lost an important ingredient for survival and growth. It is important that individuals in the group feel they are connected yet at the same time free to display their uniqueness and individuality. Overly close emotional attachment may become enmeshment, in which individuals actually feel for each other. For example, in a single-parent family composed of a mother and a preschool son, when the mother feels anxious or depressed about her son starting school, the child may likewise feel anxious and depressed. The child learns to incorporate these emotions into his individual system as a by-product of his attachment and sensitivity to his adult parent.

In contrast, disengagement occurs when members of the family are emotionally unavailable or removed from each other. In a healthy family, having a different physical appearance from others in the family does not mean one is deviant or wrong. Diversity is appreciated, within the limits of the group's ability to sustain a balance between change and tradition. Some of the following questions are useful in assessing boundaries:

- Who speaks for whom? (For instance, when an eight-year-old boy is asked about his friends and his mother answers for him, this is an indication of an enmeshed relationship.)
- Who owns the problem?
- Who is most invested and has the most to win or lose?
- Do family members enjoy friends and activities outside the family?
- Are individuals allowed to make and carry out decisions without constant "coaching" or criticism from others?
- When young adults leave home for the first time, are they allowed to make choices freely for themselves, or are they still tied to the family?

Family Communication (Behavior)

Communication provides the direct link between the person and the family system. As in individual counseling, communication behavior gives you insight into all the other components. All behaviors represent a form of communication and all communication, a form of behavior. When observing a family, it is important to look for specific patterns or typical ways of responding. (For example, who speaks to whom and in what way?) Rules about behavior and communication are designed to keep the family functioning, maintain family stability, and preserve the system. Sometimes these rules are written down (explicit), but they are more likely to be unwritten yet still understood (implicit). Rules for communication define who does what to whom and how interactions take place. Communication patterns and typical ways of responding are developed over time. Questions to address in the communication dimension include the following:

- Who speaks to whom and in what way?
- How often do members of the family interact and communicate?
- What is the quality of this interaction?
- Are interactions positive for family members (do they produce positive affect and behaviors)?
- Are certain individuals left out of discussions (possibly because they are considered outside the family's "inner circle")?
- How do members of the family get their needs met?
- How do the individual members seek attention and significance?
- Do family members gain attention in a direct fashion (asking for help or feedback) or indirectly (becoming ill at times to get recognition, sympathy, or support)?

A final area of consideration is the system's response to individual members' behavior and how the system components are used as a means of reward or punishment. The reinforcements and consequences for accepting and incorporating the group rules, upholding expected roles, and adhering to the rules allow those in control (usually the parents) to maintain the group and its level of functioning. Rewards are sometimes communicated in a concrete and tangible way (e.g., rewarding good grades in school with money or withholding allowance for failing to do chores), but more often the communication is abstract (e.g., praise: "What a great job you did on fixing the dishwasher," or criticism: "You never listen to me."). At one level these messages are designed to keep the family system in check. Sometimes messages may hold an indirect meaning and be understood on another level (e.g., "I wish you'd help out more often" could mean "You don't love me anymore, and that scares me").

For counselors, learning to listen and interpret both a message's direct or obvious meaning and its indirect or implicit one represents an important talent. In order to maintain homeostasis in the system, an individual must respond to the group in a way that maintains his or her designated role, follows the communication rules, and accepts the traditional way the family solves problems or makes decisions. Teenagers' need to grow and individuate, and their basic desire for independence and to go against the rules of the system, encourages them to violate family norms and values in perception (roles), cognition (problem solving), affect (boundaries), and behavior (communication). It is often at these times that the family will identify a specific problem or symptom of these rule violations (usually the teenager's behavior) and come to the counselor for help. In many ways this is beneficial because the conflict often stimulates the family to change and adapt, in order to survive. Members of the family may view conflict and the need for change either positively or negatively, but you can seize the moment and use it as an opportunity for growth of the individual, and you hope, of the group as well.

Table 2 provides a summary of the four components and the questions to address within each one when assessing a family system.

Table 2. Questions for Assessing Family System Components

Component	Questions
Family perception (roles)	• Are the family members' roles healthy and balanced?
	• Are the roles beneficial for each person's personal growth and development?

Family cognition (problem solving)	• How task oriented are the group members? • Are the members of the system willing and able to compromise and negotiate? • Who makes the rules and are they negotiable? • Can rules change over time? • How organized and efficient is the group? • Who makes decisions for the group and individual members? • Who has power and how is that power used? • How adaptable to change is the group?
Family affect (boundaries)	• Who speaks for whom? • Who owns the problem? • Who is most invested and has the most to win or lose? • Do family members enjoy friends and activities outside the family? • Are individuals allowed to make and carry out decisions without constant "coaching" or criticism from others? • When young adults leave home for the first time, are they allowed to make choices freely for themselves, or are they still tied to the family?
Family communication (behavior)	• Who speaks to whom and in what way? • How often do members of the family interact and communicate? • What is the quality of this interaction? • Are interactions positive for family members? • Are certain individuals left out of the discussions? • How do members of the family get their needs met?

- How do the individual members seek attention and significance?
- Do family members gain attention in a direct or indirect fashion?

Types of Family Assessments

Several comprehensive references describe the various assessment techniques available to counselors who are working with couples and families (see, e.g., L'Abate & Bagarozzi, 1993; Touliatos, Perlmuter, & Straus, 1990). As with individual assessment, techniques are varied and may be of either a formal (e.g., paper-and-pencil inventories) or an informal nature. It may be a good idea to include one assessment of each type (i.e., <u>formal and informal</u>) in the assessment process.

Formal means of assessment include measures of personality and interaction styles (e.g., Briggs & Myers, 1977); levels of marital satisfaction (e.g., Snyder, 1979; Spanier, 1976), family adaptation (e.g., Moos & Moos, 1981; Olson, Porter, & Bell, 1982); stress and coping (e.g., Lazarus & Folkman, 1984; McCubbin & Thompson, 1987), parenting and family skills (e.g., Abidin, 1990; Nash, 1984), sexual functioning (e.g., Derogatis & Melisaratos, 1979; LoPiccolo & Steger, 1974), marital communication (e.g., Bienvenu, 1970), and adjustment to divorce (e.g., Ferreiro, Warren, & Konanc, 1986; Fisher, 1981). Comparing the information gained via informal methods with the scores achieved on specific scales often requires specific training or experience. University counseling programs offering a specialty in couples and family work, as well as various family therapy training centers around the country, often provide courses, workshops, and supervision in the area of assessment. Counseling professionals enrolling in these educational opportunities often can earn graduate credit, continuing education credit, or advanced certification. Many learning experiences are also available through distance education and online instruction.

Informal assessment involves engaging the couple or family in some type of structured interview or activity, such as observation of live or taped situations where the couple or family performs some simulated task (Olson & Straus, 1972), naturalistic observation of the family in their home (Steinglass, 1979), or watching the family in game-playing situations (Ravich, 1969). Graphic representations of the family, such as genograms (McGoldrick, Gerson, & Shellenberger, 1999), photographs (Kaslow & Friedman, 1977), or family drawings (Burns & Kaufman, 1970) represent other ways of gathering data. Likewise, traditional structured interviewing techniques may be useful (Ackerman, 1958; Masters & Johnson, 1970). Among various projective strategies is storytelling (Caruso, 1988); and methods of family sculpting and choreography involve the members of the family in some creative expression of family interaction (Satir, 1983).

Assessment Techniques

The following section will examine five basic informal family assessment techniques that are likely to be useful to most counselors, regardless of their training or experience. Assessment techniques corresponding to the dimensions of a developmental differential diagnosis are described in Table 3.

Table 3. Assessment Technique Corresponding to Each Differential Diagnosis Level	
Developmental Differential Diagnosis Level	Assessment Technique
Developmental aspects (stage, age, etc.)	Genogram
Culture	Genogram
Family system components	
Roles	Typical day
Problem solving	Plan a vacation
Boundaries	Family sculpting
Communication	Draw a house

Genogram

The genogram has been widely used as a basic tool for implementing the intergenerational concept of the family systems approach and for increasing both the counselor's and family's understanding of the family system. Several family system theorists (e.g., Murray Bowen, Virginia Satir) believe strongly in the utility of drawing a graphic representation of the family. The counselor constructs a genogram similarly to a family tree, using information the family provides. As Figure 2 illustrates, a genogram displays the importance of the lines of influence from previous generations.

Figure 2. Sample genogram (7/22/02)

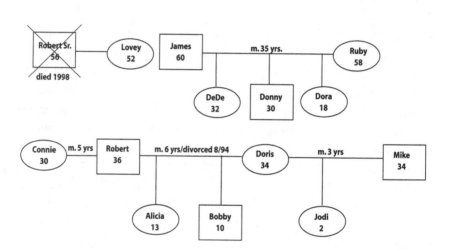

The family described in Figure 2 consists of Robert, 36 years of age, who was married for six years to Doris, 34, and divorced in August 1993. During their marriage the couple had two children: a girl, Alicia (13), and a boy, Bobby (10). After their divorce each remarried. Doris married Mike (34) and together they have one child, Jodi (2). Robert has been remarried for five years to Connie (30), and they have no children together. Robert's and Doris's families of origin are also listed. Robert is an only child whose father, Robert Sr., died in 1998 after being married to Lovey (52) for 34 years. Doris is the oldest daughter of James (60) and Ruby (58) who are both living and have been married for 35 years. Doris's siblings are DeDe (32), Donny (30), and Dora (18). As is customary, circles represent females and squares represent males.

Genograms should be completed early in the relationship-building and information-gathering stages of counseling, taking care not to overwhelm the client or clients with too many questions. In this process you would elicit the names or nicknames, ages, and birth dates of members of the immediate family, the lengths of all marriages, occupations and education level, health information (e.g., alcoholism), and descriptors for family members (e.g., having each family member think of one word that describes a particular person). Pay particular attention to such dynamic events as births, moves, job changes, family separations, health habits (drinking, overeating, gambling), and environmental stressors.

A genogram also provides information useful in the assessment of the family. For example, given information on the birth order and position of members in the family constellation, you can begin developing hypotheses regarding developmental aspects, the effects of culture on the family, and family system components. Based on the birth order and position of the children in the family, you may predict the roles that individuals are likely to have assumed (e.g., the eldest may be the most responsible and the youngest consistently the baby). The genogram also provides opportunities to identify some boundary issues and possible triangulation. (As the couple discusses an issue or concern, such as a child's negative behavior, it is common that they will form a triangle, or triangulate, on this child with roles typical of the traditional Karpman's triangle—Dad is the persecutor; the child, the victim; and Mom, the rescuer.) Family members devote attention and emotional energy to this triangle, in order to preserve the status quo and protect the system from disintegrating. Specifically, arguing about the child's behavior takes the focus off potential conflicts between Mom and Dad. If you identify such a pattern, you may draw lines to represent the connection of these three family members. Seeing this rather abstract phenomenon on paper helps family members to understand some of their past and present behavior.

The family benefits not only from the opportunity to see intergenerational influences, but also from gaining an appreciation for their history. Family cultural traditions also become evident as you ask the family about how they spend holidays, the traditions they celebrate, and other regular events that mark their lives. Values become apparent as you ask the family to describe priorities and important historical features.

After initiating the genogram, assign the family the task of completing it with other significant names and events, going back at least two generations from the immediate family. Completing this assignment often requires them to contact certain individuals in the family who have that information and ask for their help.

Draw a House

In this activity, the family is asked to draw a house for themselves (see, e.g., Ogden & Zevin, 1976). Provide large sheets of paper and markers or crayons and give the family a time limit (e.g., 10 minutes) to complete the drawing *without talking* or verbal exchanges. When time is up, ask each member to put himself or herself somewhere in the drawing (if that has not already been done). Observing the family in action provides a rich source of information, as you watch how the family communicates nonverbally, negotiates, and generally interacts during an active project. The picture also reveals the family's image of their living space and how each individual sees himself or herself in relation to that living space. During the draw a house exercise, reflect on the following questions:

- How does the family share the drawing space and the materials, including the crayons and markers?
- Does each member draw a separate house, or do they cooperate to make one large house?
- Which family member does which part of the drawing? Does Mom or Dad "provide" shelter for the family by drawing

the roof and outline of the house?
- Who participates and follows the rules?
- How does each individual negotiate to get his or her needs met?
- How does the family accommodate the "no talking" rule? How do they communicate nonverbally (e.g., glances, facial expressions, shrugs, etc.)?

Family Sculpting

Family work is often lacking in opportunities for creativity and expression, especially when the family sits passively discussing an issue in your office. Many children and adults alike enjoy getting up and moving around to express themselves. One method for engaging the family in such movement is family sculpting, a method children and adolescents are often very amenable to. In this activity, family members depict one another using the actual person, objects (chairs), or characters (puppets or dolls). The sculptor is asked to position other family members in positions that suggest distance versus closeness or activities normally undertaken (e.g., making dinner, cutting the grass). At the end of the sculpting experience, ask specific members assessment questions such as the following:
- What is it like to be in the position where you were placed?
- How does it feel to be so far away from the others?

After the debriefing, you might ask the sculptor to create the ideal family, portraying how the sculptor would like things to be. This portion of the activity is an opportunity for you to begin formulating potential goals for counseling. Family sculpting can provide important information about an individual's relationships with other members of the family and about boundaries inherent in the particular family system.

Describe a Typical Day

This interviewing technique elicits the daily activities of the family.

Ask the family to give a detailed description of a typical day, starting from the time they awake. (For example, who gets whom up in the morning? Who makes dinner? What activities are done together and apart?) As the typical day unfolds, you can ask questions relevant to the components and dimensions being assessed. Because weekdays are typically structured by work and school commitments, asking the family to describe a typical weekend day often reveals more about the family's priorities and decision making with regard to the use of free time. The values and priorities of the family and the roles of its members often become clear from this activity.

Plan a Family Vacation

Asking the family to plan a vacation together allows you to examine the family's ability to make decisions and problem solve. Designating a certain amount of "all expenses paid" money (e.g., $1,000 or $5,000) encourages decision making and careful planning. Then ask the family to decide how they will travel, what they think they should pack, what their first activity will be when they get to the destination, and the souvenirs they want to bring back. After giving the family the parameters of the activity, take an observer's role and try to remain uninvolved as the family approaches the problem. Occasionally, members of the family will try to solicit guidance from you. Because the purpose of the activity is to have the family demonstrate as authentically as possible the methods they typically use for decision making and problem solving, your involvement will influence them and reduce the amount of useful information you and they obtain.

A hypothetical family, the Smith family, is used to illustrate how these five techniques can be used in assessing a family. The following represents information gathered during the initial telephone call and the first two sessions with the family. An interpretation of the family's situation and potential goals for treatment are provided.

Assessment of the Smith Family

Mrs. Smith called to make an appointment with a counselor in our clinic. Assessment information was gathered during the counselor's return telephone conversation with the mother, an initial session with the parents, and a follow-up session with the entire family, consisting of the parents and their three children.

Initial Telephone Conversation

When the counselor asks the mother (Susan, age 33) about her concern, she states that she is worried about her eldest son, Mark, who recently has been doing poorly in school and appears angry and depressed. When asked briefly to describe Mark and the other members of the family, Susan states that Mark is a 13-year-old seventh grader who attends the local middle school. The younger son, Mitch, age 11, is in fifth grade. The youngest child, Sara, age 5, is attending kindergarten. Dad (Carl, 39 years of age) works for a small manufacturing company and must travel a lot during the week on business. When asked why she decided to call the clinic, Susan says that "we have to do something!" and that the school counselor recommended the clinic. She says she trusts the school counselor's opinion that the family can benefit from family counseling. The counselor arranges to see Susan and Carl for an initial interview and clearly explains that he would like to have the entire family (including the children) come in to the clinic for the second session so he can better understand how to help the family.

Information and tentative hypotheses the counselor makes from the phone call are the following:
Roles. Mark, the eldest child in the family, has "lost his place" as the typical firstborn and has taken on some of the middle child characteristics of being discouraged and potentially unsuccessful.
Problem solving. Susan and Carl have "agreed" to focus on Mark's problem but each has attempted to solve it in a different way.
Boundaries. Mom is enmeshed with Mark, whereas Carl is

disengaged from the family.

Communication. Given that Susan made the initial contact with the counselor, it can be assumed that she is the person most invested in Mark's problem and how it is affecting the family. Susan appears to speak for the family and is open to seeking help from outside sources. Without more information, however, it is difficult to assess the communication area.

Assessment Techniques in Session 1

During the initial session with the parents, the counselor completes a genogram to assess the developmental and cultural variables of the family.

Genogram

The counselor asks Carl and Susan to take home a copy of the genogram and to work on completing it with specific ages and dates during the week (see Figure 3). This is done both for informational purposes and to involve Carl and Susan in a joint task. The couple is asked to bring the children along for the next session.

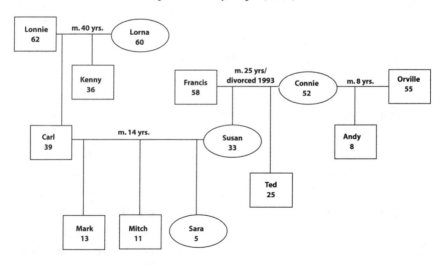

Figure 3. Smith Family Genogram (7/22/02)

Developmental and Cultural Information and Assumptions Drawn from the Genogram

From discussing Carl and Susan's family histories while beginning the genogram with them, the counselor learns the following:

1. Carl and Susan come from families where the parents have been strongly involved in religion, have married early, and have stayed married for a long time. Both parents have been married for 25 years or more.
2. Males have traditionally worked outside the home to provide for the family. The women in the family have had the responsibility for parenting.
3. Problems have been either ignored (e.g., Carl's father's alcoholism), or the women in the family have attempted to take responsibility for the situation and the problem (e.g., Carl's mother coming to school when Carl got into a fight with another student).
4. Carl and Susan are both the eldest siblings in their respective families of origin, although Susan could be considered an only child, given the eight years difference between her and her younger brother. Eldest children in both families are successful and appear to fit the traditional role of leader and most responsible among the other siblings.

Assessment Techniques in Session 2

Carl and Susan shared what they learned about their families of origin from the completion of the genogram during the week. They were each asked to share something they had learned about their family and were asked what effects, if any, they thought their family histories may have had on their current situation and problem with Mark.

Typical Day

The counselor then asked the family to describe a typical weekday and weekend. With the help of the children, Carl and Susan provided a fairly detailed account of how the family members spend their time.

Role Information Gained from the Typical Day Activity

From the schedule and activities the family described, the following patterns are clear:
1. Susan provides most of the parenting while Carl is absent.
2. Carl spends very little time with Mark, other than criticizing him about his grades, homework, and lack of motivation and work ethic concerning sports.
3. Susan and Carl have little time together to devote to their relationship.

Plan a Family Vacation/Family Drawing/Family Sculpting

Carl, Susan, and the children participated in planning a vacation, drawing their family, and sculpting the family. The following represents information and hypotheses derived from each activity:

Problem-Solving Information Observed During Planning a Family Vacation

1. Susan attempts to solve the problem directly, stating that the family has always wanted to go to Hawaii. This is where Susan and Carl had their honeymoon, and they say they have always wanted to take the children back for a family vacation. The children agree to this plan.
2. The family decides to fly to Hawaii, because it is efficient and allows more time for fun. Each of the children chooses a special activity. Mark and Mitch want to parasail as their first activity, and Sara wants to ride on a banana boat. Susan and Mark both agree that checking into the hotel first would probably be best after such a long trip.
3. After a discussion about which souvenirs to buy, Carl jokes that they might not have enough money to make it home

again. The children respond that staying there would be fine, because they could go to school on the island.

Boundary Information Obtained from Family Sculpting

1. Sara chooses to go first. She places Susan and Carl together, holding hands, with Sara at Susan's side. She places the boys next to Carl, one on each side. Sara's picture is of "one big, happy family."
2. Mark chooses to go next. He places Mitch and Sara next to Susan and Carl and himself separate from the family. He explains that he feels happy being away from all of the noise. This statement appears to upset Susan, who tries to reach out to him and bring him closer.
3. Susan places the children around her with Carl on the outside looking away, as if he were leaving for a trip. "That's how I see our family. The children and I together, with Carl always leaving on a trip," she comments.

Communication Information Learned from Drawing a House

1. Susan takes the lead and nonverbally directs the children to participate. Carl and Mark are reluctant at first, but each contributes to the drawing of the house. Carl adds a garage and driveway. Mark draws a satellite dish and computer in one of the bedrooms.
2. After a slow start, the younger children (Mitch and Sara) become enthused and create an elaborate backyard play area and swimming pool. Carl frowns and looks at Susan unhappily. Susan shrugs and begins drawing in flowers and bushes for the front yard.
3. Finally, each member of the family draws himself or herself in the picture. Susan puts herself in the front yard holding freshly picked flowers. Mitch and Sara both draw themselves in the swimming pool. Carl is unsure where to put himself and draws himself cutting the grass. Mark

places himself in his room, watching TV.

Conceptualizing the Family and the Individual System

Using the components from the BASIC ID model described earlier, Mark's family system and individual system can be described as follows.

Family System Components

Roles. Mitch (second born) has overtaken Mark (the eldest) and has assumed the position of most responsible. Mark is treated like the middle child, who gets squeezed out of the family resources for attention and perceived significance.

Problem solving. Susan makes most of the decisions and solves most family problems because Carl is frequently absent. Susan is very task oriented and works hard at keeping the family together (e.g., making doctor's appointments, getting the children to practice on time, etc.).

Boundaries. Carl and Susan have agreed to focus on Mark and his "problem." The couple has defined Mark as the focus of their energy and attention. Susan is enmeshed with Mark and appears to have trouble letting go and allowing him to individuate.

Communication. Susan speaks for Mark and is overly involved in his performance. Susan and Carl talk about Mark and worry about his "problem." There is a family rule that siblings are not supposed to talk about Mark's "problem" or make fun of him.

Mark's Individual System

Experience 1. Brother, Mitch, is praised for success (e.g., at soccer).
Perception. Mark pictures himself as incapable and left out of the family.
Cognition. "I'm not important. Nobody cares about me."
Emotion. Discouraged, depressed.
Behavior. Physical symptoms (headache), asks Mom to stay home.
Experience 2. Mom allows Mark to stay home (which serves to

reinforce Mark's system).

Potential Treatment Goals

From the information gathered thus far, it appears that this family is facing a developmental crisis precipitated by the growth and changes in their child, Mark. The parents, Carl and Susan, in attempting to solve Mark's problem of alienation from the family have indirectly made matters worse by triangulating on Mark's problem, with Carl being the persecutor and Susan, the rescuer. Without family counseling intervention, Mark will have a difficult time extricating himself from the role of victim. Treatment goals should focus on alleviating Mark's situation by attempting to influence one or more of the family system modalities of operating. The counselor could choose to focus on the perceived role that each member of the family has chosen to play and determine with Carl and Susan whether, in fact, each role is healthy for the person taking it on. Is there room in the family for individual differences? Can Mark be given some opportunities to demonstrate that he deserves to be treated as the eldest?

With regard to the family's problem-solving efforts, the family could explore alternatives to Susan needing to direct every situation. Instituting family meetings may provide a more democratic means of solving family problems. In terms of family affect, represented by boundaries, Carl and Susan could focus less energy and emotion on Mark's problem. They could benefit from nurturing and attending to their relationship, and from reinvesting themselves in it. Finally, Carl and Susan could learn to communicate their personal needs in a more direct fashion by taking time out each day to communicate, observing the rules of self-preservation and respect for each other.

The ID in Family Assessment

This final section discusses two very important influences in the assessment process not mentioned previously: the I and D components. In the traditional model I represents interpersonal relationships (e.g., divorce, remarriage, stepparenting). *D* refers to the effects of drugs and biology on the individual. In keeping with our adaptation of this model for working with families, it is important to appreciate how these two areas influence the individual members of the family.

Family Interpersonal Relationships

Families evolve as parents separate, divorce, and remarry. With each change, individuals in the family must adjust to new family members, and in many cases a new community and new surroundings. Each time a family goes through such a change, the individual and family systems are stressed by the need to cope with new roles, different methods of problem solving, potential changes in family boundaries, and new forms and methods of communication. In most cases, changes of this type represent new beginnings and opportunities. However, with each change comes a loss of some type (e.g., the loss of Dad tucking his children into bed at bedtime). We must appreciate how each member of the family is affected by this loss within his or her individual system of perception, cognition, emotion, and behavior. The process of grieving during and after a divorce is similar to the stages of grief Kubler Ross has described for death (shock, denial, anger, depression, and acceptance). Each family member may be at a different stage at different times in the divorce process. Here are assessment questions to consider:

- How has the individual coped with loss in the past?
- How much information is it appropriate to give each individual so that he or she can understand the loss and know what to expect in the future?
- How does each family member experience the loss?
- What type of support is available for individuals and the family as they go through the necessary adjustments?
- How does divorce, remarriage, or stepparenting change or influence the presenting problem?

Assessing these concerns will improve your ability to help

families cope with the changes brought on by divorce and remarriage and the challenges of stepparenting (Fisher, 1981; Ganong & Coleman, 1999; Stahmann & Hiebert, 2000).

Drugs/Biology

Drug use and alcoholism are major factors in many families' inability to function effectively. Individuals vary greatly in their use of drugs and alcohol. Likewise, individual behavior under the influence of such chemicals may range from unpredictable anger to extreme sadness and despair. Understanding the family's involvement with drugs and alcohol can greatly enhance your effectiveness and your ability to support and encourage the family or make appropriate referrals for addiction treatment. Assessment questions to consider include the following:

- Has alcohol or drugs had an effect on the parents' capabilities to handle the responsibilities of parenting?
- Have grandparents or other relatives been asked to assume the parents' roles as caregivers because of alcohol or drug abuse?
- Has the issue of alcohol or drug use become a "hot topic" for the couple? For example, is Dad's alcoholism considered a family secret? Does Mom overcompensate with gifts for missing her children's school activities?
- How are emotions expressed in the family?
- Does alcohol or drug use limit the family's ability to make decisions and solve daily problems?
- Does a parent's (or parents') alcohol or drug use limit his or her ability to meet the emotional and physical needs of the children?

Because alcohol and drug use affects so many families adversely, it is critical to address this extremely important issue and to customize treatment to specific family problems in this area (Kaufman & Kaufmann, 1992; O'Farrell, 1993; Stanton, Todd, & Associates, 1982).

Discussion and Conclusions

The Smith family provides an example of how to use the modified BASIC ID to assess the individual and family systems. The presenting problem often turns out to be more complex than it seems on the surface. Whether you work with individuals or families, the key is to gather data and information that will help you and the clients understand the problem while engaging them in such a way that they are intrigued and interested in solving the problem. From a systems perspective, we can draw the following five basic conclusions about the assessment process with individuals and families:

1. Individuals represent a system of variables or components (perception, cognition, emotion, and behavior) that interact in certain ways to keep the individual system stable.

2. A family, likewise, represents a system of variables or components (perception, cognition, emotion, and behavior) with corresponding ways of demonstrating these variables (roles, problem solving, boundaries, and communication).

3. Behavior and communication are the keys to understanding the other variables. Informal methods of assessment, such as those presented in this chapter, allow individuals and families to demonstrate their typical behavior and communication patterns.

4. Assessment, in the form of an activity, represents a means of providing data and information to the clients and counselor. A family activity also provides an opportunity for potential changes in individual or family systems.

5. Using a model such as the modified version of the BASIC ID provides a map that enables you to read the territory and make sense out of the client and family data. As you collect this data, you begin forming hypotheses about the client or family that lead to treatment goals and specific forms of intervention.

References

Abidin, R. R. (1990).*The parenting stress index* (3rd ed.). Charlottesville, VA: Pediatric Psychology Press.

Ackerman, N. W. (1958). *The psychodynamics of family life.* New York: Basic Books.

Bienvenu, M. S. (1970). Measurement of marital communication. *The Family Coordinator, 1,* 26–31.

Briggs, K. C., & Myers, I. B. (1977). *Myers-Briggs type indicator.* Palo Alto, CA: Consulting Psychologists Press.

Burns, R. C., & Kaufman, S. H. (1970). *Kinetic family drawings (KFD): An introduction to understanding children through kinetic drawings.* New York: Brunner/Mazel.

Caruso, K. R. (1988). *Projective storytelling cards.* Torrance, CA: Children's Professional Products.

Derogatis, L. R., & Melisaratos, N. (1979). The DSFI: A multidimensional measure of sexual functioning. *Journal of Sex and Marital Therapy, 5,* 244–281.

Ferreiro, B. W., Warren, N. J., & Konanc, J. T. (1986). ADAP: A divorce assessment proposal. *Family Relations, 35,* 439–449.

Fisher, B. (1981). *Rebuilding: When your relationship ends.* San Luis Obispo, CA: Impact.

Ganong, L. H., & Coleman, M. (1999). *Changing families, changing responsibilities: Family obligations following divorce and remarriage.* Mahwah, N.J.: Lawrence Erlbaum Associates.

Hammer, A. L. (1987). *MBTI relationship report: Couples counseling.* Palo Alto, CA: Consulting Psychologists Press.

Kaslow, E. W., & Friedman, I. (1977). Utilization of family photos in family therapy. *Journal of Marriage and Family Counseling, 3,* 19–25.

Kaufman, E., & Kaufmann, P. (1992). *Family therapy of drug and alcohol abuse* (2nd ed.). Boston: Allyn & Bacon.

L'Abate, L., & Bagarozzi, D. (1993). *Sourcebook of marriage and family evaluation.* New York: Brunner/Mazel.

Lazarus, R. S., & Folkman, S. (1984). *Stress, appraisal, and coping.* New York: Springer.

LoPiccolo, J., & Steger, J. C. (1974). The sexual interaction inventory: A new instrument for assessment of sexual dysfunction. *Archives of Sexual Behavior, 3,* 585–595.

Masters, W. H., & Johnson, V. E. (1970). *Human sexual inadequacy.* Boston: Little, Brown.

McCubbin, H. I., & Thompson, A. I. (Eds.). (1987). *Family assessment inventories for research and practice.* Madison: University of Wisconsin–Madison.

McGoldrick, M., Gerson, R., & Shellenberger, S. (1999). *Genograms in family assessment.* New York: Norton.

Moos, R. H., & Moos, B. S. (1981). *Family environment scale manual.* Palo Alto, CA: Consulting Psychologists Press.

Nash, L. (1984). *The parenting skills inventory.* La Canada, CA: Parenting Plus.

O'Farrell, T. J. (Ed.). (1993). *Treating alcohol problems: Marital and family interventions.* New York: Guilford.

Ogden, G., & Zevin, A. (1976). *When a family needs therapy.* Boston: Beacon Press.

Olson, D. D., & Straus, M. A. (1972). A diagnostic tool for marital and family therapy: The SIMFAM technique. *The Family Coordinator, 21,* 251–258.

Olson, D. H., Porter, J., & Bell, R. P. (1982). *FACES II: Family adaptability and cohesion evaluation scales.* St. Paul: Department of Family Social Science, University of Minnesota.

Ravich, R. A. (1969). The use of an interpersonal game-test in conjoint marital psychotherapy. *American Journal of Psychotherapy, 23,* 217–229.

Satir, V. (1983). *Conjoint family therapy* (rev. ed.). Palo Alto, CA: Science & Behavior Books.

Snyder, D. K. (1979). Multidimensional assessment of marital satisfaction. *Journal of Marriage and the Family, 41,* 813–823.

Spanier, G. B. (1976). Measuring dyadic adjustment: New scales for assessing the quality of marriage and similar dyads. *Journal of Marriage and the Family, 38,* 15-28.

Sporakowski, M. J. (1995). Assessment and diagnosis in marriage and family counseling, *Journal of Counseling and Development, 74,* 60–70.

Stahmann, R. F., & Hiebert, W. J. (2000). *Premarital and remarital counseling: The professional's handbook.* San Francisco: Jossey-Bass.

Stanton, D., Todd, T., & Associates. (1982). *The family therapy of drug abuse and addiction.* New York: Guilford.

Steinglass, P. (1979) The home observation method (HOAM): Real-time naturalistic observation of families in their homes. *Family Process, 18,* 337–354.

Touliatos, J., Perlmuter, B. F., & Straus, M. A. (Eds.). (1990). *Handbook of family measurement techniques.* Newbury Park, CA: Sage.

Chapter Six

Selecting Family Interventions

Richard E. Watts

Just as counseling approaches designed for individuals have their theory-specific techniques, family counseling approaches also have theory-specific interventions and strategies. Given the collaborative and eclectic climate of counseling at the beginning of the twenty-first century, we counselors tend not to be "theoretically loyal" when it comes to intervention selection; we select what appears most appropriate for each particular client or family. This seems appropriate given the four factors found in successful counseling outcomes: According to the research literature, 40% of clients' success is accounted for by the strengths they bring to counseling (attitudes, motivation, abilities, social support, etc.). The therapeutic alliance forged between the counselor and the client or clients accounts for another 30%. The hope and expectancy of success that is generated in counseling contributes another 15%, and 15% is attributable to the theory and techniques the counselor chooses (Hubble, Duncan, & Miller, 1999).

What should we make of the data indicating that theory or techniques account for only 15% of clients' progress? Does this mean techniques are not important? No, not at all. Effective use of counseling skills and techniques is necessary for building a strong counselor-client relationship, for engendering hope and expectancy of success, and for discovering and helping clients access their personal growth-producing abilities, assets, strengths, and supports.

In chapter 2, David Kaplan discussed four essential components of family balance (homeostasis): communication, problem solving, roles, and boundaries. Whatever presenting problem the family brings to counseling (for example, childhood depression, family developmental issues, stepfamily issues, or substance abuse problems), one or more these four components is typically an issue. Therefore, this chapter presents core family counseling strategies and interventions related to these four basic components. Note that there is nothing hard and fast about my placement of the interventions under specific components; I have placed each technique under the component for which it is most typically used. In reality, however, there is much overlap in the use of these techniques and, in practice, most of the interventions could be used for any of the four components.

You Know More Than You Might Think

You might be thinking, "I don't know very many techniques for working with families." As pointed out in chapter 3, however, if you know the basic skills of counseling, you know some of the core skills required for working with families. Several family counseling experts (Carlson, Sperry, & Lewis, 1997; Fenell & Weinhold, 1997; Sayger & Horne, 2000) have identified these basic counseling skills:
- building rapport
- gathering information/assessment
- structuring sessions
- reflecting content and feelings
- summarizing
- asking for clarification
- asking open-ended questions
- tracking patterns, themes, and sequences
- providing information
- practicing self-disclosure
- confronting

- interpreting behavior
- relabeling or creating perceptual alternatives
- addressing resistance
- facilitating behavior change
- closing and terminating therapy

Regardless of your specialty area, you are probably familiar with these skills. All forms of counseling require competent use of these basic skills, and family counseling is no exception.

Encouragement: A Foundation for Effective Counseling

Before addressing specific interventions, I would like to discuss briefly the process of encouragement in counseling. Encouragement, both as an attitude and as a set of skills, is salient for every family you work with. Your effectiveness in using both basic skills and interventions specific to family counseling increases tremendously when you take an encouragement focus in your counseling.

Alfred Adler and subsequent Adlerian counselors consider encouragement a crucial aspect of human growth and development, especially in counseling families. Stressing the importance of encouragement in therapy, Adler (1956, p. 342) states, "Altogether, in every step of the treatment, we must not deviate from the path of encouragement." Dreikurs (1967, p. 35) agrees: "What is most important in every treatment is encouragement." Moreover, Dreikurs claims that therapeutic success is largely dependent upon the therapist's "ability to provide encouragement" and failure generally is "due to the inability of the therapist to encourage" (pp. 12–13). The following are key encouragement skills (Watts & Pietrzak, 2000):
- demonstrating concern for families through active listening and empathy
- communicating respect for and confidence in families
- focusing on families' strengths, assets, and resources
- helping families generate perceptual alternatives for discouraging fictional beliefs

- focusing on effort and progress
- helping families see the humor in life experiences

Encouragement focuses on helping counselees become aware of their worth. By encouraging them, you help counselees recognize their own strengths and assets, so they become aware of the power they have to make decisions and choices. . . . Encouragement focuses on beliefs and self-perceptions. It searches intensely for assets and processes feedback so the client will become aware of her strengths. In a mistake-centered culture like ours, this approach violates norms by ignoring deficits and stressing assets. The counselor is concerned with changing the client's negative self-concept and anticipations. (Dinkmeyer, Dinkmeyer, & Sperry, 1987, p. 124)

Regardless of your theoretical orientation, you may find it useful to integrate the Adlerian perspective on encouragement into your approach to counseling. The assumptions, characteristics, and methods of encouragement help to create an optimistic, empowering, and growth-enhancing environment for clients; a place where they feel en-abled rather dis-abled (Watts & Pietrzak, 2000).

Family Interventions for Communication

Of the four basic components, I begin with interventions and strategies addressing family communication. Communication is the heart of a systemic perspective on family counseling. Honest and open communication is consistently listed as one of the foundational characteristics of healthy or well-functioning families. In fact, all the interventions presented in this chapter ultimately are communication techniques. Everything we say and do—or don't say and don't do—is communication; *we cannot not communicate.* Thus, no matter what concept we may discuss, we are ultimately addressing communication.

The following ideas and interventions are family counseling interventions whose purpose is to help families (especially the adults) improve their communication.

Communication Stances

Satir (1983) stated that communication problems occur when communication is *incongruent;* that is, when verbal communications (report) and nonverbal communications (command or metacommunication) do not agree. Examples of nonverbal communications include body position, breathing rhythm, facial expression, muscle tone, and vocal tone and intensity. In healthy communication, there is agreement, or *congruence,* between the report and metacommunication levels. Satir (1988) described four patterns of dysfunctional communication within families: placating, blaming, computing, and distracting. These patterns allow distressed people to avoid their true feelings.

Placating. Placating individuals "always talk in an ingratiating way, trying to please, apologizing, never disagreeing, no matter what." Placaters are "yes people." They talk as though they can do nothing for themselves; they must always get someone to approve of them. People with a placating style of communication do not consider themselves to be as important as others and try to get along by being agreeable (p. 85).

Blaming. Blaming individuals are fault finders. They act like dictators or bosses, as if they are superior, and seem to be saying, "If it weren't for you, everything would be all right." People with a blaming style of communication do not consider others to be very important. They are consistently critical of others and present themselves as always being right. Satir reports that the placater and the blamer are often interconnected (p. 87) in a relationship similar to that between narcissistic/borderline couples. One person strives to please (placater) and the other (blamer) is never satisfied. This cyclical "dance" is destructive for all family members, especially for the blamer and placater.

Computing. Computing persons are "very correct, very reasonable with no semblance of any feeling showing." They are "calm, cool, and collected." People with a computing style of communication do not consider either themselves or others to be very important. What is important is "the facts" of any given situation. They tend to be intellectual, rigid, and objective, and to deny their own experience (p. 89).

Distracting. Whatever distracting persons do or say is "irrelevant to what anyone is saying or doing." Their responses are never to the point. People with a distracting style of communication do not consider themselves, others, or the present situation to be important. The only thing they consider important is to avoid or abate the stress and tension in the family through distraction. They present themselves in an erratic and purposeless manner (p. 91).

As noted previously, healthy communicators do not take one of these communication stances. Rather, they communicate using congruent—open and honest—communication. The following are two of many ways to use communication stances in family counseling:

1. Explain the various stances to family members, guide the family in a discussion of the stances, and use the discussion as a bridge to teaching family members effective communication skills.

2. Applying a technique known as sculpting, you could ask each family member to take a physical pose indicative of a certain stance—placating, blaming, computing, distracting, or congruent—and to respond to each other from these stances. After the activity, ask each person to share how it felt to listen and respond to each other in these ways, leading into a discussion of congruent communication.

Basic Communication Skills

Families often develop difficulties because they lack basic communication skills; that is, family members have difficulty expressing their thoughts and feelings to each other in relationship-enhancing ways. They may avoid open and honest communication by not taking responsibility or ownership for their feelings and actions. It is therefore useful to model basic relationship-building skills in the normal course of working with a family. Some family members may also need explicit communication skills instruction, however. This is another area where you know more than you might think you do. The communication skills we teach families are very similar to the basic relationship-building attitudes and skills we all, regardless of our specialty area, use every day with clients. Using active, empathic listening and nonjudgmental acceptance; reflecting feeling and content; seeking clarification; providing feedback; asking open-ended questions; and offering affirmations are as important in building family relationships as they are in building strong counselor-client relationships. The following are communication skills we commonly teach to families.

Establishing Communication Rules

Sherman and Dinkmeyer (1987, p. 273) present some simple communication rules you can establish with a family early in the counseling process. These rules are crucial for improving communication and relationships.

- Speak only for yourself. Please don't suggest what somebody else believes or thinks.
- Speak directly to each other. Please do not try to speak to others through me or through another member of the family.
- Please do not scapegoat or blame.
- Please listen carefully and empathetically, trying to understand other people's thoughts, feelings, and experience.

Using "I" Messages

"I" messages are an effective way to help family members both express their own and hear others' feelings and thoughts. The focus of an "I" message is the expression of a feeling about someone else's behavior. The speaker addresses the actions of the other person, without attacking or belittling him or her. The process of constructing an "I" message has three steps:

    1. Describe the person's behavior without assigning blame:

"When I come home from work and the garage is messy .
. ."

2. Express how you feel about the behavior: "I feel angry and disrespected . . ."
3. Express the consequences of the behavior: "because I have to move all the stuff before I can park the car in the garage" (adapted from Friesen, 1985; Sherman, 1999).

Using Active, Reflective Listening

You can teach family members the same basic skills of active listening and reflection that you regularly use with your clients. You can explain that active listening involves listening with your entire person. As an active listener, you give the speaker your full attention, physically and emotionally, rather than focusing your energies on formulating a defense or making an excuse. Reflective listening involves attending to both the content of the person's message and the feelings underlying that message. In responding, you paraphrase the message the speaker has sent as well as the emotions embedded therein.

After explaining the active, reflective listening process to family members, demonstrate and model these skills. In addition, ask family members to practice these skills in a session so you can observe and provide feedback. It may be helpful to provide a list of "feeling words," because many clients have limited vocabularies to describe their emotions. Basic counseling texts contain many such lists (see, e.g., Carkhuff, 2000).

Using Phrases for Facilitating Communication

Allred (1976) provides some specific phrases and questions that clients can use to signal that they are open to what other family members have to say. Of course, ensuring that the client's tone of voice and nonverbal communication agree with the verbal message is always important. Allred's phrases and questions include the following:

- What is going on between us?
- What are you feeling now?
- What do you mean?
- Please, can you help me understand?
- Do I understand? This is what I think you mean. . . .
- Please go on. I am confused, will you help me understand what you mean?
- What do you think would happen if . . . ?
- Could this be what you're saying . . . ?
- What happened?
- How did you feel?
- Could you have said _____ differently?
- Could you have done _____ differently?
- What was he/she feeling when you said that?
- Could you have done anything that angered him/her?
- What is your responsibility in the relationship with him/her?
- What am I doing that angers you?
- What could I do differently to help you feel differently?
- What could I do differently to help you feel better toward me?

Processing Feedback

Sherman and Dinkmeyer (1987) recommend that when one family member provides feedback to another, the speaker should state what he or she is experiencing but make no demand for change. This strategy helps to create mutual awareness. Feedback may be either positive or negative, and the goal of giving feedback is to share what one is experiencing without criticizing or blaming. If given in a nondemanding and caring manner, feedback can make communication more open and honest. For example, a parent might state: "When you choose not to do your chores, I feel like you don't care about helping the family."

Sharing Affirmations

Most people find it much easier to criticize than to affirm. This is as true in families as in any other area of life. On the other hand, affirming one another can increase family members' self-esteem and sense of belonging. When family members look for assets, strengths, and positive changes to affirm, they communicate acceptance and concern. Teaching family members to use affirmations purposefully helps them demonstrate that they value each other and the family as a whole. Sherman and Dinkmeyer (1987) offer some examples of affirmations:

- "I like your bringing your friends home. I can see why you enjoy them."
- "I appreciate your taking time to bring your dirty clothes to the laundry room. I know I can count on you to help."
- "I enjoyed your concert. Your solo was very well done."
- "I'm very pleased with how you are responsible for yourself."

In teaching this skill to family members, ask them to look for opportunities to "surprise" each other with affirmations, rather than merely affirming or expressing gratitude after a specific event or situation. Encourage parents to try to catch their children behaving appropriately and affirm them, rather than noticing only inappropriate behavior. You can also coach family members to share two affirmations before making a negative statement.

Review of Videotapes

Videotaping sessions is useful in helping families improve their communication skills. Videotaping then playing back all or part of a session allows family members to critique their own patterns of communication, identify specific interactions that need improvement, and identify interactions that are indicative of growth and improvement. You can use the videotape to discuss general communication skills or as a feedback tool regarding a specific intervention you are using.

In summary, Sherman, (1999) describes some useful ways to help families adjust their patterns of family communication:

- Identify problematic communication patterns and messages.
- Teach and coach good communication skills such as active and reflective listening, speaking for oneself, and making "I" statements.
- Teach the use of facilitative statements to check out what another family member said or intended, rather than assuming or projecting one's own meaning onto that person.
- Challenge messages that have incongruent meanings such as "yes, but."
- Change the clients' accustomed seating arrangements.
- Select which family members come to a particular counseling session.
- Request that family members speak to each other rather than through you.
- Suggest specific content for a family discussion.
- Teach clients to inform others of their needs or feelings rather than expecting them to know without being told.

Family Interventions for Problem Solving

Adaptability and the ability to solve problems constructively is a consistently cited characteristic of healthy families. When faced with a challenge or crisis, well-functioning families pull together rather than fall apart. Well-functioning families form a support system for each family member and respond by developing adaptive and constructive coping strategies. We may think that only so-called dysfunctional families have problems resulting from adaptation and problem-solving issues. However, even well-functioning families may encounter situations that tax their ability to adapt and problem solve. The following are selected family counseling interventions whose purpose is to help families enhance their problem-solving abilities.

Challenging Maladaptive Assumptions

Family members often have both individual and systemic beliefs, values, and assumptions that hinder the family's ability to adapt and solve problems. For example, a family may have a rule that no one outside of the family is to know that one of the parents has a substance abuse problem. This rule, in conjunction with potential ramifications of the substance abuse, may substantially impede the growth and development of the family system and the individuals comprising it. The following suggestions for challenging unproductive assumptions are adapted from Sherman (1999):

- Interpret the maladaptive assumptions to clients in the form of a hypothesis or an educated guess. Doing so allows clients to perceive the assumptions in context and understand the meaning and purpose of their behavior. For example, "Could it be that you avoid dealing with the problem because you have no idea what you could do differently?"
- Help clients see the consequences of their beliefs: "Is it possible that when you insist on everything being perfect, you often wind up with 0% instead of 80% of what you want?"
- Use hyperbole or exaggeration: "Wow, if you are always so indecisive, how do you manage to get dressed in the morning?"
- Confront discrepancies between clients' beliefs and their behavior: "I'm confused. You say that family closeness is a vital family value, yet when you are angry and critical you chase your family members away."
- Introduce a new, positive behavior to expand the family's perspective: "Now that you are older, wiser, bigger, and soon to start high school, what are some new things you might want to attend to?" or "In spite all of the fighting, the members of this family are extremely caring and protective of each other."
- Reframe an existing negative idea by giving it a positive perspective: "So, when your husband makes you angry, it

mobilizes you to practice your assertive abilities instead of being passive." Reframing, often called relabeling or positive connotation, is commonly used across all four components of family balance.

- Challenge an old, maladaptive belief. For example, if a father believes in beating his children, you might ask, "You said you were a bit wild growing up. Did you stop misbehaving when *your* father beat *you* regularly?"
- Other traditional cognitive-behavioral therapy techniques, such as examining the evidence for a belief, doing a cost-benefit analysis, or engaging the family in a Socratic dialogue may also be used to challenge maladaptive individual and systemic beliefs of family members.

Parent Education

Family problems often arise because parents lack effective parenting skills. Such parents need information, direction, and support. Numerous educational materials are available for helping parents, either in individual sessions or parenting groups. These materials address such issues as parenting children at various ages and the process of blending families after divorce and remarriage (see, e.g., Albert & Einstein, 1986; Bettner & Lew, 1996; Dinkmeyer & McKay, 1990, 1996; Dinkmeyer, McKay, & Dinkmeyer, 1997; Dinkmeyer, McKay, & McKay, 1987; Dinkmeyer, McKay, Dinkmeyer, Dinkmeyer, & McKay, 1997; Lew & Bettner, 1996; Lott & Nelsen, 1995; Nelsen, 1987; Nelsen, Erwin, & Delzer, 1993; Nelsen, Erwin, & Duffy, 1995; Nelsen, Intner, & Lott, 1995; Nelsen & Lott, 1994; Popkin, 1990, 1993; Popkin, Gard, & Montgomery, 1996). Although going into detail about specific parent education interventions is beyond the scope of this chapter, Lew (1999) notes that many parent education programs cover the following key concepts:

- democratic, as opposed to autocratic or permissive, parenting styles
- giving encouragement as opposed to using rewards and evaluative praise

- understanding the purpose and goals of children's misbehavior—e.g., attention, control, revenge, or demonstrating inadequacy—and the difference between behavior resulting from the child's age or developmental level and behavior resulting from a misguided goal
- using logical and natural consequences instead of punishment in disciplining children
- importance of providing structure and limits
- communication skills training
- family council meetings

The Family Council Meeting

A family council meeting is a useful problem-solving strategy whether presented in combination with comprehensive parent education or on its own. The goals of conducting a family council meeting are these (Sherman & Fredman, 1986, p. 231):

1. To allow free communication among family members
2. To avoid emotional showdowns and violence in the family
3. To teach children and parents democratic means of settling differences
4. To operate an orderly and peaceful home

When introducing the family council meeting, it is important to point out that the process will seem difficult to implement at first because it is different from the family's usual manner of discussing issues and solving problems. Council meetings may also seem unproductive initially, until all family members learn how to use them as an effective tool for expressing concerns. On the other hand, the benefit is that it will provide the family with new problem-solving options. The following guidelines for holding a family council are adapted from Sherman and Fredman (1986, pp. 153–154):

1. Establish a fixed, regular time and place for the meeting to prevent interference or interruptions.
2. The council includes the entire family, but no one is forced to attend. However, an absentee must agree to abide by

any decisions that are made. Every effort should be made to have everyone present at every meeting.

3. Any decisions made during the meeting cannot be unilaterally broken or ignored, although they may be renegotiated at a subsequent meeting.

4. Everyone may propose agenda items. Keeping a sign-up sheet in a high-traffic place such as the refrigerator door allows agenda items to be written down immediately when they come to mind. Anything that concerns the family as a unit may be added to the agenda.

5. Parents do not ask children to make developmentally inappropriate choices during family council meetings. For example, parents would not invite a six-year-old to help decide whether they should invest in real estate or a money market account or whether the child should go to school.

6. The role of chairperson of the meeting is rotated among the family members who are mature enough to take this role. The family follows the usual rules for conducting any democratic meeting, but it is preferable to achieve a unanimous, negotiated consensus rather than a majority vote.

7. All family members must participate in carrying out the decisions made, both in spirit and word. Hairsplitting is not acceptable.

8. All family members need to feel that they have a genuine voice and that what they express will be heard, accepted, and seriously considered. A certain degree of good humor and ability to laugh at human foibles rather than at people is helpful.

9. Family council meetings are held to resolve problems, not attack people.

Because it takes learning and practice to use the family council strategy effectively, ask family members to discuss their weekly council meeting at each counseling session. The information they share provides useful issues to work on during the session. In addition, you can reinforce the rules of the family council, help families to work out implementation problems, and encourage them to continue holding meetings.

Conflict Management

Teaching families how to manage conflict is an important strategy. An in-depth discussion of conflict management training with families is not possible here, but the following guidelines, adapted from Allred (1976), Friesen (1985), and Sherman and Dinkmeyer (1987), provide a summary of key concepts. Use these guidelines as a starting point for helping families learn to manage conflict.

- Learn to recognize when a problem exists and deal with it quickly. Putting off proper conflict management often results in bitterness and resentment. One way or another, the conflict eventually will be expressed, either honestly and openly or dishonestly and indirectly.
- Identify the problem that exists. Identifying and defining the problem is crucial to setting goals and creating a plan of action.
- Stick to discussing and solving the problem at hand. Keep the focus on that one issue rather than bringing in others as a means to defend or attack each other.
- Use "I" messages to express your feelings rather than "you" messages that attack others. Expressing one's emotions, if done appropriately, is beneficial in managing conflict; unrestrained venting of anger is destructive.
- Separate the problem from the people involved. Keep the focus on behavior rather than attacking the character or personalities of other family members.
- Avoid retaliating against each other. Show mutual respect by neither fighting nor giving in. Managing conflict is based on understanding and respecting each person's point of view. Avoid responding to legitimate concerns with negative and attacking phrases such as, "Well, you're just as bad, look what you did when. . . ." "How can you be so selfish?" or

"That's a really dumb way of thinking." Respond graciously to appropriately expressed negative feedback.
- Explore the available alternatives in order to find a good solution to the conflict.
- Look for areas of agreement. Instead of looking to another member of the family to change, concentrate on what you are willing to do. Make no demands that others change. Agree to cooperate rather than bicker.
- Participate mutually and actively in selecting from among available alternatives. Managing conflict is not a contest to be won or lost. The goal should be to find a mutually acceptable solution to the problem at hand.
- Secure agreement on a solution and commit to making the selected alternative work for all family members.
- Communicate with other people in an open, spontaneous manner.

Strategic Directives

Directives are tasks you assign to family members in order to interrupt maladaptive behavior patterns. According to Haley (1976), directives are more about process than outcome. In other words, they are used more to increase motivation for change than to resolve a specific problem.

There are several guidelines to consider in designing directives:
- Whatever the task, it should be simple enough that family members can do it (unless you are using paradox and have a reason for wanting them to fail).
- The task should be appropriate to the family's financial situation and time constraints.
- Directives must be designed and delivered in ways that take into consideration the culture of the family and the personalities of individual family members.
- Although you are giving the family a task to do, completing the task may be less beneficial for the family than the process

of negotiating how to accomplish it. From this viewpoint, the directive becomes something for the family to talk about instead of their problems or their past. It also provides an issue for counselor-family discussion.

- If your goal in assigning a directive is to intensify your relationship with the family, give the family a relatively simple task. If your primary goal is to bring about organizational change, assign a task that requires more thought.

According to Haley (1976) and Keim (2000), directives may be straightforward or indirect. Straightforward directives are ones in which you act like a coach, asking clients to take specific actions and behave in a particular manner. Your influence is overt and clearly identifiable to the clients. It is clear that you expect the clients to follow your directive. Keim (2000) offers an example of a straightforward directive: A female counselor directs a male client to apologize to his wife in order to repair the marital relationship. Later, when the counselor asks the man why he apologized, the client says that the primary reason is that he realized he was wrong but adds that the counselor's suggestion that doing so would help his marriage was influential. The counselor's influence was overt and the goal of the directive was clear to the client.

Indirect directives are instances where you influence clients to take action but do not openly or directly ask them to do so. In this case, your influence is covert and not clearly identifiable, and your goal is not immediately clear to the family. Indirect directives do not put as much pressure on clients to follow through. They are useful when you want clients to consider an idea without being overly concerned that you will respond negatively if they reject it. Haley (1976) offers an example of an indirect directive: An overprotective mother is denying her child the opportunity to make choices or experience the consequences of his actions. The goal of counseling is to help Mom disengage from her son. Anticipating that she would not respond positively to a straightforward directive to stop overprotecting her son, the counselor asks her to spend the next week hovering over her child. To follow the directive would require Mom to exhibit even more overprotective behavior than she already has been. The counselor's goal is that the mother will refuse to do more and state that the child should do more for himself.

Be aware that both directives and the paradoxical procedures discussed in the next section of this chapter are powerful and often intrusive interventions. The Ethical Code for the International Association of Marriage and Family Counselors clearly addresses this matter: "Due to the risk involved, members should not use intrusive interventions without a sound theoretical rationale and having thoroughly thought through the potential ramifications to the family and its members" (International Association of Marriage and Family Counselors Ethics Committee, 1993, p. 74). Thus, directives and paradoxical procedures must be used judiciously and carefully.

Paradoxical Interventions

According to Sayger and Horne (2000), the purpose of paradoxical interventions is to alter the current pattern of interaction in the family, to "block dysfunctional sequences by using indirect and seemingly illogical means" (p. 55). Friesen (1985) suggests that paradoxical interventions not be used as primary interventions for change, but rather "as a fallback when other methods have failed" (p. 106). Although paradoxical techniques can be powerful, they "are not as commonly used as many other types of interventions" (Keim, 2000, p.189), and many counselors have either abandoned paradoxical strategies entirely or "present them humorously and are honest about their intent" (Nichols & Schwartz, 2001, p. 361). Following are brief descriptions of three prominent paradoxical strategies:

Prescribing the symptom. Ask the clients to continue or expand the problem or symptom that brought the family to counseling. There are two ways to present this strategy. If you offer a *compliance-based prescription,* you want the family to comply and, in so doing, be forced to respond differently to the problem. For example, if the presenting problem is that one of the children is sad all the time, you might tell the child to try to feel depressed several times a day and ask the family to encourage the child to be sad. The goal is that the family will stop their ineffective efforts to cheer up the child and the child won't feel guilty for not being happy. If you offer a *defiance-based prescription,* you hope the clients will rebel against it. In the example of the sad child, you might ask the child to continue being sad because it helps his brother (with whom the sad child is competitive) feel superior. Because you want the child to rebel against the prescription, you would present it in such a way as to encourage the child's defiance (Nichols & Schwartz, 2001, p. 360).

Restraining progress. In this defiance-based intervention, you caution the family about change and ask them not to change, to progress very slowly, or to worry about relapsing when improvement occurs. If the intervention is successful, the family responds by rebelling against the request and changing in ways that solve the presenting problem (Keim, 2000).

Pretending. When using this compliance-based intervention, you ask the identified patient (usually a child) to playfully act as if, or pretend, that he or she has symptoms. Other family members are instructed to pretend to help the "symptomatic" family member. The goal of pretending is that clients will demonstrate some control over behavior that they have labeled as uncontrollable (Madanes, 1981). For example, Madanes asked a child who complained of recurring stomachaches to pretend to have the problem. The child's grandmother was directed to pretend she believed the child and to do what she would normally do when the child had stomachache. She held the child, prayed the rosary, and put drops of oil in his nose. Madanes prescribed this pretense for one week, and by the end of the week, the stomachaches no longer occurred. The prescription enabled the child to receive the affection and attention he desired from his grandmother, which she enjoyed providing, but without the symptom (Thomas, 1992).

Keim (2000, p.190) provides the following wise counsel regarding the use of paradox in counseling:

> Paradoxical interventions should be used only by experienced [counselors] or by those under direct supervision of an experienced clinician. Paradox must not

be used with people who have difficulties understanding motivations of others or who have thought disturbances. It should be employed only in the context of a strong therapeutic relationship in which the benevolent intentions of the therapist are beyond question.

Solution-Focused Questions

Solution-focused counselors seek to change clients' behaviors and attitudes from a problem-and-failure focus to a focus on solutions and successes. In the process the clients discover and develop latent assets, resources, and strengths that they may have overlooked when they were focusing on problems and limitations. Here are brief explanations of some interventions or questions taken from selected solution-focused sources (Cade & O'Hanlon, 1993; DeJong & Berg, 1998; de Shazer, 1985, 1991; Littrell, 1998; Metcalf, 1995; Murphy, 1997; O'Hanlon & Weiner-Davis, 1989; Quick, 1996; Sklare, 1997; Walter & Peller, 1992).

Pre-session change question. Between the time they make an initial appointment and their arrival at the counseling session, the family often engages in a flurry of activity. To focus the family on the changes they have already made, you could ask, "Between the time you called to make the appointment and your arrival here today, have you made any movement toward a solution to your problem?" If movement has occurred, follow up by asking, "What do you need to do to keep this going?"

Miracle question. Ask the client to fantasize about a solution to the problem: "Suppose tonight while you are asleep a miracle happens and the problem is solved. When you awake in the morning, what will be different in your life that will let you know the miracle occurred and the problem is solved?" You can follow up with the *first sign question:* "What do you need to do to start implementing some of this miracle, not all but some of it?"

Exception-finding questions. Almost every problem has a solution. Exception-finding questions help identify times when the solution is occurring. There are at least two ways to ask such questions: (1) "Are there times when the problem does not occur? How are things different at those times?" and (2) "Are there times, even now, when some of the solution, even a small part, is already occurring?" Only a small piece of the solution is needed. Take this small piece and expand, expand, expand.

Scaling questions. Solution-focused counselors use scaling questions in numerous ways. These questions are very adaptable and useful for obtaining various types of information, especially assessment and progress self-evaluations. Some examples include these:

- "How committed are you to solving this problem? If I were to talk to _____, how would he/she answer?"
- "What will this person need to see you do in order to recognize that you have moved up the scale [e.g., from a 3 to a 4]?"
- "How motivated are you to change?"
- "How hopeful are you that you can change?"
- "How ready are you to stop coming to counseling sessions?"

Coping questions. In some chronic situations (e.g., terminal illness, permanent disability, HIV/AIDS), no resolution is possible. In these cases, asking coping questions may help clients become aware of strengths and abilities that can help them cope with the difficult situations. For example, "How do you cope with . . . ?" This question can be used to explore simple coping abilities (e.g., "How were you able to get out of bed?") and more advanced ones (e.g., "How were you able to get to the counseling appointment?").

Narrative Therapy Procedures

Narrative therapists seek to help clients rewrite the stories of their lives, to liberate themselves from their problem-saturated narratives and create new stories about themselves that re-envision their pasts, presents, and futures. The following brief explanations of narrative therapy interventions useful with families and individuals are taken from numerous sources (Eron & Lund, 1996; Freedman & Combs, 1996; Morgan, 2000; White & Epston, 1990; Zimmerman &

Dickerson, 1996).

Externalization. Narrative therapy emphasizes that people are not the problem; the problem is the problem. Externalizing questions are used to separate the problem from the people affected by it. Such questions begin the deconstruction of the "problem-saturated" narrative, in which clients cannot see themselves or their lives apart from the problem, by objectifying the problem as external to the people involved: "What does Depression whisper in your ear?" "What does Blame have you doing to each other?" "What conclusions about your relationship have you drawn because of [the externalized problem's] influence?"

Looking for unique outcomes. Similar to "exception-finding questions" used in solution-focused counseling, unique outcome questions seek to identify times when clients are able to avoid the effects of the problem, and ask them to elaborate on how they are able to do so. Within the clients' account of a unique outcome lies the text whereby alternative narratives or stories can be developed. Some examples of unique outcome questions include, "Can you remember a time when [the externalized problem] tried to take you over, but you didn't let it? What was that like for you? How did you do it?" Similar to the way you would use the miracle question in solution-focused counseling, you can also phrase unique outcomes in future tense: "What will be different when you are standing up to [the externalized problem]?"

Preference questions. Preference questions seek to make sure that the client indeed preferred the unique outcome over his or her typical experience: "Was the way you handled the situation better or worse?" "Was this more or less like the way you want things to be?" "Was that a positive development or a negative one?"

Landscape of action questions. When you discover an event, thought, action, belief, or the like that does not fit with the client's dominant story, asking landscape of action questions can help you explore the unique outcome in detail. These questions often begin with *who, what, where,* or *when* to help you explore the particular details of the unique outcome: "Where were you when this happened?" "When did it happen?" "How long did it last? "What happened just before and after?" "How did you prepare yourself?" "Did you tell anyone about it? If so, what did he/she say?" "Have you done this before?" "What steps led up to this?"

Landscape of consciousness questions. These questions invite a client to reflect on the meaning of the event or unique outcome he or she has described. Together you and the client explore the meaning of the unique outcome in terms of the person's desires, intentions, preferences, beliefs, hopes, personal qualities, values, strengths, commitments, plans, characteristics, abilities, and purposes. Some examples include, "What do you think that says about the hopes you have for your relationship with your daughter?" "What personal values does the choice you made demonstrate?" "How would you describe your relationship with your wife at the time _____ happened?" "What did it take in order to do that at this point in your life?" "When you took this step what were you intending for your life?" "What does it say about you as a person that you would do this?" "Can you help me understand more about what that says you believe in or value?" "What do you think that says about your [abilities/skills/knowledge]?"

Circulation questions (thickening the alternative story). When you discover a unique outcome, you can develop it further via landscape of action questions. In discussing the unique outcomes, you invite clients to explore the meanings they give to these events, then to link these meanings into an *alternative* or *unique outcome story*. Circulation questions are helpful for exploring and describing the history of the alternative story by asking how the clients would "circulate" the new story among their friends and relatives. Some examples include, "Now that you have reached this point in your life, who else should know about it?" "Who would be least surprised to hear you say this?" "I guess there are a number of people who have outdated views of who you are as a person. What ideas do you have about updating these views?" "If I wanted to discover some more about this skill of yours, who (other than you) would be able to tell me about it?" "What do you predict will happen in the coming [months/years]?"

Consulting your consultants. This practice involves interviewing clients and eliciting and documenting their "alternative knowledge."

As an alternative model for closure, during the last session you can ask the clients, "If other people seek counseling for the same reasons you did, may I share with them the important discoveries you have made?" In this "consulting" process you (1) consult the clients as authorities on their own lives, (2) deem their pre-existing and newly acquired knowledge and abilities effective and worthy of respect, and (3) consider clients' ideas significant enough to be documented and circulated to others.

The following brief case example may be helpful in understanding how the narrative procedures fit together. Mary and Bill came to me for counseling, stating that "all we do is fight and blame each other for our problems." We agreed to explore the problem and then externalized it. They chose to name it "Blaming," and we explored what Blaming was doing to their relationship. We then looked for unique outcomes—times when they were able to keep Blaming from taking over their relationship—and discussed how things were different then. We also discussed how things would be different for them when they were consistently able to stand up to Blaming. They agreed that their preferred relationship would be one where they did not let Blaming take control. Next, we explored in detail, via landscape of action questions, those times when unique outcomes occurred and how they occurred. This led us to reflect on, via landscape of consciousness questions, the unique meanings that each partner gave the outcomes. The couple began to see that there were alternative perspectives and choices to the Blaming narrative that so dominated their relationship. We then began to create an alternative story of their relationship and, using circulation questions, discussed to whom they might want to circulate this new story, how these people would see the alternative story played out in the couple's relationship, and what the others' reactions might be. Through these discussions we strengthened the couple's alternative story and their concomitant choices and behaviors. Finally, as we neared the end of our sessions, I asked Mary and Bill if I could share with future clients the important discoveries they had made. As the experts of their lives, they felt good about recalling the knowledge and abilities they brought to bear in creating a new relationship story and agreed to allow me to use their "counseling story" to help others.

Family Interventions for Boundaries

According to Minuchin (1974), boundaries within a family are the means by which members perceive their function within the system. A crucial task of the marital subsystem is the development of boundaries that allow the couple to satisfy their psychological needs and protect them from the intrusion of in-laws, children, and others. The clear functioning of the marital subsystem boundaries is crucial for the healthy functioning of the entire family. Boundaries between other subsystems within the family system are equally necessary. Parents must be in charge and lead the family as a united coalition. Parents must establish clear generational divisions and neither over-control their children nor relinquish their adult responsibilities as parents. In families with well-functioning boundaries, parents avoid interfering in sibling conflicts, children do not take on parental or spousal responsibilities, and extended family members (e.g., in-laws) are not involved in family conflicts.

Minuchin (1974) identified three basic types of boundary functioning: clear, enmeshed, and disengaged. Well-functioning families have clear boundaries. *Clear boundaries* are flexible and allow family members to experience both personal autonomy and belongingness and togetherness. There is a balance between closeness and separateness. With *enmeshment,* family members tend to become overdependent or overinvolved in each other's lives, and personal autonomy is sacrificed as the individuality of members is lost. The boundaries between subsystems become so blurred that there are no clear lines of responsibility and authority. Consequently, members do not properly and consistently understand their place and function in the family system. At the other end of the boundary continuum is *disengagement,* where the family has extremely rigid boundary functioning with a resultant lack of closeness. Thus, family members are isolated and appear unrelated. Although personal autonomy is high, family members receive little nurturing, support, and guidance.

Consequently, individuals from disengaged families often have difficulty forming significant relationships outside the family because they have not experienced the formation of significant relationships within the family. All families have some degree of enmeshment or disengagement, and these relational patterns do not necessarily imply dysfunction. When enmeshed or disengaged boundary functioning is continual or habitual, however, they become problematic. The following selected family counseling interventions can help families improve their boundary functioning.

Enactment

The enactment process enables you to observe and influence dysfunctional family interaction patterns. An enactment may occur as you observe typical family interaction patterns in a session or may be prompted by questions you ask. According to Minuchin and Fishman (1981), the enactment process involves three steps, or *movements:*

1. Observe spontaneous family transactions during a session and decide which maladaptive patterns to focus on.
2. Next ask the family to do what they would normally do to try to correct the problem. This leads the family to play out the maladaptive interactions more specifically as you observe. During the process you question, challenge, and nudge the family to "test the limits" of their functioning.
3. Then suggest alternative transactions (i.e., doing something different) and have the family act them out.

Enactments challenge the family's experience of reality. Colapinto (2000) notes that the enactment process typically challenges family members' explanations for their own and others' behavior, their perspectives, their role and function in the family, their view of problems, and their role in a solution.

An enactment may be dramatized or as simple as telling an underinvolved parent, "Talk to your son about your concerns; I don't know that he understands your position," while keeping the overinvolved parent out of the interaction (Colapinto, 2000, p. 157). The real power of enactment resides not in the emotional content of the situation but rather in the very fact that family members are being directed to behave differently (i.e., change their function) in relation to each other. By prescribing and monitoring family transactions, you assume control of a crucial area—the rules that regulate who should interact with whom, about what, when, and for how long (Colapinto, 2000, p. 157).

Boundary Making

Colapinto (2000) describes boundary making as a special case of enactment in which you discover and engage areas of interaction that are open to certain members but closed to others. Several techniques address this area:

Cognitive constructs. Cognitive constructs are phrases or directions that make clear the boundary problem and indicate how to create a new boundary. For example, when a family member tends to speak for other members, you might comment, "You're helpful, aren't you? You take his memory" (Minuchin & Fishman, 1981, p. 147). Minuchin and Fishman suggest that counselors invent their own boundary-making phrases or metaphors and present a number of examples:
- You take his voice.
- If she answers for you, you don't have to talk.
- You are the ventriloquist and she is the puppet.
- If your father does things for you, you will always have ten thumbs.

Boundary intrusion: Early in the counseling process, you can introduce a rule about boundary intrusion: "In this room, I have only one rule. It is a small rule, but apparently a very difficult one for this family to follow. It is that no person should talk for another person or tell another person how he or she feels or thinks. People should tell their own story and own their own memories" (Minuchin & Fishman, 1981, 149). You can use variations of this rule to enforce boundaries and firmly remind family members that intrusion into other members' psychological space is "disobeying the rule." Minuchin and Fishman note that many overt and covert forms of boundary encroachment can be blocked by this method.

Detourers, allies, and judges. Sometimes you may see boundary issues where a problematic relationship between two people is maintained by a third person who serves as "detourer, ally, or judge" (Minuchin & Fishman, 1981). The involvement of the third party prevents the two family members in conflict from addressing their problem. In such a case, you have several options: (1) You can arrange to see the original two family members without the third person in order to enable them to work on their issues without interruption; (2) you can direct the third person not to interrupt (using "the rule") or ask him or her to leave the room; (3) you can invite the third person to join you in observation of the dyad, thereby separating the third person from the two in conflict (Friesen, 1985).

Concrete spatial maneuvers. Minuchin and Fishman (1981) suggest the use of concrete spatial maneuvers to change boundary functioning. The use of space is indicative of psychological events or emotional transactions among people. By repositioning family members and yourself in a session, you can change the spatial relationship between family members or between yourself and the family. This technique has the advantage of being clear, intense, and nonverbal. Two examples from Minuchin and Fishman follow:

- **Moving family members to change boundaries.** If a husband and wife sit separated by a child, you might ask the child to exchange seats with a parent so the parents can talk directly instead of across the child. If you make the directive clear and explain the rationale, family members usually will comply. If necessary, you could move to lessen the distance between yourself and the person from whom you request the change, in order to make resistance more difficult (Minuchin & Fishman, 1981, p. 150).

- **Using yourself as a spatial boundary maker.** Minuchin and Fishman (1981) suggest the strategy of using your "arms or body to interrupt eye contact in an overinvolved dyad," thus acting as a spatial boundary maker. They continue, "This maneuver can be accompanied by a change in the position of chairs so as to handicap the sending of signals, and it may be further reinforced by a statement like, "You are talking to your brother; you don't need your father's help," or, "Since you know this event better because you were there, consult your memory instead of using your mother's" (p. 150).

Family Interventions for Roles

The term *role* refers to the socially expected behavior for a person occupying a certain place in a particular family system. Both formal and informal roles exist in all families. Formal and traditional roles are assigned, and certain role-congruent behaviors are expected in conjunction with them. Examples of such roles are parents as caretakers or breadwinners and children as students or helpers. Norm expectations provide guidelines for thinking, feeling, and behaving in ways that are acceptable for a particular role. Informal roles, on the other hand, are assigned to members in order to meet the family's social and emotional needs.

Family roles are not necessarily dysfunctional. In fact, the performance of roles is a significant indicator of how well a family is functioning. The chief criterion in distinguishing between adaptive versus maladaptive role functioning is the flexibility and creativity of the family. In well-functioning families, roles are flexible and easily interchanged, and family stressors are handled creatively. Many families presenting for counseling, in contrast, have rigid and inflexible roles, and family stressors are handled by rigid, inflexible, and cyclical patterns of behavior. For example, when a family loses a parent due to death or divorce, the family roles must be adjusted to compensate. If the family roles are rigid and inflexible, the necessary adjustments to this developmental crisis are not typically forthcoming, and the family may develop more severe problems. Another reason that family members take on roles in the family is to help them feel significant, but this may also contribute to the presenting problem. In the preceding example, one of the older children may begin taking on more responsibilities in the home to help the family adjust. If the situation is not carefully monitored by the remaining adult in the family, the child may take on far too much responsibility and assume the role of surrogate spouse or parent.

Troubled families consistently have members occupying maladaptive roles. Children may be assigned or choose to take on roles inappropriate to their age, sex, or personality characteristics. A child may take on a parenting role, a sexual role, or the role of the "family pet" (the child everyone takes care of and who has no responsibilities). Often a family member will be assigned the role of scapegoat, or identified patient. The person in this role is blamed for all the family's problems and is typically the reason the family seeks counseling; that is, the person the family wants "fixed." Children assigned to the scapegoat/identified patient role often recognize that they are supposed to be a problem child and act on this expectation, seeking to use it to their best advantage.

In addressing family roles during counseling, it is important to give due consideration to the influence of cultural and ethnic norms. Knowledge of diverse family customs, traditions, and values—and what these variables mean to a particular family—is crucial both for understanding family role functioning and for choosing appropriate interventions.

Interventions addressing communication, problem solving, and boundary functioning are often used to address role functioning as well. For example, Satir's communication stances have been adapted to address the roles family members take in dysfunctional families, especially ones with substance abuse issues (Friel & Friel, 1988). The family counseling interventions may be useful in enhancing family members' understanding of their roles and role functioning.

Family Photographs

Sharing family photographs in a counseling session can be uplifting as the pictures recall happier times for the family. They can also provide a springboard for discussing communication patterns, structure and boundaries, or roles within the family. Sherman and Fredman (1986) ask each family member to bring to the session a specific number of family photographs (perhaps six) that say something significant about family relationships, without giving any further instructions. During the session (or sessions if desired), they impose a time structure so that every family member gets an opportunity to share his or her pictures. Each member of the family in turn presents the chosen photographs and shares why they are significant. In guiding a discussion of the contents of each photograph, the counselor can ask process questions pertaining to communication patterns, family structure, and family members' roles. This technique can be a useful way to engage clients who may be reluctant to begin work in counseling.

Affirming Existing Roles

Discovering and affirming the strengths and abilities that families possess is crucial in creating a positive counseling environment. As noted earlier, roles are not necessarily problematic; certain roles may be functional and appropriate, even in families receiving counseling. It is important to affirm and strengthen existing roles that function well. For example, you might comment, "Mom and Dad, I appreciate the way you strive to be kind, fair, and firm when you discipline your children."

Role-Change Directives

Role-change directives assign or prescribe new positions or roles in the family in a direct manner. For example, "Jane [the over-responsible critic], can you this week accept being in charge of planning fun for the family? And Joe [the irresponsible fun lover], could you accept being in charge of the work assignments this week?" (Sherman, 1999, p. 123).

Reframing Existing Roles

Reframing is used with all four components of family balance. In reframing existing role behavior, your goal is to help family members see the potentially positive aspects of role behavior they perceive as negative. For example, imagine that a couple complains that their daughter continually "butts into" their conversations. In exploring this issue, you discover that the parents often have hostile conversations and that the child typically intrudes when she begins to sense tension in the relationship. You might clarify, "It seems to me that Sherry is trying to be a peacemaker when battles break out between you two." After reframing the role more positively, you might work to help families improve their communication, problem solving, and boundaries.

Prescribing Role Reversals

There are at least two ways to use role reversals with families:
- Similar to the way you would use the reversal technique in Gestalt therapy, you can ask each family member to assume a role opposite to his or her typical one. This provides members with numerous new possibilities for behaving. For example, you might ask the peacemaker to become more assertive and the dominating personality to be more accommodating. Encourage family members to act as if they were that kind of person and have some fun exploring their new role (Sherman & Dinkmeyer, 1987).
- Ask family members to role-play being one another in a session, taking on another member's part. This experience can help clients to see how other family members perceive them and to understand each other better. Sherman (1999) also suggests that role reversals be done outside of sessions as an experiment. For example, "the overadequate parent

[mother] can be sent on 'vacation,' and the father and children, who are constantly berated for their lack of performance, can take charge of the household in mother's absence" (p. 123).

Blocking Maladaptive Role Behavior

This intervention is similar to aspects of boundary making. Here you interrupt, or "block," inappropriate roles or role behavior by prescribing or coaching new patterns of behaving. For example, you might say to a parent, "Rather than criticizing again, could you put your pointed finger behind your back and try something new?" or "Could you identify something that your son did right" (Sherman, 1999, p. 123).

Conclusion

Issues of communication, problem solving, boundaries, and roles regularly arise in counseling families. In this chapter I have presented several techniques related specifically to issues around these basic components of family balance. These are only a few of the many strategies and interventions used in family counseling, so I provide the following reading list to suggest other resources you may find useful in expanding your knowledge base.

Brock, G. W. (1992). *Procedures in marriage and family therapy* (2nd ed.). Boston: Allyn & Bacon.

Haley, J., & Hoffman, L. (1967). *Techniques of family therapy: Five leading therapists reveal their working styles, strategies, and approaches.* New York: Basic Books.

Heitler, S. M. (1990). *From conflict to resolution: Skills and strategies for individual, couple, and family therapy.* New York: Norton.

Hinkle, J. S., & Wells, M. E. (1995). *Family counseling in the schools: Effective strategies and interventions for counselors, psychologists, and therapists.* Greensboro, NC: ERIC/CASS.

Minuchin, S., & Fishman, H. C. (1981). *Family therapy techniques.* Cambridge, MA: Harvard University Press.

Nelson, T. S., & Trepper, T. S. (Eds.). (1993). *101 interventions in family therapy.* New York: Haworth.

Nelson, T. S., & Trepper, T. S. (Eds.). (1998). *101 more interventions in family therapy.* New York: Haworth.

Patterson, J., Williams, L., Grauf-Grounds, C., & Chamow, L. (1998). *Essential skills in family therapy: From the first interview to termination.* New York: Guilford.

Sherman, R., & Fredman, N. (1986). *Handbook of structured techniques in marriage and family therapy.* New York: Brunner/ Mazel.

Sherman, R., Oresky, P., & Rountree, Y. (1991). *Solving problems in couples and family therapy: Techniques and tactics.* New York: Brunner/Mazel.

Watts, R. E. (Ed.). (2000–2002). *Techniques in marriage and family counseling* (Vols. 1 & 2) Alexandria, VA: American Counseling Association.

References

Adler, A. (1956). *The individual psychology of Alfred Adler: A systematic presentation in selections from his writings.* H. L. Ansbacher & R. R. Ansbacher (Eds.). New York: Harper Torchbooks.

Albert, L., & Einstein, E. (1986). *Strengthening your stepfamily.* Circle Pines, MN: American Guidance Service.

Allred, G. H. (1976). *How to strengthen your marriage and family.* Provo, UT: Brigham Young University Press.

Bettner, B. L., & Lew, A. (1996). *Raising kids who can.* Newton Centre, MA: Connexions Press.

Cade, B., & O'Hanlon, W. H. (1993). *A brief guide to brief therapy.* New York: Norton.

Carkhuff, R. R. (2000). *The art of helping* (8th ed.). Amherst, MA: Human Resource Development Press.

Carlson, J., Sperry, L., & Lewis, J. A. (1997). *Family therapy: Ensuring treatment efficacy.* Pacific Grove, CA: Brooks/Cole.

Colapinto, J. (2000). Structural family therapy. In A. Horne (Ed.), *Family counseling and therapy* (3rd ed., pp. 140–169). Itasca, IL: Peacock.

DeJong, P., & Berg, I. K. (1998). *Interviewing for solutions.* Pacific Grove, CA: Brooks/Cole.

de Shazer, S. (1985). *Keys to solution in brief therapy.* New York: Norton.

de Shazer, S. (1991). *Putting differences to work.* New York: Norton.

Dinkmeyer, D. C., Dinkmeyer, D. C. Jr., & Sperry, L. (1987). *Adlerian counseling and psychotherapy* (2nd ed.). Columbus, OH: Merrill.

Dinkmeyer, D. C., & McKay, G. (1990). *Systematic training for effective parenting of teens* (2nd ed.). Circle Pines, MN: American Guidance Service.

Dinkmeyer, D. C., & McKay, G. (1996). *Raising a responsible child* (rev. ed.). New York: Fireside Books.

Dinkmeyer, D. C. Sr., McKay, G., & Dinkmeyer, D. C. Jr. (1997). *Systematic training for effective parenting* (4th ed.). Circle Pines, MN: American Guidance Service.

Dinkmeyer, D. C. Sr., McKay, G., Dinkmeyer, J. S., Dinkmeyer, D. C. Jr., & McKay, J. L. (1997). *Systematic training for effective parenting of children under six.* Circle Pines, MN: American Guidance Service.

Dinkmeyer, D. C., McKay, G., & McKay, J. L. (1997). *New beginnings: Skills for single parents and stepfamily parents.* Champaign, IL: Research Press.

Dreikurs, R. (1967). *Psychodynamics, psychotherapy, and counseling.* Chicago, IL: Alfred Adler Institute of Chicago.

Eron, J. B., & Lund, T. W. (1996). *Narrative solutions in brief therapy.* New York: Guilford.

Fenell, D. L., & Weinhold, B. K. (1997). *Counseling families: An introduction to marriage and family therapy* (2nd ed.). Denver, CO: Love.

Freedman, J., & Combs, G. (1996). *Narrative therapy: The social construction of preferred realities.* New York: Norton.

Friel, J., & Friel, L. (1988). *Adult children: The secrets of dysfunctional families.* Deerfield Beach, FL: Health Communication.

Friesen, J. D. (1985). *Structural-strategic marriage and family therapy.* New York: Gardner.

Haley, J. (1976). *Problem-solving therapy.* San Francisco: Jossey-Bass.

Hubble, M. A., Duncan, B. L., & Miller, S. D. (Eds.). (1999). *The heart and soul of change: What works in therapy.* Washington, DC: American Psychological Association.

International Association of Marriage and Family Counselors Ethics Committee. (1993). Ethical code for the International Association of Marriage and Family Counselors. *The Family Journal: Counseling and Therapy for Couples and Families, 1,* 73–77.

Keim, J. (2000). Strategic family therapy: The Washington school. In A. Horne (Ed.), *Family counseling and therapy* (3rd ed., pp. 170–207). Itasca, IL: Peacock.

Lew, A. (1999). Parenting education: Selected programs and current and future needs. In R. E. Watts & J. Carlson (Eds.), *Interventions and strategies in counseling and psychotherapy* (pp. 181–192). Philadelphia: Accelerated Development/Taylor & Francis.

Lew, A., & Bettner, B. L. (1996). *A parent's guide to understanding and motivating children.* Newton Centre, MA: Connexions Press.

Littrell, J. M. (1998). *Brief counseling in action.* New York: Norton.

Lott, L., & Nelsen, J. (1995). *Teaching parenting the positive discipline way.* Fair Oaks, CA: Sunrise Press.

Madanes, C. (1981). *Strategic family therapy.* San Francisco: Jossey-Bass.

Metcalf, L. (1995). *Counseling toward solutions.* West Nyack, NY: Center for Applied Research in Education.

Minuchin, S. (1974). *Families and family therapy.* Cambridge, MA: Harvard University Press.

Minuchin, S., & Fishman, H. C. (1981). *Family therapy techniques.* Cambridge, MA: Harvard University Press.

Morgan, A. (2000). *What is narrative therapy?* Adelaide, South Australia: Dulwich Centre Publications.

Murphy, J. J. (1997). *Solution-focused counseling in middle and high schools.* Alexandria, VA: American Counseling Association.

Nelsen, J. (1987). *Positive discipline.* New York: Ballantine.

Nelsen, J., Erwin, C., & Delzer, C. (1993). *Positive discipline for single parents.* Rocklin, CA: Prima.

Nelsen, J., Erwin, C., & Duffy, R. (1995). *Positive discipline for preschoolers.* Rocklin, CA: Prima.

Nelsen, J., Intner, R., & Lott, L. (1995). *Positive discipline for parenting in recovery.* Rocklin, CA: Prima.

Nelsen, J., & Lott, L. (1994). *Positive discipline for teenagers.* Rocklin, CA: Prima.

Nichols, M. P., & Schwartz, R. C. (2001). *Family therapy: Concepts and methods* (5th ed.). Boston: Allyn & Bacon.

O'Hanlon, W. H., & Weiner-Davis, M. (1989). *In search of solutions: A new direction in psychotherapy.* New York: Norton.

Popkin, M. (1990). *Active parenting of teens.* Atlanta, GA: Active Parenting.

Popkin, M. (1993). *Active parenting today.* Atlanta, GA: Active Parenting.

Popkin, M., Gard, B., & Montgomery, M. (1996). *1 2 3 4 parents! Parenting children ages 1 to 4.* Atlanta, GA: Active Parenting.

Quick, E. K. (1996). *Doing what works in brief therapy: A strategic solution focused approach.* San Diego, CA: Academic Press.

Satir, V. (1983). *Conjoint family therapy* (3rd ed.). Palo Alto, CA: Science and Behavior Books.

Satir, V. (1988). *The new peoplemaking.* Palo Alto, CA: Science and Behavior Books.

Sayger, T. V., & Horne, A. M. (2000). Common elements in family therapy theory and strategies. In A. M. Horne (Ed.), *Family counseling and therapy* (3rd ed., pp. 41–61). Itasca, IL: Peacock.

Sherman, R. (1999). Family therapy: The art of integration. In R. E. Watts & J. Carlson (Eds.), *Interventions and strategies in counseling and psychotherapy* (pp. 101–134). Philadelphia, PA: Accelerated Development/Taylor & Francis.

Sherman, R., & Dinkmeyer, D. (1987). *Systems of family therapy: An Adlerian integration.* New York: Brunner/Mazel.

Sherman, R., & Fredman, N. (1986). *Handbook of structured techniques in marriage and family therapy.* New York:Brunner/Mazel.

Sklare, G. B. (1997). *Brief counseling that works: A solution-focused approach for school counselors.* Thousand Oaks, CA: Corwin Press.

Thomas, M. B. (1992). *An introduction to marital and family therapy: Counseling toward healthier family systems across the lifespan.* New York: Merrill/Macmillan.

Walter, J. L., & Peller, J. E. (1992). *Becoming solution-focused in brief therapy.* New York: Brunner/Mazel.

Watts, R. E., & Pietrzak, D. (2000). Adlerian encouragement and the therapeutic process of solution-focused brief therapy. *Journal of Counseling and Development, 78,* 442–447.

White, M., & Epston, D. (1990). *Narrative means to therapeutic ends.* New York: Norton.

Zimmerman, J. L., & Dickerson, V. D. (1996). *If problems talked: Narrative therapy in action.* New York: Guilford.

Chapter Seven

Assessing Family Interventions

Steven Benish

The initial challenge in writing an assessment chapter is to keep counselors interested in what might seem to be a very dry subject. Having experience as a clinician in private practice, a workplace personnel consultant, and a school counselor, I understand the reluctance and apprehension that many counselors have concerning outcome and process assessment measures. It conjures up bad memories of being in graduate school statistics courses and research procedures labs, with a dizzying array of complex equations, difficult computer programs, and mind-boggling statistical analyses. Few of us normally deal with such complex computations on a daily basis, and I have yet to hear, "I'll take multivariate regression for $200, Alex."

Rest assured, this chapter will be practical and geared for the everyday use of counselors, therapists, and other clinicians. The focus will be on practical assessments, everyday language, and nothing that sounds like a complex formula more familiar to nuclear physicists than therapists. I will discuss two types of assessments in this chapter: process assessments and outcome assessments.

A *process assessment* looks at the process of counseling, specifically how satisfied or dissatisfied the client is during the sessions. We have all had the experience of counseling someone, thinking we were doing a wonderful job, and then having had the client drop out or bluntly inform us, "You're not hearing what I want you to hear." Therefore, it is important to encourage ongoing feedback from clients about the counseling process.

The second type of assessment I will present is outcome assessment. An *outcome assessment* measures progress or improvement in clients' functioning as a result of the counseling intervention. Outcome measures can measure general happiness, interpersonal relationship improvements, or any other factors that are goals of counseling.

With the understanding that this chapter will be practical and applied, I believe that it is only fair to give you an idea of my counseling background. As I stated earlier, I have been a school counselor, workplace violence prevention consultant, marital counselor, private practice therapist, and crisis counselor. Having had no formal graduate training in family systems therapy, I dismissed this approach in my early clinical work, probably because I was overconfident in my training and abilities and was intimidated by a theoretical orientation that I did not understand. Only when I became frustrated because some clients did not make progress in individual counseling did I start to realize the impact that the family system was having on personal or family progress. A case example is a client named Jill, a 15-year-old high school sophomore who was disrupting classes, skipping school, acting out in the hallways, and using substances. A concerned teacher referred Jill to me, the school counselor. After a few sessions, Jill's conduct in school improved significantly. However, she would regress the next week by acting out again, with no plausible explanation. Finally, Jill confided that because her parents were divorced, she stayed with her mother one week and her father the next. On the weeks of her in-school disruptions, she stayed with her father whose late-night partying with friends kept Jill up until morning. Thus, she would arrive at school tired and irritable from lack of sleep and feeling angry toward her father. What seemed to crystallize the problem in this situation was the assessments we performed after each session. I noticed a pattern of Jill doing well, then poorly on alternate weeks. This allowed Jill and me to see the pattern of what was happening and to bring her parents into the counseling process to help her.

How Do We Know That Counseling Works?

There is ample evidence that both individual and family counseling are better than no treatment for most problems (Lambert & Bergin, 1994), and that most treated clients are better off than 80% of people who do not seek treatment (Miller, Duncan, & Hubble, 1997). These findings have been confirmed through more than 40 years of outcome research indicating that therapy does make a positive difference in families' lives. However, it is important to use an outcome measure rather than assuming automatically that counseling is working. With the advent of managed care in the 1980s, professional counselors are now called on to be more accountable for counseling outcomes. Not all counseling is effective, and not all techniques or approaches work for all clients. This is why, even though we know that counseling generally works, we need to measure outcomes for each client or family in sessions with us. We must know that our clients are satisfied and, more importantly, that they are improving. We are bound ethically to discontinue treatment if the client is not making progress, and outcome measures help us to make decisions to continue counseling, terminate treatment, or refer the client to another professional.

Why Should We Assess Outcomes?

Why should we use a formal intervention assessment when, as trained clinicians, we believe we know when clients are making progress? One reason is that we usually overestimate our effectiveness with clients, and a standardized client measure is the most reliable and valid means of assessing true effectiveness for change (Hubble, Duncan & Miller, 1999). A second reason for formal assessment is the changing climate in counseling and psychotherapy, including the powerful forces of managed care. Managed care is a business that requires positive results for reimbursement of professional services, and as such, needs proof of the effectiveness of your work. Most of us who have been in private practice or worked in an agency are familiar with the difficulties of dealing with managed care companies, and utilizing a quality assessment tool is one way to show that your counseling is effective. A third reason for assessment is that evidence of progress gives the client hope, and hope in the client accounts for about 15% of therapeutic change (Lambert, 1992). A fourth reason for assessment is that it allows the client and counselor to alter course when the client is not making progress; it serves as a tool to help steer the ship of counseling. By teaming up to fix the problems, the counselor and client could create a stronger therapeutic alliance.

I had the opportunity to sit down with several managed care employees and managers and to ask them what would help a clinician become a preferred provider or receive approval for extra sessions of therapy. The insurance managers provided several answers, but the one factor that came up most often was "show us that you are an effective clinician by providing an outcome measure to quantify your effectiveness." These men and women who make decisions that affect the livelihood of counselors stated that they were far less likely to utilize the services of a counselor who did not utilize outcome measures. There are currently 400,000 mental health providers licensed to serve the American public, approximately double the number needed (Hurst, 1997). This puts counselors in the unfortunate position of competing with each other for clients, due to the oversupply of therapists. Those who are able to show a quantifiable positive result from their therapy will survive. Those who do not unfortunately will perish in the current marketplace.

In the past, insurance companies and other third-party payers looked at psychotherapy as a service and used level of training (e.g., M.A., Ph.D.), years of experience, and certification/licensure as the criteria for payment. Due to the pressure placed on insurance carriers to reduce costs, third-party payers are now looking more strongly at outcomes (Hubble et al., 1999). They are constantly asking whether the client achieved an objective improvement in functioning. These are the reasons why we need to use empirically sound, objective assessments.

When Should We Assess Outcomes?

Because we know that most improvement in therapy occurs early in treatment (Hubble et al., 1999), it is very important to conduct assessment before treatment, during treatment and, if possible, following the closure of treatment. Most families will show improvements in overall or specific functioning within the first several sessions, or they will not improve at all. It is important to know this, because if a client has not improved, you will need to alter your approach or refer the person to a different practitioner.

Continuous assessment is vital to the process. An example is Kevin and Rachel, a married couple in their thirties. They came to counseling stating that they had "communication problems." After four sessions, my impression was that they were making great progress, and I believed that they were both happy. The process and outcome measures revealed something very different, however: Rachel was happy with the progress, but Kevin was not. When we probed the meaning of this discrepancy, we realized that Kevin and Rachel's stated goals were different and that we were not working on the issues important to Kevin. Had I not used the measurements, I would eventually have terminated therapy with both Rachel and I thinking that we had been successful and Kevin feeling dissatisfied in the marriage, thus leading to a actual result of failure in therapy. This case illustrates the advantage of using an assessment tool to measure satisfaction and change in therapy.

What Qualities Are Important in a
Family Outcome Instrument?

Several factors relate to the essential qualities of a good assessment tool: ease of use (utility), cost effectiveness, reliability, and validity.

Utility often becomes a deciding factor, because counselors are so busy counseling, getting reimbursement, and performing administrative tasks that they cannot spend an inordinate amount of time doing assessments. An assessment with high validity, high reliability, and cost effectiveness will be completely useless if no one uses it because it takes too long to administer, interpret, or score.

Cost effectiveness is also essential in the current climate of counseling. Most third-party payers do not reimburse for process or outcome measures, so the counselor has to pick up the tab. This means the assessment must be relatively cheap and reproducible without substantial cost.

The other important factors of reliability and validity are well known to most counselors. In simple terms, *reliability* refers to whether an assessment consistently produces the same results for the same situation, and *validity* refers to whether the assessment measures what its authors claim that it measures. Suffice it to say here that reliability and validity are absolutely necessary components to any assessment. They are necessary though not sufficient aspects of a quality instrument.

Which Process Assessments Are Helpful for Counseling Interventions?

Process assessments are different from outcome assessments in a number of ways. Process instruments measure the counseling relationship and the process of counseling, whereas outcome instruments measure results and changes that have occurred as a result of counseling. Process instruments focus on the dynamics occurring within counseling sessions, examining the counseling process as it unfolds in the office with clients. Process instruments give you feedback on the clients' perceptions of the counseling process, thus helping you to adjust the therapeutic process in response. You can learn how family members perceive the process differently or similarly, and then recognize patterns and alliances within the family. Using process instruments might also help you prevent early dropout from therapy by providing clients with a safe method of giving feedback.

Four important factors in selecting an instrument were explained earlier in this chapter: ease of use (utility), cost effectiveness, reliability, and validity. Cost effectiveness and ease of use are even more important in a process assessment. If you have already spent substantial time and cost on an outcome assessment, you have even less time and money to spend on a process assessment. For these reasons, I favor using a simple assessment for measuring process.

The Session Rating Scale (SRS; Johnson & Miller, 2000) is a simple, 10-item process assessment that measures clients' experience during counseling sessions. The areas measured are acceptance by the counselor; respect from the counselor; understanding, honesty, and sincerity of the counselor; agreement on goals; agreement on tasks; agreement on treatment; pacing of the session; and feeling of hope. On a Likert-type scale from 0 to 4, the client rates his or her perceptions of the 10 processes addressed by the questions. The SRS should be given toward the end of each session to gauge any processes that are helping or hindering the counseling session.

A case example might be helpful to illustrate the use of the SRS. I was counseling a couple and their 15-year-old son, who was showing signs of oppositional-defiant disorder. The family had shown signs of improvement initially, based upon their outcome scores and their observational reports, but progress had slowed since then. The results of the SRS showed that although the parents were happy with the processes and results, their son was unhappy with the goals and tasks of treatment. Not coincidentally, his growing unhappiness with the goals and tasks of treatment coincided with the stalling of progress. In the next session, the family and I discussed this situation and changed the goals and tasks of treatment to satisfy all members of the family. After these changes were made, the family rapidly resumed progress toward their therapy goals.

Which Outcome Assessments Are Best for Family Interventions?

Four components of family balance are most helpful cornerstones in measuring progress in family counseling: boundaries, roles, communication, and problem solving. *Boundaries* refer to one's relations with other family members and range from enmeshment to disengagement. The optimal placement for boundaries on this continuum is in the middle: interdependence without enmeshment. This placement allows both intimacy and a feeling of individual identity (individuation), and it provides emotional distance without feelings of isolation or aloneness.

Roles are defined as responsibilities that an individual takes on (voluntarily or not) to maintain homeostasis. Roles can be divided into healthy, functional roles (those that maintain a healthy homeostasis) and unhealthy, dysfunctional roles (those that make the person pay a price for maintaining the family homeostasis). Examples of healthy roles are parent, child, and in the right situation, gatekeeper. Examples of unhealthy roles are scapegoat, flag bearer, the parentified child, and when a parent takes on the role of the helpless child.

Communication is the ability to openly express feelings and thoughts directly to other family members without fear of reprisal, criticism, or other adverse reactions. Healthy communication patterns in a family are displayed through open, nonjudgmental listening and expression of thoughts and feelings without fear of this openness damaging family relationships.

Problem solving is the ability to resolve efficiently and effectively family conflicts and problems that arise within or outside of the family setting. Problem solving can be handled individually or, more effectively, as a team approach with the family members working together to solve problems.

Now that we understand the operational definitions of the four cornerstones, we can discuss the assessment that most effectively measures them. The most comprehensive and arguably the best tool for assessing these areas of the family system is called the Family

Adaptability and Cohesion Evaluation Scale (FACES), developed by Dr. David Olson at the Department of Family Social Science at the University of Minnesota. Dr. Olson developed this instrument based on his circumplex model of marital and family systems. This model bridges the distance between research, theory, and practice (Olson, Russell, and Sprenkle, 1989). The circumplex model is often used as a relational diagnosis because it focuses on integrating the four cornerstones, which are relational in nature, and it is designed for assessment, treatment planning, and measuring outcomes (Olson, 1996).

FACES offers the advantage of solid reliability and validity. It shows high positive correlations with other well-developed inventories, such as the Self-Report Family Inventory (Beavers & Hampson, 1990), the Family Assessment Measure (Skinner, Santa-Barbara, & Steinhauer, 1983), and the McMaster Family Assessment Device (Epstein & Bishop, 1993).

FACES operates on the basic premise that healthy couples and families are more balanced (compared to unhealthy couples and families) in three basic measures: family cohesion, flexibility, and communication. *Family cohesion* is defined as "the emotional bonding that family members have toward each other" (Olson, 1999, n.p.), which in the circumplex model covers the areas of boundaries, decision making, space, coalitions, and emotional closeness.

Cohesion is measured in terms of separateness versus togetherness and ranges from very low (disengaged) to moderate (separated) to moderate/high (connected) to high (enmeshed). The circumplex model advocates a balance between extremes. For example, if Mother, Father, Daughter, and Son are in counseling to work on family issues, the ultimate goal would be for them to have a balance of cohesion (connected to separated) rather than being at the extremes of enmeshed or disengaged. When you see scores tending toward enmeshed or disengaged showing up on the FACES report, you would then begin to work with the clients on how to bring their cohesion to a middle point and to help the family change intrafamilial patterns that interfere with healthy, balanced relating. Integrated togetherness and separateness are simultaneous goals. All relationships strive for closeness and intimacy without the loss of individuality. This dance of intimacy is often a fine line that ebbs and flows in a healthy relationship, righting itself through the efforts of the family members when an unbalance occurs.

Family flexibility refers to "the amount of change in its leadership, role relationships, and relationship rules" (Olson, 1999, n.p.). It encompasses roles, negotiating styles, discipline/control, and family rules. Again the goal is to achieve balance, this time between flexibility and stability. Too much flexibility will leave the members feeling that their situation is chaotic, and too little flexibility will leave them feeling confined or controlled.

The circumplex model rates the family's flexibility from very low (rigid) to moderate (structured) to moderate/high (flexible) to very high (chaotic). Again, a balance between these states is the goal. Families tend to maintain the status quo and not to allow new rules to be implemented. This rigidity may cause problems as adjustments and changes become necessary through the family life cycle. A balanced family system tends to be the most functional over time, according to the circumplex model. A balanced family has a democratic parental leadership, with some child input into the system and consistency in both roles and rule enforcement. An appropriately flexible family has an egalitarian leadership style and a democratic decision-making process that openly involves the children.

An unbalanced family situation may be either rigid or chaotic, either not surprisingly causing tension and angst for its members. The chaotic relationship has inconsistent or strangled leadership with impulsive and erratic decision making, coupled with inconsistent and undefined roles that result in confusion. In a rigid relationship, there are highly defined roles but one member is overly controlling, preventing negotiation or democratic decision making and leaving very little possibility for role changes.

The circumplex model also rates *communication,* which is seen as critical for movement on the other two dimensions of cohesion and flexibility. Because communication is viewed more as a facilitating factor, it is somewhat distinct from the other two factors and is used in a different way. The areas measured in regard to communication are self-disclosure, speaking skills, clarity in speaking, listening skills, and respect and regard. Self-disclosure in the circumplex model refers to sharing information and feelings about oneself and the familial relationships. Speaking skills are focused on speaking for oneself rather than others. Listening skills are measured via empathy and attentive listening, and respect and regard are measured through the affective dimensions of communication and problem solving.

The circumplex model and the FACES instrument use a three-dimensional model and linear rather than curvilinear measures, consistent with Olson's findings (Olson, 1991). Again the emphasis is on balanced scores on the three dimensions of cohesion, flexibility, and communication.

A case example might be helpful at this point to illustrate the usage of the instrument. Bob and Elaine came to counseling with their two children, complaining of hostility, incongruence, and instability in their marriage and child rearing. After examining the results of their FACES inventory, their therapist could see that their flexibility scores were too high, leading to a chaotic household. Communication was minimal, and the cohesion scale was low on emotional closeness. As the therapist worked with Bob and Elaine on these issues, the couple began to talk about their childhood experiences: Bob had a controlling, distant father whom he had hated, and Bob reacted to this upbringing by swearing not to control his kids. He was trying so hard to be non-controlling that he was leaving a power vacuum in the family and was repeating the pattern of non-communication that his parents had displayed with him. Elaine wanted more emotional closeness and would shut Bob out when he did not respond. Bob would react to her rejection by becoming more aloof, and the pattern would continue. The counselor helped Bob and Elaine to understand what they were trying to avoid in their relationship and how to communicate their intent more clearly, rather than assuming that each knew what the other was thinking.

The basic goals of the circumplex model are to reduce the symptoms and problems in a family that are fed by current interpersonal dynamics (Olson, 1999). A corollary goal is to teach the couple or family how to manage change and how to restore balance in cohesion, flexibility, and communication. Many families initially may be resistant to making changes and, as many experienced counselors know, will likely desire that *other* family members change their behaviors. It is important to educate clients on the dynamics of the family system and to help family members who are resistant to change. You can accomplish this by helping a family member to understand how his or her actions affect the system and how other family members react to them. Doing this reinforces an internal locus of control over one's problems, rather than a feeling of being victimized by others' actions. Family members need to understand that systemic changes sometimes result in greater distress temporarily, as members react and adjust to others' behavioral changes; once the family has adjusted to these changes, the situation will become more stable again.

Conclusion

Inventories and measurement instruments can be helpful additions to your work with families. Given the multidimensional dynamics and complex relationships involved in each family, a measurement instrument can help you sort out and identify specific target goals for therapy, measure changes from therapy, and provide insight for clients on what changes are needed.

It is important to use instruments as tools toward positive change rather than as tools to find the "cause" of problems, because blaming problems on one family member is correlated with early dropout of clients from therapy (Wolpert, 2000). Additionally, enlisting all family members' cooperation in the interpretation of scores can add meaning to test results. The therapist-client relationship accounts for 30% of change in therapy (Miller et al., 1997, Lambert, 1992), so it is important to use a collaborative approach with the family when integrating the test results into counseling and therapy.

As counselors, we know that assessments are not panaceas but can be effective tools in helping us learn family therapy and integrate it into our practices. Think of assessment not as a burden that causes extra work, but as a tool to help clients achieve better results. Assessments ultimately increase the health and legitimacy of the counseling profession, because when used properly they improve clients' outcomes.

When we recall our reasons for entering the counseling field in the first place, most of us remember wanting to help people through difficult times in their lives. Many of us, idealists who wanted to improve the world through a helping career, have oscillated between achieving these goals and occasionally feeling frustrated by a lack of progress toward them. Incorporating family systems theory and using assessments in your practice will not negate the frustrations you face as a counselor but will give you tools to help others improve their lives. Your quest toward these goals is valid, noble, and attainable. With the appropriate tools at your disposal, you can enrich others' lives.

References

Beavers, W. B., & Hampson, R. B. (1990). *Successful families: Assessment and intervention.* New York: Norton.

Epstein, N. B., & Bishop, D. S. (1993). The McMaster Family Assessment Device (FAD). In F. Walsh (Ed.), *Normal family processes.* New York: Guilford Press.

Hubble, M. A., Duncan, B. L., & Miller, S. D. (1999). *The heart and soul of change: What works in therapy.* Washington, DC: American Psychological Association.

Hurst, M. W. (1997). *How to use emerging communication technologies to streamline and improve care management and delivery.* Paper presented at the Behavioral Informatics Tomorrow Conference.

Johnson, L. D., & Miller, S. D. (2000). The Session Rating Scale, Revised Version 2. Retrieved November 1, 2001, from http://www.talkingcure.com/measures.htm.

Lambert, M. J. (1992). Psychotherapy outcome research: Implications for integrative and eclectic therapists. In J. Norcross & M. Goldfried (Eds.), *Handbook of psychotherapy integration* (pp. 94–129). New York: Basic Books.

Lambert, M. J., & Bergin, A. E. (1994). The effectiveness of psychotherapy. In A. E. Bergin & S. L. Garfield (Eds.), *Handbook of psychotherapy and behavior change* (pp. 143–189). New York: John Wiley and Sons.

Miller, S. D., Duncan, B. L., & Hubble, M. A. (1997). *Escape from Babel: Toward a unifying language for psychotherapy practice.* New York: Norton.

Olson, D. H. (1991). Three dimensional (3-D) circumplex model & revised scoring of FACES. *Family Process, 30,* 74–79.

Olson, D. H. (1994). Curvilinearity survives: The world is not flat. *Family Process, 33,* 471–478.

Olson, D. H. (1996). Clinical assessment and treatment interventions using the circumplex model. In F. W. Kaslow (Ed.), *Handbook of relational diagnosis and dysfunctional family patterns* (pp. 59–80). New York: John Wiley and Sons.

Olson, D. H. (1999). Empirical approaches to family assessment [Special issue]. *Journal of Family Therapy.* Retrieved November 1, 2001, from http://www.lifeinnovations.com/studies/fip0.html.

Olson, D. H., Russell, C. S., & Sprenkle, D. H. (1989). *Circumplex model: Systemic assessment and treatment of families.* New York: Haworth Press.

Skinner, H. A., Santa-Barbara, J., & Steinhauer, P. D. (1983). The Family Assessment Measure. *Canadian Journal of Community Mental Health, 2,* 91–105.

Wolpert, M. (2000). Is anyone to blame? *Clinical Child Psychology and Psychiatry, 5,* 115–131.

Chapter Eight

Closure Issues with Families

Steven E. Craig and Gary H. Bischof

In the recently heralded book *Tuesdays with Morrie,* Mitch Albom (1997) writes about his rekindled mentorship and friendship with his college professor. Albom learned that his former professor, whom he affectionately called "Coach," had been diagnosed with a form of Lou Gehrig's disease. Though Coach's body withered away, his soul continued to grow. In the later pages of the book, to which we can do no justice in this brief paragraph, Albom talks of the days leading up to Coach's death. As he sits with Coach, Albom makes a statement that concisely describes Western culture's perspective of death: "I don't know how to say goodbye" (p. 185).

For many in our Western culture, goodbyes are awkward to say the least. Society has taught people that goodbyes are endings. As counselors, however, we are convinced that closure of the counseling relationship constitutes both an ending and a beginning. On the one hand, closure signifies the ending of the present counseling relationship. On the other hand, many family counselors conceptualize closure as the start of a working relationship between counselor and family that may be summoned in future times of crisis or during a difficult life transition. Some (Heath, 1985; Lebow, 1995) have likened this to the relationship people share with their family doctor. People may go extended periods of time without seeing their physician, yet the relationship remains open in times of need.

Surprisingly, a review of the literature reveals sparse coverage of closure issues in family counseling. For Brock and Barnard (1999, p. 115), closure means "to end actively." The assumption is that closure, when ideally implemented, consists of a *collaborative* venture between client and therapist. Clearly, situations exist in which families may prematurely discontinue counseling for reasons including financial constraints, lack of compatibility between therapist and clients, or geographic inconvenience. But, regardless whether closure is client initiated, counselor initiated, premature, or naturally determined after problem resolution, it deserves careful consideration from counselors who work with families. Although closure may be considered the final stage of counseling, we believe that it is also a *process,* the elements of which take place throughout counseling.

In this chapter, we will discuss the common tasks of closure, including how closure in family counseling is different from closure in individual counseling, indications of a family's readiness for closure, working toward closure, elements of the closure session, innovative methods to facilitate closure, considerations after the final session, and unilateral termination, both client initiated and therapist initiated.

Common Tasks of Closure

A select group of authors (Bell, 1975; Brock & Barnard, 1999; Lebow, 1995; Papero, 1995; Treacher, 1989; Wilcoxon & Gladding, 1985) have attempted to expand counselors' understanding of closure of a family counseling relationship. Lebow (1995) provides a comprehensive description of the closure process for family counselors that we have found especially helpful. His closure tasks and a brief description of each follow:

    1.**Track progress.** You spend considerable time defining goals for the counseling process with your clients. Before closure can occur, you and your clients must collaboratively assess the degree to which treatment goals have been achieved.

2. **Review the course of counseling.** Lebow considers this task to be a continuation of tracking the family's progress. In this step, you assist family members in reviewing the major events of counseling, encouraging them to share their perceptions of those things that have been most and least helpful. This task also allows counselors to share their perceptions as well.

3. **Highlight gains.** Families who achieve their stated goals often give the credit to their counselor and neglect to recognize their role in the success. It is important to make a concerted effort to highlight the gains the family made during counseling and to credit these changes to the efforts of family members.

4. **Generalize learning to the "real world."** Lebow suggests that family counseling is most effective when family members are able to apply the skills they have learned to real-life situations. These skills may include behavioral skills (assertiveness), affective skills (working through grief), or psychodynamic skills (insight about themselves). Assist families in developing a maintenance plan that will ensure they will continue practicing the skills following closure.

5. **Internalize the therapist.** Throughout counseling, family members will often discuss among themselves what they believe you might say or do when they are facing a dilemma. During the closure process, encourage clients to practice this skill so that they will have internalized some of your perspectives and ideas by the time the counseling relationship ends. Families who receive constructive feedback from you as they practice internalization are likely to develop confidence in their abilities to solve future problems without having to seek further counseling services.

6. **Learn from past endings.** All people have experienced endings during their lifetime. Approach the closure process with sensitivity to the various ways in which family members have experienced endings in their individual pasts, with special consideration to how these experiences might affect the closure process.

7. **Say goodbye.** Lebow considers this task one of the most difficult for counselors. Families need the opportunity to express their appreciation for your assistance and to acknowledge the attachment that has likely developed. After all, the relationship may have existed for a considerable length of time, and the family has trusted you with intimate information. Although some families may end counseling abruptly, you must still be willing to work through your own feelings and accept the family's way of ending the relationship. Ultimately, you are responsible for ending the relationship in the most positive and healthy manner possible.

8. **Discuss conditions for returning.** Assist the family in devising guidelines for their possible return to counseling. By normalizing the possibility of future difficulties, you prepare the family to expect setbacks. As such, Lebow suggests that you help families determine a set of conditions under which they would return.

9. **Make appropriate referrals.** In select cases, appropriate referrals may be warranted; for example, to a psychiatrist or primary care provider for a medication evaluation, to self-help groups, to individual counseling, or to supplemental marital therapy. You may also need to make a referral when a family's problems exceed your professional training or competence.

10. **Define your post-therapy availability.** This task is related to task 8, in which you and the family collaboratively determine the conditions for their return. It is important to make clear when and under what conditions you will be available for future consultations or sessions. For example,

if you are in private practice, you cannot necessarily guarantee that you will be available at the same time and day if the family wishes to return. Thus, the limits of your availability should be made clear during the closure phase of counseling.

Rather than viewing these tasks as a linear, strictly sequential process, Lebow (1995) suggests conceptualizing them as an agenda needing coverage during appropriate phases of counseling. We have learned that an agenda, though helpful as a guiding framework, is rarely sufficient for every family. Inevitably, families will present with unique characteristics or expectations that make strict adherence to an agenda unrealistic. As each counseling relationship draws to a close, you will not necessarily need to address all of these tasks with every family. The list is helpful to keep in mind, however, as a guideline for reaching successful closure with couples and families. Now that we have taken a look at some of the common tasks of closure, let us also review some ways in which closure in family counseling is different from closure in individual counseling.

Individual versus Family Closure

The closure process with a family presents some unique challenges that further distinguish the process of family work from individual counseling. Unlike when you counsel an individual, with a family you must contend with a number of participants and subsequently a variety of perspectives. Occasionally, family members will have discrepant views regarding their readiness to end counseling. When this happens, it is especially important to process each family member's reaction to closure of the counseling relationship and to become skillful in handling participants' discrepant views. One strategy is to negotiate a compromise among participants, a process that validates each person's perspective while also modeling effective conflict-resolution skills for the family. For example Patterson, Williams, Grauf-Grounds, & Chamow (1998) discuss a couple who disagreed on their readiness for closure. After a period of counseling, the husband felt he and his wife were communicating more effectively and was prepared to discontinue counseling. In contrast, the wife felt she and her husband could benefit in other areas, especially their sexual relationship, and she wished to continue the weekly sessions. After validating both partners' perspectives, the counselor facilitated a compromise that resulted in sessions being continued on a biweekly rather than weekly basis. This enabled the couple to continue counseling on a less intensive basis to address issues related to their sexual relationship.

Now that you have a clearer understanding of how closure with families is different from closure with individual clients, we will discuss some more specific ways to assess a family's readiness for closure.

Indicators of a Family's Readiness for Closure

I (SEC) once had a girlfriend in the fourth grade who, upon my calling to tell her I wanted to break up with her, replied, "I didn't know we were going out." I'm certainly hopeful I establish a better relationship with my clients than I did with my first girlfriend! Aside from the damage this incident did to my ego, it illustrates an important point about the process of closure. Before you can ascertain a family's readiness for closure, you must first understand where they are going. Said otherwise, you must be clear on the family's stated goals and objectives for coming to counseling. Failure to identify goals clearly can result in an ambiguous ending that leaves both counselor and family feeling empty and dissatisfied.

The assessment of a family's readiness for closure is a vital task in family counseling. So how do family counselors determine when is an appropriate time to end the counseling relationship? To answer this question, we need to take a look at some behaviors that suggest a family is ready for closure. Most theorists, including those highlighted in chapter 3 (Adler, Perls, and Lazarus), have their own perspectives about how change occurs and how counselors can have some assurance about when to discontinue counseling. However, Bell

(1975) has identified five key indicators that a family may be ready for closure of the counseling relationship, and these indicators are useful for family counselors across various theoretical foundations. According to Bell, family work is complete when the family

1. resolves or learns to cope effectively with symptoms
2. demonstrates enhanced cooperation, independence, and humor
3. displays more open styles of family interaction
4. reports increased feelings of security
5. demonstrates increased flexibility in their family roles

Treacher (1989) has devised an approach for assessing closure readiness based on Minuchin's structural theory of family therapy. According to Treacher, three questions are integral to assessing a family's readiness for closure:

1. What is the status of the family's presenting problem? (e.g., improved; worsened; improved to an acceptable level according to all participants)
2. What structural changes have taken place? (e.g., boundaries; hierarchical changes)
3. What changes in individual and family beliefs have occurred? (e.g., role definitions; overgeneralizations).

Families that indicate a resolution of the presenting problem, demonstrate positive structural changes, and display a shift in cognitive beliefs are probably ready for closure.

Other potential indicators of a family's readiness for closure lie in their observable behaviors and your personal feelings. Such client behaviors as an increase of small talk, noncompliance (no-shows, cancellations), decreased motivation, and more positive affective tone all may signal readiness for closure. We have also observed greater courage and confidence in families who are nearing the closure phase of counseling. Finally, if you are finding yourself feeling consistently bored, tired, or disinterested because the major work seems to have been completed, you may consider initiating a discussion about the family's readiness for closure.

Certainly, the preceding indicators are helpful. We have found another way of assessing the appropriateness of closure, however: We ask the family if they're ready. Because counseling is a collaborative process, and because we work under the assumption that clients know themselves better than we know them, we invite families to participate in deciding whether or not counseling will continue.

Working Toward Closure

Several strategies may be employed to ease the transition toward closure, especially in cases where the family expresses some reluctance to end counseling or where family members have discrepant views about their readiness for closure. A common approach is to increase the time between sessions to provide the family with more opportunities to implement the skills they have learned in counseling and to help them gain confidence that they can solve problems successfully on their own. Thus, if you have been meeting weekly with a family, you might suggest meeting every other week. Sometimes as therapy begins to wind down, families naturally implement this strategy by canceling or rescheduling appointments. You can reframe this phenomenon positively by suggesting to the family that it indicates less reliance upon therapy. If problems resurface as the time between sessions is extended, you can take a one-down approach and apologize for pushing the family too hard. Alternatively, you can normalize relapses by presenting them as opportunities to learn more about the problem and to develop longer-lasting solutions.

Another helpful strategy when you extend the time is to suggest that the couple or family meet on their own without you at the usual therapy day and time. This could be done at home or at some other agreed-upon neutral place. Doing so may reinforce the family's ability to solve problems independently and emphasize the value of setting aside some time to check in with one another. Clients often report talking about what their therapist might say regarding their circumstances during their family meeting, thus highlighting the internalization of the therapy experience in their collective lives. For example, one family met at a restaurant for pizza at the usual counseling time and checked in with one another about how the past week had gone. They found doing so helpful, and on returning for their next session, reported that they would likely continue meeting periodically for pizza and a family discussion when counseling was over. Exploring successful meetings of this kind with the family can help clarify how they worked through issues on their own, and offers you opportunities to praise family members for their positive contributions. Unsuccessful meetings might indicate the need to continue regular sessions and may reveal issues that still need to be addressed.

In cases that do not involve severe problems such as violence or abuse, it is often helpful to normalize minor relapses or even to predict relapse. Presenting the natural process of change as "two steps forward, one step back" can help reassure people that a minor relapse is not a crisis. You can even ask couples to predict what their next argument will be about, or explore with a family what it would mean to them if their teenage boy stayed out past curfew and how they would handle it. Adolescents might be encouraged to test their parents' new teamwork by trying to play one parent against the other. Such strategies help to normalize setbacks and can place minor relapses in proper perspective. Discussion of these issues also allows you to emphasize the importance of handling problems effectively and that life will not be problem free. The closure of counseling also presents clients with an opportunity to share their experiences of the counseling process, and this is addressed next.

Reflective of the changing nature of the relationship between you and a family as closure approaches, you can elicit from the family perspectives on your performance and what they found useful or feel could have been improved in the counseling process. Such information enables you to improve your skills and reinforces the things you are doing well. Inviting honest feedback puts clients in the position of being experts and acknowledges that they have something to offer you. Soliciting feedback also provides an opportunity to address any matters that that the client might have found annoying or irritating and establish a clear sense that there is no unfinished business. For counselors with little experience working with families, hearing what was helpful about the counseling or the counselor's style can bolster confidence and may increase self-efficacy.

Elements of the Closure Session: Goodbye for Now

Perhaps Carlson and Carlson (1999, p. 49) say it best, "Transitions are like speed bumps: You need to slow down while approaching them." Our experiences supervising counselors in training have shown us that many counselors have a tendency to rush the process of closure. Consider the last major transition you can recall. Perhaps it was a relocation to another city. Maybe it was a new marriage. Maybe you recently faced a divorce or a new career. Transitions are stressful experiences mentally, emotionally, and physically. The same can hold true for the closure of a counseling relationship. The primary responsibility for easing the transition lies with you.

Earlier, we referred to Lebow's (1995) tasks for the closure process. During the last few sessions before closure, many of these tasks become more prominent and important. For example, the last few sessions should include a review of treatment goals and events, an attempt to help families internalize the therapist, time to process endings and how each participant is feeling about closure, a review of gains made and the role each member played in these successes, and definition of post-treatment availability. Seligman (2001) gives five guidelines for the closure phase of counseling. Though she intended these guidelines for individual counseling, we have modified them for work with families. Let's take a look at how Seligman's guidelines may be helpful for family work:

1. Allow at least three weeks to process closure. This allows both you and family members time to share your personal reactions about the process.
2. Expect various, surprising reactions. Although many families may show little emotion at the initiation of

closure, other reactions, such as anger, hurt, or disappointment, may emerge later.

3. Expect various, surprising reactions in yourself. You too may experience different emotions related to closure and should anticipate the possibility of feeling anger, frustration, excitement, or disappointment. Personally, we can both attest to the disappointment and confusion we have experienced when some families have prematurely terminated without notice. I (SEC) recall feeling disappointed over one family's unexpected decision to discontinue counseling. For about ten weeks, I had been seeing a blended family who, in my estimation, had made significant strides but could likely benefit from continued counseling. The family called during the week to inform me that they had decided to end the counseling relationship, without giving any reason for their decision. I was confused and disappointed. Through consultation with colleagues, I became aware that my feelings were most likely a result of my own struggle to accept the family's way of ending the counseling relationship. When families terminate counseling, counselors' tendency is to personalize their decision. Experience has taught me that when this occurs, it is important to self-assess and determine whether I might have done something to thwart the process. On the other hand, it is equally important for me to consider the possibility that the family members have gotten what they need from the counseling experience and are simply ready to apply what they have learned.

4. Elicit feedback from clients about the process. Instead of asking for general feedback, attempt to elicit reactions to specific moments in the counseling experience. Because clients are often reticent to criticize, work hard to create a safe environment where clients feel comfortable enough to speak candidly about their experiences.

5. Try to leave clients with positive feelings and a sense of self-efficacy about the counseling experience.

Empowerment is crucial during the closure phase of counseling. Clients have a tendency to express gratitude during closure. Although it is important to acknowledge their appreciation, it is also crucial to find ways to return the responsibility for their success to the family members.

In the next section, we identify some creative ways to empower the family and solidify change. These are activities you might use during the last few sessions of the counseling relationship.

Innovative Methods to Facilitate Closure

The purpose of the following activities is twofold. First, they may ease the transition for all participants. Second, and perhaps most important, they provide a way to highlight the changes a family has made by allowing all the members to participate actively. Efforts to empower families during the closure process can facilitate their belief in themselves. Your encouragement may help them regain faith in themselves, recognize their strengths, and develop the "courage to be imperfect" (Dreikurs, 1967, p. 43). We have successfully used experiential activities to focus the final session on the changes made during counseling. The following examples from our clinical experiences illustrate how you might use these strategies.

Sand Tray

Several years ago, a blended family consisting of a stepfather, mother, and 14 year-old son came to see me (SEC) for counseling. After many sessions the family found that they would soon face an adjustment period when two other stepchildren would be moving into the home. The 14-year-old had reacted in ways that understandably were a concern for the parents: vandalism, defiance toward teachers and his parents, and a sudden drop in grades. Given the context of this family's situation, I decided to provide an opportunity for this family to work together on an experiential activity that could highlight some of the positive changes they had made in counseling. My instructions went something like this, "Using any of the figurines and materials available for the sand tray, construct something that displays what you have learned during our time together." (For a detailed review of sand tray therapy, see Mitchell & Friedman, 1994). In watching the family, I noted that their level of cooperation had increased. Of special significance was the cooperation between the son and his stepfather, a relationship that until then had been largely distant because, as both parents admitted, the mother had been overinvolved and the stepfather underinvolved in the day-to-day responsibilities related to childcare.

When the family had finished, I used the following questions to highlight their presenting problem (the adolescent's misbehavior), the changes they had been able to make, and the role each family member played in resolving the problems. Only through observing the family in an activity like the sand tray could I notice these positive changes, highlight them, and subsequently encourage the family and reinforce their ability to problem solve. Similar goals can be achieved through media such as family art activities, games, and role-playing.

Here are useful questions for processing the sand tray activity:
1. If you were to provide a title for your sand tray creation, what would it be?
2. How is your creation reflective of the changes you have made?
3. If you could change one thing about your creation, what would it be?
4. When problems come up for your family in the future, how will you address them?

Sculpting

Pioneers of family therapy, such as Virginia Satir and Bunny Duhl, introduced the use of sculpting with families. Briefly, sculpting involves family members physically positioning themselves and others to represent the relationships and roles in the family. Sculpting provides an active, experiential, and often powerful means of assessment and intervention with a family. Families who have used sculpting earlier in treatment can recreate the way their family was sculpted at the start of therapy, then all create new sculptures to represent how they see their family currently. Even if they have not used sculpting previously, they can do "before and after" therapy sculpts. Again, this strategy highlights the gains a family has made and provides a present-centered opportunity to process and underline the contributions of each family member in bringing about the positive changes. To set a future orientation, ask the family to portray ongoing changes they hope will continue or to anticipate and plan for minor relapses.

I (GHB) have also used line sculpts to depict clients' perspectives on progress in therapy. For example, using the idea of a continuum, with one side of the room representing the time before therapy started or when things were at their worst, and the other side of the room representing complete resolution of the problem, I ask family members to place themselves along the continuum to show where they see the problem now. We explore their reasons for choosing a certain spot and, true to a systems approach, acknowledge different perspectives on progress. I typically also orient the discussion toward the family's progress and what they can do both to maintain the gains and to continue progress.

As an example, I used line sculpts at the beginning and again near the end of treatment with a single mother and two teenage boys who had presented with concerns about sibling aggression and vague suicidal threats by the younger son. As closure approached, for each major problem we had addressed in counseling, the family members placed themselves along a continuum of progress. Although there were minor differences in their perspectives, the tangible difference between their positions on the continuum at the beginning of therapy versus near the end of treatment reinforced that the entire family felt significant positive changes had been made. The tone of the exercise was playful, a significant change from their affect at the beginning of therapy, and the activity also seemed to help them give themselves credit for the contributions they had made.

Football Scaling Grid

Another intervention I (GHB) have used to help a family identify progress at the end of therapy involves the use of a handout showing a representation of a football field. There is blank space on the left side for the family to write down the goals or problems that have been the focus of therapy. To the right is the football field, marked off in 10-yard intervals, with an end zone on the far right, representing a "touchdown"; that is, resolution of a problem or full attainment of a goal. Family members indicate where they were on each presenting problem when they came in and where they are now. I encourage them to jot down what they or others have done to accomplish change and, for partial successes, to identify what would help them advance a bit farther toward resolution of the problem or attainment of the goal. This variation of the scaling question used in solution-focused therapy approaches provides an enjoyable pictorial means to summarize the gains made in treatment. Typically, family members feel encouraged when they see this visual representation of the progress they have made, even though most don't reach a touchdown for all their issues. You could give out a handout like this for family members to complete independently as a homework assignment prior to the final session. I have also done a similar intervention on a chalkboard or dry-erase board, having various family members indicate their perspectives using different symbols or colors.

I used this strategy with a family of four who had presented with complaints that the teenage daughter was defiant and disrespectful to her parents and had frequent hostile conflicts with her younger brother. The family was involved in various sports and seemed to like visual images, so I opted to use the football scaling grid in our final session as a way to highlight the considerable gains they had made and identify how they could maintain and further the work they had done. In advance of the session, I drew a football field on a dry-erase board and identified the major areas we had focused on in counseling. In the session, I gave each family member a different colored marker and, for the various problem areas, they rotated the order in which they marked their perspectives. I encouraged them to think for a moment about where they would place their progress on a line prior to calling out a yard marker. Each member noted significant progress on most areas, and their different perspectives on some of the problems led to helpful discussions about their various views of the changes made. Seeing the progress on the board, the son remarked, "Hey, we've done pretty good!" The father had tended to be cautious about acknowledging improvements during counseling, and the other family members were surprised at the significant progress he identified on the football grid. We went on to generate a list of specific things that each member had done to contribute to the family's progress and another list of steps that would maintain and further these gains. I provided these lists to the family as their "game plan" for continued progress and for review should a minor setback occur.

Use of Rituals

Rituals have been defined as collaborative, symbolic acts that address multiple meanings on behavioral, cognitive, and affective levels (Roberts, 1988). In terminating family counseling, rituals can be used to bring together therapeutic themes and to mark the closure of therapy. Rituals and certificates also can ease the transition from treatment to no treatment. The following sections highlight the use of rituals and certificates during the closing stages of therapy.

Evan Imber-Black (1999, pp. 207–209), a well-regarded and creative family therapist and trainer, offers an example of a ritual that assisted the family of Karen, a severely mentally retarded 22-year-old, when she left home. The family consisted of the parents, Karen, and her 20-year-old brother. The school Karen attended had been encouraging transition to a group home as a viable option, but the family had been reluctant to consider this. Conflict between Karen and her parents escalated as attempts were made to plan for the move to the group home. Using themes and language that had developed as counseling had progressed, the therapist devised a ritual that would mark Karen's young adulthood, promote the family's confidence in her and themselves, and highlight ongoing connectedness among the members.

The parents and brother each were asked to choose a gift for Karen to take with her to her new home, a gift that would remind Karen of them and ease her adjustment to her new setting. Karen, in turn, was asked to select a gift for each family member. The gifts were not to be bought but rather something that belonged to them or that they had made. They were asked to bring these gifts to the next session and to keep secret what the gifts were.

The family arrived and appeared excited and happy in a way the therapist had not seen before. They had also agreed on a definite date for Karen to move out, something that they had not been able to do before. There was a lot of secretive laughter as family members went about preparing their gifts. Each person was instructed to share his or her gift and provide a brief explanation of its meaning. The recipient was instructed to respond simply "thank you." This format placed all family members on more even ground, given Karen's limited verbal abilities, and focused on the giving of the gifts while limiting discussion.

Karen's father offered his gift first, his favorite frying pan with which he made Sunday breakfast on a regular basis. Karen had been learning to cook, and he had not let her use it for fear that she would ruin it. Karen beamed and said "thank you." Her mother gave her perfume and a pair of earrings that had belonged to Karen's grandmother, explaining that Karen was now grown up enough to have them (she had never allowed her to wear earrings previously). Teary-eyed, Karen said "thank you." Her brother, who was also moving out to go to college, gave Karen his pet bird and a box of birdseed. He had had pets over the years and had been responsible for them, whereas Karen had not. He promised to teach her to care for the bird before she moved out.

Karen then gave her gifts. To her mother she gave her favorite stuffed animal with which she still slept, saying that she could not sleep with it in her new home. To her father she gave a photograph of herself and several young men, which had been taken on one of her visits to the group home. She said to her father, "These are my new friends." To her brother she gave her clock radio, a prized possession that had been a Christmas present, saying, "Don't be late for school!" Two weeks after the session, Karen moved into the group home, and a month later her brother left for college. The family ended therapy and at one-year follow-up reported that both children had adjusted well to their new settings and were visiting for the holidays. The mother had also returned to school to train for paid employment.

I (GHB) have also used a therapist-devised ritual for closure with a client. During the first session, which took place in the psychiatric wing of a local hospital, this middle-aged African American female had remarked after telling some of her story that I must think she was "a nut." I responded by assuring her that I did not think she was a nut but asked, if she were a nut, what kind she would be. She responded that she would be a Brazil nut. We utilized this metaphor at various times throughout her therapy, likening the thick, hard shell of the Brazil nut to her difficulty in allowing anyone to be very close, as well as to times when she might want to protect herself appropriately, the unique and rich taste of the Brazil nut to her talents and sense of self, and so on. For our final session, to her surprise, I brought in some Brazil nuts and nutcrackers, and we broke apart and ate Brazil nuts while discussing the gains she had made, the skills she had developed, and how she might maintain the progress she had made. This ritual also tapped her sense of humor, an important resource for her, and she thoroughly enjoyed this encounter during a closure session about which she had been feeling uneasy.

Other variations on the use of rituals for closure may involve having clients bring in symbols of the progress the family has made or of the efforts it will take to maintain their gains. Family members might also be asked to consider the specific things they and other family members have done to promote change, and to share these at a final session. Closure rituals generally necessitate a fairly formal final session and might not be appropriate in all cases. Also keep in mind that rituals should flow naturally from and be related to the themes and issues that have evolved over the course of therapy.

Use of Celebrations and Certificates

One of the most important tasks in reaching closure is for family members to highlight and underscore the positive changes that they have worked to achieve, and to reinforce that the identified client and the entire family are indeed different than they were when therapy started. A useful way to do this, particularly when the problem has been child-focused, is through the use of celebrations and certificates. These interventions come from narrative approaches to therapy (see, e.g., Freedman & Combs, 1996; White & Epston, 1990). Narrative therapy is based on theories of social constructionism and emphasizes the "stories" that are developed about people and circumstances. By deconstructing dominant, problem-saturated stories and reauthoring or building up more positive alternative stories, the therapist and family collaboratively work toward initiating and reinforcing change.

Narrative therapists frequently use questions in therapy to *externalize* the problem; that is, to place a problem that the client might view as an internal flaw or defect outside of the person (White & Epston, 1990). An example would be inquiring about times the client won the battle against depression and how he or she did so. Particularly in cases when a problem is child-related, externalization may also take on the form of personification, in which the problem is given a name and viewed as a force that the child and family can unite against and strategize about how to defeat. For instance, bed-wetting might be termed "Sneaky Wee," or problems with temper tantrums might be framed as times the child allows the "Tantrum Monster" to outwit him or her.

You can then make use of these externalizations to create official written documents or certificates for presentation to the child and family upon conclusion of counseling. These words appear on an official certificate signed by yourself and others, if appropriate. The text from an actual certificate (White & Epston, 1990, p. 194) offers a good example:

☉ Beating Sneaky Wee Certificate ☾

This certificate is granted to

_____

in recognition of his success at putting Sneaky Wee
in its proper place.
_____ has turned the tables on Sneaky Wee. Sneaky Wee
was running out on him. Now he has run out on Sneaky Wee.
Instead of soaking in Sneaky Wee, he is soaking in glory.

Celebrations of positive change can occur along with the presentation of certificates or separately. They serve similar purposes of highlighting changes and congratulating family members for the efforts they have made to bring about those changes. Serving cake or cookies—or some other celebration that fits the family's culture—is a way to celebrate and mark the distinctions between the way things were when the family started in counseling and how they are now. A celebration can provide a fun and positive context for reinforcing the positive contributions of each family member, and can be used to identify helpful keys for maintaining progress. Narrative therapists also emphasize the importance of the identified client rallying others in his or her life who will support and strengthen the person's newly developing "story." Celebrations can serve the purpose of bringing those people together, uniting them in honoring the changes the client has made, and recommitting them to continue to assist in defeating the problem. For example, a closure session for a teenage girl on probation might involve her family members, probation officer, and school counselor. Each of these individuals could be invited to share in the celebration of her growth by noting signs of progress and identifying how he or she will support the girl's ongoing efforts to lead a new, responsible life.

Other strategies may be employed to reinforce the new status of the client. The client or family may become "experts" in solving similar problems for others, and may even be included later as consultants in others' therapy. Narrative therapists also report on the development of support groups for people who have overcome a specific problem. For example, in some areas, clients who have struggled with anorexia have formed an Anti-Anorexia League (Freedman & Combs, 1996). This group offered a ready-made support system for those making the transition out of therapy, creating a new "audience" to reinforce their new status. They have also developed educational programs and projects to counter dominant cultural messages about body image and anorectics themselves.

After the "Final" Session

A useful termination should include some discussion about indications that a return to therapy is warranted. As mentioned previously, the family should have a plan to deal with predictable setbacks. In addition, you might agree with the family upon some conditions, such as a designated time frame or number of attempts to solve a recurring problem, after which the family would contact you again. As an example, sex therapist Barry McCarthy (1999, p. 298) has developed a relapse prevention plan for problems of low libido that includes the following behavioral conditions for returning to therapy: "If two weeks go by without sexual contact, the higher-desire spouse assumes responsibility for initiating a sexual date within the week. If the person does not do this, the lower-desire spouse takes responsibility to initiate a pleasuring or erotic date within the next week. If that does not occur, they schedule a therapy appointment. This promotes therapeutic adherence."

Another strategy for post-therapy follow-up is to offer the family the option of an initial phone consultation during which you can remind them of what has been helpful in the past or offer specific suggestions to address the problem at hand. Based on the results of this consultation, you may then suggest a return to counseling. There is a fine line between being available to clients in crisis and empowering them to become increasingly self-reliant.

Some counselors routinely utilize pre-planned booster sessions to reinforce change and provide a sense of ongoing but less formal contact. Booster sessions are typically scheduled at three- or six-month intervals (Lebow, 1995). These sessions allow you to assess how well the family has maintained their prior gains, to renew old skills and insights, to reinforce the positive changes the family had made previously, and to instill hope and optimism. Booster sessions also provide a mini-evaluation of the need for a brief return to therapy. In some cases, particularly when a family is feeling reasonably good about progress but desires to maintain some connection with therapy, I (GHB) have scheduled a session for two or three months in the future, with the understanding that the family may call and cancel if they feel that things are going well. Some clients report feeling an added sense of security and confidence from knowing they have an appointment scheduled, even if they opt not to use it.

Unilateral Termination of Therapy

Closure is ideally a collaborative process between counselor and family. We do not do our family work in an ideal world, of course. Outside forces such as managed care restrictions and financial constraints may affect the length of treatment, even when both the therapist and family would like to continue. Other circumstances, such as the client or therapist moving or changing jobs, may necessitate an end to treatment before treatment goals have been reached. In many cases, treatment ends abruptly when the couple or family simply doesn't return. In other cases, the counselor may unilaterally recommend discontinuation of conjoint treatment for clinical reasons. These last two situations will be discussed in the following sections.

Client-Initiated Termination

Anyone working with families has experienced the frustration of getting a call from a family member indicating that he or she is canceling an appointment and doesn't plan to reschedule. At other times clients simply do not show up and stop treatment without explanation. Some researchers suggest that client-initiated termination is more frequent in couples and family counseling than individual counseling (Lebow, 1995). Compared to the stable alliances common in individual counseling, alliances in family work are often more precarious, and more attention is often given to facilitating alliances among family members rather than between the counselor and the family. Sessions are frequently difficult and anxiety provoking because family members must face complaints about one another. A family approach involves multiple clients, who often vary in their motivation and desire to be in counseling A strong reaction to counseling from one family member may lead to abrupt termination. With the pace of modern life, it may become increasingly difficult to rally several family members to commit to a regular appointment time. For these reasons and others, some families opt to discontinue treatment suddenly. Finally, some cases of couples or family counseling hinge upon whether a partner wants to stay in the relationship or whether a family member plans to maintain contact with others in the family. Typically, a client's decision to leave the relationship or distance himself or herself from family members leads to the discontinuation of treatment.

In addition to understanding clients' reasons for termination, we do well to consider our own responses to premature terminations. Counselor reactions to client termination vary but often include blaming the family, blaming ourselves, and wondering what we might have done differently. It is important to remind ourselves that sudden terminations do not necessarily equal dissatisfaction with treatment. In a case study of premature termination related to my wife's dissertation (Helmeke, Bischof, & Sori, in press) a couple canceled their session and informed the therapist that they would not be returning. Due to the nature of the study, a follow-up interview was conducted. We learned, much to our surprise, that the couple had actually found counseling helpful, liked the counselor, and noted that the sessions had assisted them in clarifying that it would be best to separate for a while. Counselors seldom have access to clients' perspectives on why they stop family work, but many report instances of clients who had discontinued therapy suddenly returning later (Patterson et al., 1998).

One of the challenges when clients leave treatment abruptly is to reach some sense of closure. Some family counselors advocate encouraging clients to return for a final wrap-up session and even informing clients at the beginning of counseling in a treatment disclosure statement that a concluding session is recommended or expected. Other alternatives are to attempt to ascertain the reasons why the clients stopped counseling through a phone call, and to present a case for returning to counseling if you believe there is more work to be done.

Our view is that it is not advisable to pursue families unduly when they have indicated a desire to terminate treatment. It is helpful to follow up initially by phone and to leave a message if possible. Because parents are typically responsible for making final decisions about continuing or discontinuing family counseling, we attempt to contact them first. Multiple calls may be warranted if there is no way to leave a message. After a few weeks, whether or not you have left a message, a letter is warranted. The letter should be positive, highlight the gains the family has made, and leave the door open for the family to decide to return in the future. It is also prudent to inform the family that you will be closing their case if you don't hear from them by a certain date, typically about two weeks from the date of the letter. Doing this helps make the status of the counseling less ambiguous. These strategies provide you and the family with at least some closure to the counseling experience. I (GHB) recall the admonition from my first clinical supervisor that "if you let families go easily, they will be more likely to return easily."

Therapist-Initiated Termination

There are likely to be occasional times when you decide unilaterally that treatment should be discontinued. Such instances include when families have become dependent upon counseling and are anxious about going it alone, or when they seem to be using therapy as an excuse not to have to make real changes in their lives. Some of the strategies we discussed earlier about making a transition from regular sessions to closure apply here (e.g., spacing out sessions, preserving therapy hour without the therapist, etc.). Another strategy may be to limit the number of remaining sessions. Although the ultimate decision to end counseling may be a collaborative one, you may actively initiate open discussion about working toward a close of treatment in these kinds of cases.

Other clinical issues may suggest a need to terminate family treatment. One example is when there is an ongoing threat of family violence, and the perpetrator, victim, or other family members minimize or deny the violence. In such a case, continuing family treatment might actually increase the risk of further violence as the family members face issues more directly, leading to possible repercussions following treatment sessions. I (GHB) faced this situation in one memorable case. A couple who were cohabitating agreed that no physical violence had occurred in more than two years, but the male partner continued to deny and minimize his coercive threats and destruction of property. These behaviors had serious repercussions not only on his relationship with his partner but also the relationship between both adults and the female partner's eight-year-old son from a previous relationship. The male partner also began to dictate the structure of treatment sessions, demanding conjoint sessions and refusing to cooperate with the structured individual time within sessions that I was suggesting. I could not in good conscience continue treatment in this manner. I explained my rationale and referred the couple to individual or group treatment for domestic violence, with the possibility of conjoint treatment thereafter. The male was extremely unhappy with my decision, but the female seemed quietly pleased at seeing someone establish clear limits with her partner.

Conclusion

This chapter has addressed an often-neglected stage and process of family work. Closure of counseling, at its best, is a collaborative, mutually agreed upon process that contains elements throughout the counseling process as well as specific tasks to be addressed in the final stage of therapy. Work with families offers some unique challenges and opportunities related to ending counseling successfully.

In this chapter we have addressed common tasks associated with effective closure and have identified key issues at various points as counseling draws to a close. We have also included core elements of the closure session itself and have offered innovative interventions that involve the entire family and facilitate the process of successful closure. We have also suggested clarifying your availability after the final session and establishing guidelines for a return to counseling. Finally, we have discussed some of the issues involved when termination of counseling is initiated unilaterally.

Like much of our work with clients, there is probably more we could have said and other issues we might have addressed. But as we know, all things must come to an end. So, we say goodbye and wish you good endings. And if you are having difficulties you can't seem to handle on your own, you can call. . . .

References

Albom, M. (1997). *Tuesdays with Morrie: An old man, a young man, and life's greatest lesson.* New York: Doubleday.

Bell, J. E. (1975). *Family therapy.* New York: Aronson.

Brock, G. W., & Barnard, C. P. (1999). *Procedures in marriage and family therapy* (3rd ed.). Boston: Allyn and Bacon.

Carlson, R., & Carlson, K. (1999). *Don't sweat the small stuff in love.* New York: Hyperion.

Dreikurs, R. (1967). *Psychodynamics, psychotherapy, and counseling.* Chicago: Alfred Adler Institute of Chicago.

Freedman, J., & Combs, G. (1996). *Narrative therapy: The social construction of preferred realities.* New York: Guilford.

Hackney, H., & Cormier, S. (1994). *Counseling strategies and interventions* (4th ed.). Boston: Allyn and Bacon.

Heath, A. (1985). Ending family therapy—Some new directions. *Family Therapy Collections, 14,* 33–40.

Helmeke, K. B., Bischof, G. H., & Sori, K. (in press). Dropping out of couple therapy: A qualitative case study. *Journal of Couple and Relationship Therapy.*

Imber-Black, E. (1999). Creating meaningful rituals for new life cycle transitions. In B. Carter & M. McGoldrick (Eds.), *The expanded family life cycle: Individual, family, and social perspectives* (3rd ed., pp. 202–214). Boston: Allyn & Bacon.

Lebow, J. (1995). Open-ended therapy: Termination in marital and family therapy. In R. H. Mikesell, D. Lusterman, & S. H. McDaniel (Eds.), *Integrating family therapy: Handbook of family psychology and systems theory* (pp. 73–86). Washington, DC: American Psychological Association.

McCarthy, B. (1999). Relapse prevention strategies and techniques for inhibited sexual desire. *Journal of Sex and Marital Therapy, 25,* 297–303.

Mitchell, R. R., & Friedman, H. S. (1994). *Sandplay: Past, present and future.* Florence, KY: Taylor & Francis/Routledge.

Papero, D. V. (1995). Bowen family systems and marriage. In N. S. Jacobson & A. S. Gurman (Eds.), *Clinical handbook of couple therapy.* New York: Guilford.

Patterson, J., Williams, L., Grauf-Grounds, C., & Chamow, L. (1998). *Essential skills in family therapy: From the first interview to termination.* New York: Guilford.

Roberts, J. (1988). Setting the frame: Definition, functions, and typology of rituals. In E. Imber-Black, J. Roberts, & R. Whiting (Eds.), *Rituals in families and family therapy* (pp. 3–46). New York: Norton.

Seligman, L. (2001). *Systems, strategies, and skills of counseling and psychotherapy.* Upper Saddle River, NJ: Prentice Hall.

Treacher, A. (1989). Termination in family therapy—Developing a structural approach. *Journal of Family Therapy, 2,* 135–147.

White, M., & Epston, D. (1990). *Narrative means to therapeutic ends.* New York: Norton.

Wilcoxon, S. A., & Gladding, S. T. (1985). Engagement and termination in marital and familial therapy: Special ethical issues. *American Journal of Family Therapy, 13*(4), 65–71.

Chapter Nine

Diversity Issues in Family Work

Fran Steigerwald

I begin this chapter with a historical perspective of multiculturalism and diversity issues within the counseling profession. My hope is to challenge counselors who conduct family work to adopt a personalized approach to cultural self-understanding and skill development through personal introspection. Case examples, questions, and introspection exercises provide self-examination opportunities that can form the basis for cultural competency. In order to maximize the impact of this chapter, I encourage you to keep a working notebook or journal.

In this chapter I also look at societal expectations of the family and family tasks. I examine and challenge societal preferences for particular structures and appearances that influence our concept of a "normal" family or "normal" family functioning. In addition, I examine how you can gain knowledge and understanding of the culture of the families you counsel. I provide some basic cultural information and sources for further exploration to help you gain these needed pieces. Finally, I discuss multicultural practices and strategies that can enhance your family work and propel you forward on your journey to becoming a culturally competent family counselor.

Where Multiculturalism Began: History and Challenge

The Civil Rights Movement of the 1960s exploded the myths of America as color blind and as a giant melting pot, shaking societal complacency about race and culture. The movement empowered minorities to speak out and define themselves as an essential and recognizable part of a pluralistic society, needing and benefiting from inclusion into the mainstream. At the same time, the movement challenged the power base of White privilege and entitlement, forcing people to self-examine what they judged as "right" and to include multiple perspectives and a diversity of worldviews. The Civil Rights Movement began the growth and understanding needed for the inclusion of all citizens into the mainstream of society.

At the same time, the feminist movement began to give voice to women and women's issues. Sexism, the unequal distribution of power between men and women in American society, and the dissatisfaction of many women with the traditional, restricted female roles began to be highlighted and addressed. Awareness, discussion, and initiation of expanding and changing women's roles changed the function and form of the family and of society. Diversity among families challenged the uniform, traditional model of family as having a working father, a stay-at-home mother, and two children, all of whom look the same. Issues of women's power; reproductive rights; domestic violence; and emotional, physical, and sexual abuse became family issues that needed to be addressed and worked through in family counseling situations.

Wrenn's 1962 challenge to counseling professionals to recognize ourselves as "culturally encapsulated counselors" (p. 444) began a critical examination of professional issues, assessment biases, and culturally restrictive practices with the goal of understanding equality and multicultural issues. A few professionals dismissed this challenge and held firm to the power base that affirmed their entitlement to set standards for others. Many, however, were troubled to think that their professional efforts were directed to defining and upholding a universal stereotype of "healthy family functioning," acceptable behavior, or "normalcy." Many were aghast to think that our profession encouraged people to conform to societal constructs proposed and perpetuated by the dominant White middle-class male perspective. Many counseling professionals began examining the counseling process itself. White, middle-class male values and behaviors that perpetuated personal, organizational, and institutional sexism and racism seemed to be the operational standard. Continuing dialogue and examination among enlightened professionals uncovered bias against, misdiagnosis of, and underserving of minorities and diverse populations. The rapid ideological and demographic changes in society over the past 40 years have added fuel to this cultural movement and necessitated moving multiculturalism into the forefront of the counseling profession as an important and timely topic.

What do the terms *diversity* and *multiculturalism* mean in the new millennium? *Diversity* is defined in the *American Heritage Dictionary* (Pickett et al., 2000) as "a point in which things differ." This raises the question, differ from what? At least when applied to people, the implication is different from the norm, the dominant White middle class, the majority way of being, thinking, looking, sounding, acting, and loving. Predominant in this difference is the concept of culture, which Bucher (2000) has defined as a "way of life, including everything that is learned, shared, and transmitted from one generation to the next . . . languages, values, rules, beliefs, and even material things we create" (p. 2). Bucher also uses the term *cultural landscape,* "referring to the different lifestyles, traditions, and perspectives that can be found in the United States and throughout the world" (p. 2); this landscape is in a state of constant change.

Exercise One

Spend a few minutes thinking about the larger society in your life today. Think about the people you come into contact with or see or read about in the media. Does your panorama of society contain more ethnic minorities; gender role differences; socioeconomic diversity; people with disabilities; and people of various ages, religions, beliefs, values, and sexual orientations than the society

---

your parents or grandparents experienced at the same points in their lives? Does this perception help you understand Bucher's concept of a changing cultural landscape?

The changes in the U.S. cultural landscape can be quantified. The U.S. Bureau of the Census (1997) estimates that the racial and ethnic minority population in the nation will reach 47% by the year 2050, meaning that the percentage of Whites will drop to 53% or less. Another factor to consider in these statistics is the growing number of people who do not want to be defined by race and refuse to list any category, who mark the category "other," or who have multiple heritages that defy categorization. La Raza, a nonprofit Hispanic advocacy group formed in 1968, reported an increase from 22.4 million Hispanics living in the United States in 1990 to 35.3 million in 2000, with more than one third of this population being under 18 years of age. Not only states having historically high Hispanic populations, but also states in the Midwest have experienced dramatic rises in the Hispanic population. Within the 10-year period between the two most recent censuses, Wisconsin's Hispanic population rose by 107%, Iowa's by 153%, and Minnesota's by 166%.

Another factor contributing to the changing cultural landscape in the new millennium is technology. McLuhan's (1967) term *global village* refers to the shrinking of the modern world as technological developments bring the people of the world together, increasing contact and awareness across cultural differences and highlighting the need for understanding of these differences.

Cultural isolation and bias have more opportunities to be challenged as diverse worldviews come into contact. It is each person's challenge, and our profession's ethical responsibility, to decide whether to choose to hold on to narrowly defined perspectives of "acceptable" standards of living and being, or whether to learn to appreciate and celebrate diversity. The heightened awareness of diversity and diversity issues, as well as altruistic concerns for the effectiveness of counseling as a true helping profession, propel and continue counselors' quest for professional self-examination. It has taken more than half a century of dialogue and honest and brave introspection, collectively as a profession and individually as human beings, to arrive where we are today. Almost every text and counselor training component touches on multicultural issues and gender sensitivities. Less and less frequently are these issues being relegated to last chapters or afterthoughts, and more and more they are being incorporated into theories, understandings, and strategies. Multicultural competency and skill training has begun. Cultural sensitivity has become a way of being as a counselor, not just a garment that is put on when certain clients walk into our offices. There are still, however, many counselors who lack knowledge and understanding of the life circumstances of the culturally diverse families with whom they work and who see their clients only from their culturally bound perspective. Multicultural awareness and appreciation is our profession's challenge for the millennium.

This challenge is not an easy one. We are often slow to stretch our comfort zones of life. It is very hard to view objectively, let alone challenge, the values we hold very close. Our culture, personal perspectives, and worldviews are part of what define who we are. The process of arriving at a true understanding is complex, difficult, and frustrating, especially when we may not even think to challenge the majority ways of thinking and doing. The easier road through life may appear to be not examining or challenging these issues, but this road is one of stagnation.

Exercise Two

Take some time now to reflect on your life. Read the following statements, then either close your eyes and reflect on or write down your responses:
- When you look around your home, what images do you see? What do people look like? How similar are they to you? Stuff, lots of it, very similar
- When you go out into your neighborhood to shop or take a walk, what images do you see? What do people

---

similar to me - neighborhood, some diversity
linden - very diff

look like? How similar are they to you?

- When you go to your place of work, what images do you see? What do people look like? How similar are they to you? *more diverse*

- When you go to your church, mosque, or temple, what images do you see? What do people look like? How similar are they to you? *very very similar*

- When you choose to have a party, what images do you see? What do people look like? How similar are they to you? *more diverse*

- When you go out to socialize with large groups of people, what images do you see? What do people look like? How similar are they to you? *similar*

- How diverse are the people in your daily life? What do you think about your level of contact with diversity? Does or could this level influence your personal perspectives and your professional cultural competency? *↑ w/ LMHS. a ton. Makes me more aware*

Usually, it is not until people feel discomfort in their lives that they consider new ways of doing and being. The shrinking global village necessitates change and causes discomfort for many, as they experience increased opportunities to meet diverse people and have their standards and rules challenged. Cultural sensitivity begins with contact and awareness, but it must also be accompanied by a willingness to change and be challenged. When pain and discomfort create personal introspection, the status quo begins to be shaken up and the process has begun.

The same process also occurs within family dynamics. Jackson (1957) studied the family as a unit and was the first to observe its resistance to change, which he coined *homeostasis*. The families with whom he worked were suffering from dysfunction, but their resistance to change, which produced negative feedback loops, provided the family with a sense of stability. A goal of family counseling became challenging that homeostasis, shaking up the family, and introducing positive feedback to bring the family into a state of heightened awareness. So, too, a goal of multicultural counseling is for the counselor to examine his or her own ways of thinking and judging and to introduce new, positive awarenesses and approaches.

Counseling in general and family counseling specifically will make little progress in the new millennium if cross-cultural differences are ignored or misdiagnosed. Family sessions may be ineffective if the counselor lacks an understanding of cultural perspectives. We counselors are growing and becoming more aware as a profession, yet we are not as good as we can become. What we need today is a willingness to subject ourselves and our profession to critical examination and strategic development.

Family and Society: Cultural Diversity Issues

If there is anywhere where diversity issues are magnified and manipulated, it is within and among families and in family counseling. The dramatic struggles within families to balance individual versus group needs, autonomy versus conformity, and tradition versus moving to new ways of being are played out on the family stage as culture and values are transmitted from generation to generation. In the past, the goal of family counseling was often to help all families adopt or conform to societal expectations and norms, with little thought to individual families' cultural backgrounds. Today, family counselors acknowledge the complexities of cultural backgrounds and help families understand and negotiate societal and cultural influences. How do family work and multiculturalism interrelate? This section is divided into six areas of reflection that can help to explain the interaction of family and multicultural counseling.

The Role of Family in Perpetuating Society

The importance of family is intrinsically understood in our society, because the family's main charge is the development of healthy individuals in order to continue society (Duvall & Miller, 1985). When a child is born or brought into a family, the societal expectation is that the family will nurture and raise the child for optimal growth in body, mind, and spirit. The most crucial task of a family is the development and socialization of children into mature, healthy, and productive members of society. Duvall and Miller propose a family life cycle that organizes the family's developmental tasks. These tasks include providing physical maintenance, such as food, clothing, shelter, and health care; maintaining order with rules, roles, and boundaries; teaching responsibility, the division of work, and the allocation of assets; developing appropriate conceptual abilities, motivation, and morale; giving and receiving affection; achieving an appropriate balance of dependence and independence and conflict resolution patterns; and the reproducing, socializing, and releasing of family members into the larger society. It is the family that gives children the skills that will allow them to operate effectively in society.

This relationship between family and society can be fraught with anxiety. The belief that when society is in difficulty the family must not be meeting its obligations results in placing blame on the family. The demise of the family has often been blamed for causing the demise of society. Reiss and Lee (1988) wrote about the stability of the family, "The last 50 years have apparently changed the marriage relation from a permanent and lifelong state to a union existing for the pleasure of its parties. The change thus swiftly wrought is so revolutionary, involving the very foundations of human society, that we believe it to be the result not of any temporary condition" (p. 309).

The interesting thing about this statement is that it was made in 1887 and referred to changes in family life between 1837 and 1887. Gordon (1988, p. 17) stated, "For at least 150 years, there have been periods of fear that 'the family'—meaning a popular image of what families were supposed to be like, by no means a correct recollection of any actual 'traditional family'—was in decline; and these fears have tended to escalate in periods of social stress."

In order to focus on this particular issue, you may wish to ask yourself these questions:

- Is the family an agent of society? If so, to what extent?
- What is the relationship between individual family

differences and autonomy versus societal expectations?

- As family counselors, to what extent are we also agents of society, perpetuating societal standards that are based on the majority rule?

Societal Expectations of the Normal Family

Societal norms exist concerning what a normal, traditional family looks like. Deviations from these standards are often framed and examined as problematic. Although the importance of the family goes unquestioned, the structure of the family, what a normal family looks like, is often questioned and may be at the basis of some reactive thoughts about family diversity. Individual and societal problems have tended to be examined in the light of family-of-origin structure, using White middle-class traditional norms as indicators of optimal functioning. Many social problems and issues have been seen as failures of the family, due to deviations of the family from the expected structure. Family research has examined the impact of family structure and functions upon the development of children. A number of studies have found that the more a family deviates from expected structural norms, the more it is questioned (Jacobson & Gurman, 1996; Morrison, 1995; Saucier & Ambert, 1986). Paramount is the notion of what a "normal" family looks and acts like, assuming, of course, that "normal" families rear "normal" children (Walsh, 1993). Inherent in this discussion is the judgment that if a person or a family does not measure up to the dominant standard, then it is deficient and therefore inferior (Thomas & Sillen, 1972; Westley & Epstein, 1969).

The concern over what the family structure should look like and what family values are correct made its way into the popular political arena in the 1990s when former Vice-President Dan Quayle criticized the popular television show "Murphy Brown" for featuring a forty-something unwed mother. Many across the country echoed his beliefs that family values were eroding and made the causal connection between diverse family structures—often specifically families without live-in fathers—and social upheaval, poverty, lack of morals, crime, and violence (Whitehead, 1993).

Many researchers over the past three decades (Offer & Sabshin, 1974; Skolnick & Skolnick, 1992; Stacey, 1990; Walsh, 1989) discussed the inherent problems of referring to family normality without a clear understanding of the term. There are numerous ways to define "normal." *Normal* can be used in terms of referent health, as in an absence of symptomatology or disease. *Normal* can be defined as a statistical majority, in which case divorce is the statistical norm, as 50% of all U.S. marriages end in divorce, and when unfiled separations are included, the estimate reaches 66% (Martin & Bumpass, 1989). *Normal* can be used as a template for ideal or optimal functioning, as when a height and weight chart is used to assess an infant's growth. *Normal* can also be used in reference to developmental processes within the family life cycle, as when we say that it is normal for adolescent children to begin to separate from their parents (Walsh, 1989). *What is normal*

Normal can also be used to perpetuate the culturally restrictive myth of a normal family being White; containing a biological mother and father with 2.3 children (preferably a boy and girl), a dog and a cat; living in a home that they own; and having an annual income in excess of $30,000. It would serve the family counselors who are examining bias and underutilization of counseling by minorities to re-examine the term *normal* and all its entrapments and inherent judgments in our conceptualization of diverse family clients.

May (1998) helps clarify this conceptualization:

The concept of the traditional nuclear family continues to permeate our thinking and our interventions. This concept leads to distinction between traditional and alternative families. The distinction is dubious, both historically and morally.

Historically it attributes a sense of false universality to a family type that is a relatively recent creation and that is continuously in change. This false historical attribution is then used to give legitimacy to certain family types and not others, independent of the special consequences of each family on the lives of the people within the families. (p. 296)

Here are some questions that you may wish to examine:
- Is one "type" of family judged better than another by our society, by your family, by yourself? If so, what effects do these judgments have upon those families and members that do not fit within the acceptable "type"?
- Think about diversity among families in structure, appearance, race, creed, physical characteristics, roles, rules, operational dynamics, sexual orientation, and socioeconomic status. Who sets and promotes those standards?
- How do these implied standards affect our work as culturally competent counselors?

Family as the Vehicle of Both Culture and Worldview

The family is the vehicle that both carries culture forward to the next generation and teaches values, prejudices, worldviews, and cultural identity. We need to examine our tolerance levels for cultural variations within the family itself. McGoldrick (1993) defines *family culture* as a person's context, including rules, beliefs, rituals, thoughts, language, class, religion, geographic and ethnic background, and family history and experiences. Understanding family culture is essential to understanding development and identity and the perspectives that clients bring into a counseling session.

Worldview and *racial/cultural identity development* are two multicultural concepts that can help counselors contextualize clients in their culture. *Worldview* is a personal orientation to and perception of the world. It is taught and cultivated within the family framework of values. The work of Ibrahim (1985), Kluckhohn and Strodtbeck (1961), Pedersen (1988), and Sue and Sue (1999) formulated the value-orientation model of worldview. In this model, worldview can be described using the four life dimensions of time, activity, social relations, and relationship with nature, which are culturally appropriate for all persons. The premise is that various cultures view these four dimensions differently. Variations on these dimensions are to be understood and accepted from a personal cultural perspective, rather than being judged as problematic or symptomatic. Differences in worldview among family members can be examined and discussed without applying inherent bias.

Time. Does the family promote a past, present, or future orientation to time? Many cultures value and respect past history, others value living in the moment, and still others place emphasis on planning for and anticipating the future. What values and beliefs within the family emphasize a particular orientation toward time? How do individual family members view time? How are differences in their views handled?

Activity. Where does activity fit in this family's life? Is it a doing, becoming, or being family? How are work, leisure, introspection, and quiet time valued? Some cultures and some families value one position over the other. What values and beliefs within the family emphasizes a particular orientation toward activity? How do individual family members view activity? How are differences in their views handled?

Social relations. How are social relations defined in the family's life? Are they linear (leaders and followers), collateral (consultant and collaborative), or individualistic (each is in control of his or her own life)? What type of social relations are valued and respected within the family? How do individual family members view social relations? How are differences in their views handled?

Relationship with nature. What is the family's relationship to nature? Does nature predestine and determine life? Is life lived in harmony with nature? Or is nature a challenge to be mastered and controlled? What values and beliefs within the family emphasize a particular orientation toward nature? How do individual family members view their relationship to nature? How are differences in their views handled?

Inherent in each of these four dimensions is a personal or cultural belief about control and responsibility, including whether control is externally or internally oriented, who has the control and responsibility, and how it is used (Rotter 1966). These beliefs begin to formulate a pattern of cultural assumptions about the world. Each dimension can be valued and understood in the context of culture and worldview, rather than the context of family judgment and labeling.

Ivey, D'Andrea, Ivey, and Simek-Morgan (2002) present the concept of worldview in another way: You and your clients are constantly making meaning in the world. The way you frame the world and what it means to you is a story you tell about what you experience and observe throughout your life. Not only do you make meaning of this complex world, but so do counseling and therapy theorists. The stories told by existential-humanistic, cognitive-behavioral, psychodynamic, and multicultural theorists are different and sometimes competing, but they provide rich ways for you and your clients to think, feel, and act differently now and in the future (p. 2).

Racial and cultural identity is a unique and developing dimension that many researchers have studied and determined to be developmental (Atkinson, Morten, & Sue, 1989; Cross, 1971; Hardiman, 1982; Helms, 1984; Ponterotto, 1988; Ruiz, 1990). Over time and through reciprocal social interaction experiences, individuals can change their racial and cultural identities. Cultural development has various levels, statuses, or stages that a person may cycle through or choose to remain at. These various stages or statuses are not fixed and rigid, but they do provide a theoretical foundation for recognizing differences within groups and movement among stages. Individual family members may simultaneously be experiencing various stages of cultural identity or acculturation to the dominant culture.

The racial/cultural identity model developed by Atkinson, Morten, and Sue in 1989 provides a framework for conceptualizing and discussing these different stages. Their work defines five stages that oppressed people, people of color, may go through in developing an understanding of their cultural identity within a dominant group:

1. **Conformity.** The person values the dominant group and deprecates his or her own group.

2. **Dissonance.** The person is aware of inconsistencies between the dominant group's values and his or her own.
3. **Resistance and immersion.** The person deprecates the dominant group, appreciates his or her own, recognizing oppression.
4. **Introspection.** The person becomes concerned about the appreciating and deprecating process and may see group views as interfering with individual autonomy.
5. **Integrative awareness.** The person appreciates his or her own self and cultural group while appreciating selected aspects of the dominant group.

Hardiman (1982), Helms (1984), and Ponterotto (1988) all developed White identity-development models based upon the assumptions that racism permeates society and that cross-cultural connections influence the dominant White culture. Helms' (1984) six status levels are the most widely cited and used in research:

1. **Contact status.** The person is satisfied with his or her current status and is unaware of racism.
2. **Disintegration status.** The person feels anxious and disoriented because of racial dilemmas.
3. **Reintegration status.** The person idealizes his or her own racial group and is intolerant of others.
4. **Pseudo-independence status.** The person expresses intellectual commitment to his or her own group and deceptive tolerance of others.
5. **Immersion/emersion status.**
   The person engages in a personal search for the meanings of racism and entitlement
6. **Autonomy status.** The person makes a commitment to relinquish entitlement and racism.

There is a continuum in how tolerant families are of diversity within the family itself. At one end of the continuum, all family members must look, walk, talk, and act alike. A monoculture of sorts exists within the family and everyone must be the same to be accepted. At the other end of the continuum, individuality of expression, appearance, and thought is so emphasized that each member is unique and the family so disconnected that it appears to have no family culture at all. Somewhere between these two extremes fall the majority of families and their worldviews.

There is also a continuum in how tolerant families are of divergence between their family's culture and the dominant societal culture. At one end of the continuum, the family may foster a strong racial pride within the family, independent of societal values. At the other end, the family rule may be to become acculturated to the dominant culture, to fit in and blend in. Alternatively, multiple stages and racial identities may coexist within the same family. Similar continuums of tolerance for diversity exist for gender roles and expectations within the family, for immigrant parents and their first-generation children, for interracial families, for multigenerational households, for blended families, and for families with alternative lifestyles.

Here are some questions to ponder:
- How is the culture within a family influenced by the greater societal cultural norms?
- Are cultural norms influenced by individual family cultures?
- How are individuals, families, and society interconnected?
- How does an understanding of worldviews and racial identity development assist you in being a culturally competent counselor?

Cultural Self-Awareness

A culturally competent counselor needs to be aware of his or her own family culture and how it may influence counseling relationships, especially when working with a family whose culture is different. A sound therapeutic relationship is necessary for effective counseling to take place. Counselors' basic training and skill development center upon that concept. Counselors are charged with creating conditions wherein rapport can be built and congruent relationships established, using empathy, unconditional positive regard, and genuineness (Rogers, 1957). Even if the counselor practices these fundamental skills, however, the interaction between the family and the counselor can be fraught with major misunderstandings, especially if cultural differences between the counselor and the family are not considered or acknowledged. Understanding and valuing the importance of culture begins with an understanding and valuing of one's personal cultural foundations. "Counselor, know thyself" has been an imperative to professionals to be vigilant about self-awareness and professional development and continually to examine themselves and their theoretical orientations. Knowing how your own family has affected your development and the formulation of your culture is important to cultural competency. Knowing and understanding your family's myths about what is normal, your family's tolerance for diversity among its members, your learned biases and judgments, your worldview, and your racial/cultural stage of identity development forms the foundation for cultural competency. Complete the following exercise to examine your family culture and how you conceptualize family culture.

Exercise Three

Read over the following exercise and allow yourself sufficient time and introspection to tell the story of "My Culture" by writing down your responses to these questions.
- When did you first realize that you were _____ [YOUR RACE]? When did you first realize that you were _____ [YOUR GENDER]?
- What story or stories are connected with those times?
- What do you think and feel about your race? Your gender?
- Are there other stories connected to your emerging awareness?
- What are your central beliefs, values, or rules of life? How did you get them?
- What is most important to you?
- What are your religious or spiritual beliefs?
- What roles do you assume in your life? Where did these come from?

- What are your interactions and boundaries with others in your family and outside of your family? How did you come to learn them?
- What were you taught within your family about people who were different from you?
- What were your interactions like with diverse populations?
- How does your gender influence your life views and choices?
- How do your gender and sexual orientation conform to or differ from those of your family?
- Is there a physical characteristic that has a defining role in your life?
- What is your worldview? Your orientation to time, activity, social relations, and relationship with nature?
- Do you see yourself recognizing your own racial development in your life?
- Do you see yourself as a cultural person? Can you appreciate your cultural formation?
- What is the importance of family in this process? Share your cultural story with someone you value, someone who will listen and appreciate your story. Afterwards, ponder these additional questions:
- What was this sharing like for you?
- How do your family dynamics affect your culture?
- What have you come to understand about yourself as a cultural person?
- How do you feel about others as cultural beings?
- How has this exercise helped you increase your cultural sensitivity and understanding?

Knowing and valuing your own culture helps you to understand and value the culture of others. Understanding how intrinsic and complex your own culture is can help you eliminate bias and racism in your family work.

Cultural Bias in Family Counseling Theories

Multiculturalism was not considered in the development of many family counseling theories. European or White North American and male references formed the basis of many traditional counseling theories and interventions. The client's context was often ignored, even to the point of excluding family considerations. Cultural competency urges you to examine theoretical perspectives from a multicultural context in order to effectively meet the needs of your clients (Ivey et al., 2002).

Exercise Four

Understanding the importance of family, family culture, and the need to consider the multicultural implications of your theoretical approach, you are preparing to meet a new family for family counseling.

Before You Meet the Family

A woman named Susan phones your office to set up an appointment for her entire family. The secretary prepares an initial intake, providing you with the following information:

Susan and Marty are the parents of Joe, age 13, and Faye, age 12. They have lived in a middle-class suburban development since Joe was born. Susan is a full-time nurse for a local cardiologist and Marty is a pharmaceuticals salesman for a national drug company. Susan states that they have always been very open and free in communicating with each other and with their children. Their children have responded in a fun-loving, spontaneous manner until about six months ago. Susan states that nothing significant has happened or changed in their family. She and Marty have a solid, loving relationship. However, the children are now showing signs of moodiness and

---

isolation from the family. They want to stay in their rooms and not participate in fun family activities the way they used to. Their children have been having some difficulty in school; their grades have dropped from As to Bs and Cs, and some minor altercations (unexplained spats with their classmates) have been reported between classes. The classroom teacher suggested family counseling. Susan's mother, who teaches in a middle school, has told Susan that this is normal adolescent behavior and that she should not overreact to these small things. Susan says, however, that they have been very involved parents and do not want to ignore what may become a larger problem.

Before You Meet the Family

You are giving some thought to this family. You want to be prepared and you also like to "center" yourself before they come in. Take some time here to formulate answers to the following questions:

- From the small amount of information you have, what ideas do you have about this family? *What experiences are common b/n kids → behavior*
- How will you help set the tone for a sound therapeutic relationship with this family? *open comm, let them talk / explain them 1st*
- Would you do anything different in this family session than you would in your "typical" first family meeting? *no. just ensure all have opp to talk*
- Are there any special areas you might like to explore? *all p.o.v.s*
- In general, how are you feeling about seeing this family? *a challenge !* *go to why/ if conns. necessary*

The Family Walks In

Susan and Marty are both women.

What reaction do you sense within yourself? *expected* Thoughts? Feelings? Would you make any changes in your strategy? *new dimension - what's it like for kids?*

Susan is a Black woman and Marty is a White man.
What reaction do you sense within yourself?
Thoughts? Feelings? Would you make any changes
in your strategy? *same*

Susan wheels in her husband, who is quadriplegic.
What reaction do you sense within yourself?
Thoughts? Feelings? Would you make any changes
in your strategy? *no*

Susan and her husband Marty are both White; they
introduce you to their two Asian children.
What reaction do you sense within yourself?
Thoughts? Feelings? Would you make any changes
in your strategy? *no*

Susan and Marty are Hasidic Jews.
What reaction do you sense within yourself?
Thoughts? Feelings? Would you make any changes
in your strategy? *no*

Think about your reactions. Try not to judge
them as good or bad, but rather as indicators of where
you are and where you may have to go with these
issues. You may have had reactions ranging from "I
had no reaction whatsoever," to "I was unsure where
to go with this family when I saw that they were____,"
to "Finally, I had something to hang my diagnostic
hat on," to "I froze and needed time to regain my
composure," to "I don't want to work with those kinds
of families." What can you learn about yourself
through these reactions? What would you like to do
with these reactions?

↓ surprise/closure. Excited @ all opps, inc.
influence of family structure on children.
give them safe space to talk, but don't assume
diversity is issue.

Diversity challenges all of us. Look at the range of reactions to diversity issues I listed at the end of the exercise: numbness, defensiveness, fear, quick assumptions, panic, relief, self-consciousness, and avoidance. Our reactions tell us about our comfort level in working with diverse families. They also give us a measure of how culturally competent we are as professionals. They point to our fears, our biases, our prejudices, and our potentially racist thoughts. The recognition of diversity may give some counselors an immediate, simplistic place to begin to examine the problem issues, even though there may be no correlation between this and the problem. Culturally encapsulated counselors are quick to make judgments and diagnose a family based on their appearance or differentness alone. Faced with our reactions, we have options: to flee, to choose not to work with diverse families, to deny our reactions while remaining distant and disconnected from our clients, or to stay and work through these pesky signals and become competent, caring counselors who are able to help families change, navigate in a racist environment, and develop in positive ways.

Here are some questions to ponder:

- What are the limitations of the theories we use?
- Do they assume that certain attitudes and values are to be universally held and impose these upon families with differing cultures?
- How does understanding the individual's and family's cultural influences differ from looking for symptoms of dysfunction?
- How can professional diagnosis and treatment perpetuate culturally biased universal standards or stereotypes?

Culturally competent family counseling approaches the family with deep respect. Conceptualization, assessment, and treatment of families are undertaken as collaborative adventures. A broad, inclusive understanding of the diversity of human interaction replaces the narrow, restrictive interpretations that constrain families as well as counselors.

Universals in Family Functioning

The concept of healthy family functioning varies greatly among cultures and within families, yet research is beginning to examine family strengths and dimensions that can be applied to most cultures. According to Dancy & Handal's (1980) model, the key determinants of children's adjustment and satisfaction is not the appearance of the family, but the critical variables of family processes such as conflict resolution, problem solving, and family interaction. Strength-based models that appreciate each family's uniqueness and its functions regardless of its structural appearance lend themselves to cultural competency.

Strong, healthy families and a strong, healthy society are universally valued. According to Stinnett and DeFrain (1985), in studies of family strengths, six dimensions consistently were reported: commitment, communication, appreciation and affection, time spent together, ability to cope with stress, and spirituality. These dimensions were reported in strong families across all boundaries of appearance and diversity.

Anderson and Sabatelli (1999) found five family characteristics that have a positive influence upon the family system: common purposes and tasks, a sense of family history, emotional bonding, strategies for meeting the needs of individuals and the family as a whole, and firm yet flexible boundaries within and between family subsystems. Families that exhibit these qualities are able to adapt and adjust the family's rules, roles, communications, and patterns of interaction and to incorporate diverse family structures. Ivey and colleagues (2002) summarize this perspective clearly:

> Although the list of examples of cultural differences could go on, it is important to note the fundamental assumptions that ground our work as culturally competent family counselors and psychotherapists. In order to work ethically and effectively among culturally diverse families, we must (1) be aware of our own ethnic/racial heritage, (2) be alert to the ways in which sociopolitical factors and scientific

norms influence the field and our own theory and therapy approach, (3) demonstrate empathy for members of other cultures, (4) realize that ethnicity may be an essential ingredient in a treatment plan, and (5) not assume homogeneity within groups but instead remain keenly alert to the significant variations of each client and family while noting the broad characteristics that differentiate ethnic/racial groups. (p. 403)

Cultural Knowledge and Understanding of Diverse Families

Counselor-client differences on any of the dimensions of race, gender, sexual orientation, age, ethnicity, religion, disability, or family structure may give rise to a cross-cultural counseling experience. Sue, Arredondo, and McDavis (1992) proposed multicultural counseling competencies and standards to address these experiences. Three of the standards follow:

1. A counselor is aware of his or her own cultural values and biases.
2. A counselor is aware of the client's worldview.
3. A counselor is knowledgeable about culturally appropriate intervention strategies.

The first and second sections of this chapter have assisted you in self-examination through cultural exploration, racial identity development models, an outline for worldview awareness, and family "picture" work. At this point the imperative needs to move from "Counselor, know thyself" to "Counselor, know thy clients." The same strategies can be applied to this imperative. When working with diverse families, it is important to have an understanding of the experiences, heritages, backgrounds, and characteristics of the specific cultural groups with which you work. It is equally important to understand oppression and the significant impact it may have on development.

Ridley (1995) defines *racism* as "any pattern of behavior that tends to systematically deny access to opportunities or privileges to members of one racial group while perpetuating access to opportunities and privileges to members of another racial group" (p. 28). According to Ridley, racism may be overt, covert intentional, or unintentional, but all are insidious forms of victimization. Racism and the various other-isms all imply *oppression,* that is, "the systematic, institutionalized, and socially condoned mistreatment of a group in society by another group or by people acting as agents for society as a whole" (Yuen, 2000). Oppression has residual effects, which it is important to recognize and understand in order to avoid judgmental and inferential errors, misdiagnosis, or inappropriate treatment (Ridley, 1995).

Discrimination of any kind—whether on the basis of race, gender, sexual orientation, ethnicity, disability, age, or other characteristics—limits the opportunities of the group labeled "inferior" and creates barriers to their advancement, while supporting and giving access to the "superior" group. Therefore, repeated exposure to discrimination may pose risks and cause harmful effects in the oppressed. Discrimination and oppressive circumstances interfere with a person's ability to live life fully, make choices, and exert control in building a meaningful life (Yuen, 2000).

Being marginalized and experiencing discrimination and oppression may have these effects:
- reduced access to social benefits, such as approval, popularity, rights, privileges, power, opportunity, knowledge, and advantages
- increased social risks, including victimization through violence, suspicion, blame, the assumption of guilt for crime or other harmful actions, rejection, alienation, isolation, and economic exploitation (Kids Help Phone website, 2001).

Oppression may become internalized in people who are oppressed, affecting the way they view and value themselves and how families value their members. Low self-esteem, depression, difficulties with interpersonal relationships, substance abuse, behavioral disorders, child abuse, domestic violence, helplessness, and suicide all may be symptoms of internalized oppression (Aponte & Wohl, 2000; Harper, 1988; Ho, 1990; Hughes & Demo, 1989;

McIntosh, 1984). Families that regularly suffer discrimination may carry into counseling sessions a distrust of the counseling process itself, exhibiting resistance, hostility, defensiveness, and suspicion. They may view the counselor as representing the oppressive majority group (cultural transference), as an oppressor, or as an authority figure. Anger, fear of reprisal, and inability to be genuine often result and confound the helping process. Cultural countertransference refers to the emotional response of the counselor being projected back onto the family. This may occur if the counselor is unaware of the cultural transference process or of his or her personal prejudices and stereotypes. Countertransference places the clients in a double bind of loss, whether they accept or reject the counselor's projection (Ridley, 1995).

For example, a counselor may immediately assume that a Black client's anger is Black rage. Countertransference occurs when the counselor dismisses it, minimizes it, or is afraid of it and as a result avoids any issues that could arouse it. The clients continue to lose because their issues are not dealt with therapeutically. Culturally incompetent counselors who have high power needs or high dependency needs or who experience "White guilt" may be condescending and paternalistic. This attitude may cause the clients to become enraged or passive, learned helplessness to be reinforced, and the ability to problem solve to be jeopardized. The therapeutic process and outcomes are impaired as a result (Vontress, 1981).

In order to understand a family's cultural perspectives, you can examine their worldviews and where they are in their development of racial identity, as well as encouraging them to tell their cultural stories. Outside of sessions, it is important to read, take workshops, do research about particular cultural dynamics, understand and examine yourself as a racial and cultural being, involve yourself in diverse cultural relationships and experiences, seek consultation and supervision about diversity issues, investigate institutional barriers, and learn to be an advocate for diverse clients (American Counseling Association, 1992). Ridley (1995) cautions counselors not to be blind to racial and cultural issues, but at the same time not to be overly color conscious, filtering every issue through the lens of race. In addition, Paniagua (1996) recommended four areas to consider when working with families from the four major non-White cultural groups in the United States (i.e., African Americans, Native Americans, Asians, and Hispanics):

1. Focus on the extended family, because all four cultures value the inclusion of multiple family members in counseling sessions.
2. Examine the levels of acculturation within the family, because in all four cultures it is not uncommon to have dissimilar levels of acculturation among family members, and you will need to take this into consideration in your therapeutic processes and interactions with the family.
3. Consider the similarities and dissimilarities between yourself and the family, because these differences will influence assessment and treatment. The family needs to value the interactions, processes, and outcomes of the counseling relationship. Your cultural sensitivity, cultural competence, and credibility enhance the process.
4. Address the problems of bias in tests and assessment guidelines. Following are ten guidelines for minimizing bias in family assessment:
   - Examine your own bias and prejudice.
   - Be aware of the effects of racism.
   - Consider socioeconomic issues.
   - Minimize sociocultural gaps between yourself and the family.
   - Assess for the presence of culturally related syndromes (DSM-IV).
   - Ask culturally appropriate questions.
   - Consult folk healers.
   - Be cautious in using mental status exams.
   - Use the least biased assessments first.
   - Consider language differences.

Another important consideration is to avoid the pitfall of stereotyping on the basis of race or cultural group. Each person and family is unique and has its own culture. To assume that a particular family possesses certain traits and values because of their race, creed, age, gender, or ethnicity is culturally naïve.

Williams (1999, p. 130) summarizes culturally competent considerations:

> Multicultural family therapy can be complex and challenging. Family counselors working ethically with ethnic or racial families must understand myriad cultural issues and be able to assess the impact of these issues on family processes. Levels of acculturation, ethnic/racial identity, cultural modes of interpersonal interaction, spirituality, social and class status and its relationship to race and racism, and gender and racial discrimination are potentially salient cultural issues.

Exercise Five

Please study this case, then reflect upon the questions that follow it.

Case Study

As part of your work at a university counseling center, you do pro bono work with people in the community. A children's services department in rural Appalachia has contacted you to counsel a 10-year-old boy named Joey. School officials have described Joey as big for his age, unruly, and conduct disordered. The teacher and principal are working to get this child evaluated and reassigned to a school for severely behaviorally handicapped children. You are advised that Joey broke a child's arm in kindergarten, which school officials describe as having started all the problems. Since then he has been described as a clown and troublemaker, constantly distracting others in the classroom and frustrating the teachers.

You want to see the entire family together but you have been told that "Dad," Joey's stepfather, definitely will not come in for counseling. You try to get the other family members to come in for sessions,

---

but you are only able to see Joey, his mother, and his aunt together about three times. The mother is 26 years old, very quiet and docile. The aunt, Mom's older sister is assertive and tells you that she is there to protect her sister from the system taking away her kids. She explains that this happened to her. She adds that her baby sister doesn't read, so she doesn't want her signing away all her rights. You try to reassure them and discuss informed consent and confidentiality issues.

In the initial session you learn that Joey is very mischievous at home as well as in school. He has a younger brother, age six. Joey is constantly getting him riled up through fighting and horseplay. Mom says it never stops. He takes hours to settle down at bedtime, jumping from bed to bed and kicking the furniture repeatedly, until Dad comes home from work around 11 p.m. and threatens to punish him. Mom says she and her husband do not beat Joey, instead punishing him by denying him videos, grounding him, or making him stand in the corner. They live in Dad's trailer with two of his older sons, ages 19 and 21, who both work and spend little time at home. They do, however, help with a lot of chores. Mom is emphatic that there are no drugs or alcohol in the house but says that her parents and the six siblings in her family of origin are all alcoholics.

Mom explains that Joey hit the kid in kindergarten after his maternal grandmother told Joey a family secret when she was drunk. Joey had assumed till then that the man he had lived with all his life was his Dad. Grandma told Joey that his real Dad was in prison and that this man was not his real father but only his brother's. Mom says she knows that was wrong for his grandma to tell him this and thinks that this is when he started being angry.

Mom doesn't know what else to do about Joey's problems. Most of her interaction with her two boys seems to be negative; she describes it as mostly yelling and screaming. She says that she goes to bed with a migraine headache several times a week. She describes her nerves as being shot and explains that she had received some "nerve pills" in the past but was denied a refill of the prescription because the clinic doctor said she could depend on them too much.

You encourage Mom to get a physical. You discuss parenting issues with her, such as natural and logical consequences, and emphasize stressing the positive with the boys and trying to ignore some of the negative behavior. You encourage her to spend positive time with the children. You set up numerous appointments with the entire family, but Mom repeatedly breaks the appointments, giving as excuses that she has to bake a birthday cake that month, she doesn't have a car, she can't find a parking space at the university, or her headaches and backaches are bad. She sends Joey with his case worker. They have few resources and pay $2 for the session, usually in small change.

You continue to see Joey because Children's Services provides transportation. Through sand-tray work and game playing you recognize that Joey needs to be in control and to win. He seems to like power and getting people upset. He becomes joyful and silly when he gains power. Joey is beginning to talk to you about some of his real feelings of anger and guilt. You want to see the family together, because you know this is where the work really needs to be done.

↑ power
↑ control

[handwritten left margin]

research, ask mom/Joey for more ideas/day

[handwritten left margin]

Exercise Five continued

You get a call from Children's Services saying that Joey's mom called them. She and Joey's Dad want to stop counseling altogether because they say Joey comes home worse after his sessions with you.

Questions

Take some time to reflect on this family. Refer back to the guidelines for working with diverse families, then answer the following questions:

- How does this family's culture differ from your own? Jot down some ideas. *SES, mixed*
- What do you know about the Appalachian culture? *SES*
- What potential problems can you see? *know little*
- How could you have "joined" with this family?
- How did the differences between the family culture and the culture of the university counseling center inhibit progress? *educated vs. uneduc*
- What could you do to learn more about this family and their culture? *research, from them*
- What do you think is causing the mother's resistance?

I had the opportunity to work with this family years ago, and they taught me more about becoming a culturally sensitive counselor than any other experience I have had. I am forever grateful to them. I had worked closely with my supervisors to try to understand Mom from her perspectives on life but felt that I never had gotten a real handle on her life. I became frustrated and judgmental. I, too, understood exhaustion and frustration. I had raised four children as a single parent. When my kids were all in their teens, there were days when I did not think I or they would make it. I baked birthday cakes and still went to therapy. I circled parking lots 12 times but still kept appointments. I hated myself for even making these comparisons, but I still did. I thought that I had worked really hard to be understanding of Mom's culture. I had told her numerous times in the few counseling sessions we had had simply to focus on the positives and ignore the negatives. This did not seem to have any effect. When Mom pulled Joey because she felt that I was making him worse, my ego flared and I was hurt. Even though I was embarrassed by these feelings, I was able to discuss them with my supervisor.

When I got my ego under control, I phoned Mom. I told her that I would love to continue to see Joey, but that I would support her decision as his parent. I believed that she and her husband loved Joey and wanted only what they thought was best for him. I said I would be available if they ever needed me, and I supported their right to decide this. An hour later I got a call back from Mom stating that her husband liked what I had said and he wanted the family to continue. Her voice sounded lighter than I had heard it before.

I was encouraged. I relaxed and got creative, asking her if we could put our heads together to try and find ways to keep regular appointments and make some progress. I told her that negotiating the university parking situation was overwhelming for most of us. She described the rural area where she lived, and I found a Rural Action building in her area that would allow me to use a counseling office. Dad still declined to attend, but we had his complete support. I met the family on their turf bright and early twice a week. I'd start with Mom and Joey but would work with whoever came. I intuitively dressed down in an effort to bond with Mom and provide a safe environment. I concentrated on supporting Mom. I felt as if I was trying to gain the trust of a small, frightened child, but gradually she opened up. She shared her culture with me by telling me family stories and bringing in crafts and willow baskets that she and her husband made, displaying the skills that were passed down from generation to generation. Mom described her trailer and the land around it and how much they loved it.

Finally, feeling safer, she began to talk about all the drinking in her family when she was growing up. She had made a promise to herself that she would not drink because of her two children. Finally, she got up the nerve to ask me what *positive* and *negative* meant. She had not understood the words I had used so frequently in my pursuit of teaching good parenting. I had never realized that. One sacred session she shared with me how her father had disciplined her and her siblings and got them all to do their chores. "You see, he'd line all us kids up against the wall. I was the baby and the last one. He got his shotgun out and held it here, to my head, and told the rest they'd better git goin' or he'd blow my head off." I cried with her, and for the first time I finally saw what it meant to understand life from my client's perspective . . . from her culture, her worldview, her values. I was working with a miracle and I had not known it. She didn't drink. She took care of her family's basic needs. She wasn't doing any of the things that were done to her as a kid. She drove. She could bake a birthday cake! These were miracles! I'd missed them all, and worse yet, I'd devalued them all by looking through my own White professional middle-class eyes and my ideas about what a normal family was. Once I was able to value her life and her work, and see her strength in holding this family together, things changed. Can you imagine how she must have felt in the beginning coming to me for counseling? I was part of the system that worked against her family and took kids away. She had to find me in a complex university setting without being able to read. I was an interloper into rural Appalachia . . . a Northern White "educated" woman who was going to tell her how to run her life and family. I might as well have worn a neon sign around my neck that glowed, "I AM THE EXPERT ON YOUR LIFE! TRUST ME!" Joining with Mom was the key to finally doing some solid work with this family. Trust starts with respect and valuing. Previously these had just been words to me. I had thought that I knew their meaning, but until I connected with this family, I knew only their surface meanings. This family taught me how to be a culturally sensitive family counselor.

Many traditional family therapy approaches do not have cultural sensitivity as an important foundation. Many systems counselors would not have seen this family because Dad would not come. Many theoretical models repeat the "social norms" and enforce male-oriented power dynamics, assuming theoretical values are universal and need to be imposed upon others of diverse cultures. What is the label *resistance* really all about? Examine it through the eyes of culture. This is where we need to look at theoretical perspectives with the lens of cultural sensitivity and see their limitations. Multicultural family counseling works toward empowering families to cope with their lives as they perceive them. We need to use creativity and professional dialogue to find effective ways to meet the families with which we wish to join.

Multicultural Strategies for Family Work

Skills and strategies such as active listening, forming a therapeutic bond with the family, unconditional positive regard, and an understanding of systems theory are necessary in all family counseling sessions. Certain additional multicultural strategies are necessary when working with diverse families. In their highly respected work, Sue, Arredondo, and McDavis (1992) cite several general multicultural skills and abilities that a counselor should possess for competency in working with diverse populations:

- the ability to send and receive both verbal and nonverbal messages appropriately
- the ability to exercise institutional intervention on behalf of the client
- the ability to seek out and work with healers or spiritual leaders
- the ability to speak the language of the client, make an appropriate referral, or arrange translation
- the ability to use assessments and tests with expertise, understanding their cultural limitations
- the ability to work sensitively with people who have experienced oppression and discrimination and, where possible, to eliminate oppression and discrimination
- the ability to educate clients about processes and outcomes

In additional writings, two other abilities are added to the preceding list (Ivey et al., 2002):

- The ability to determine whether the problems that are addressed in counseling are the result of external factors,

such as racism and oppression
  • The ability to educate clients about their rights

One of the more challenging aspects of working with diverse families is the conceptualization and management of resistance. Ridley (1995) points out that counselors need to be able to understand resistance therapeutically, not take it personally, and be able to employ resistance management strategies skillfully. Some of these strategies are refocusing attention on the clients; confronting normative resistance, contradictions, and inconsistencies; exposing clients to the concept of secondary gains; and reframing control needs.

Recently, specific interventions for use with culturally diverse families have appeared in the literature. Goldenberg and Goldenberg (1998) stress the importance of understanding the family's social and political context; developing a structure for working with institutional and community resources; formulating, supporting, and prioritizing concrete goals and solutions through problem solving; teaching effective communication techniques; empowering and strengthening the family to gain control of their lives; protecting the integrity of the family; reducing conflict and building flexible boundaries; and mobilizing the family to work together.

When working with families in which generational conflicts are exacerbating acculturation differences, Szapocznik and colleagues (1997) have proposed using a model called bicultural effectiveness training (BET). BET helps family members to realize the pressures that living in two cultures exert on them by having each member share his or her experience in a respectful way. Understanding the need for some flexibility and the harmful effects of rigidity aids the family in adjustment.

Assertiveness training (Alberti & Emmons, 1995; Cheek, 1976), relaxation techniques and stress inoculation and management (McNeilly, 1996; Meichenbaum, 1994), and storytelling are additional strategies and techniques that counselors have employed effectively to foster positive mental health in diverse families and to develop techniques for clients who have been disempowered.

Advocacy is a relatively new concept in working with diverse families. Kenney (2001) states that advocacy begins the moment you begin to examine honestly and openly the concept of race in our society. Advocacy requires going out to schools, churches, and community agencies to ensure that your clients have available to them resources for their growth and enhancement. It requires counseling professionals to challenge political forces that keep people oppressed and deprived.

Exercise Six

Family Diversity Self-Assessment Checklist
The following Family Diversity Self-Assessment Checklist is adapted from the cultural competency work of Sue, Arredondo, & McDavis (1992) and Sue, Bernier, et al. (1982) and the feminist empowerment work of Worell and Remer (1992). I suggest you use this list periodically to re-examine your commitment to cultural competency.

Self-Awareness
1. How aware am I of my own family's culture, values, and attitudes? *more so than before
Catholic, conserv, middle class, midwest*

2. How aware am I that my own family culture, values, and attitudes can create biases that influence the process of forming a therapeutic relationship with a family in counseling?

    1-10 → 8.5 , I know, just not always how

3. How am I able to understand, value, and communicate sensitivity for cultural backgrounds that are different from my own? *let them teach me
    show interest*

4. How do I consciously work on being open, receptive, and comfortable with a wide range of family cultures and values? *acknowledge differences*

---

5. What do I understand about how my image of a "normal family" can lead to discrimination, hindering progress and work?

need open mind

6. How do I work to examine and eliminate any discriminatory attitudes, judgments, and beliefs I may have about families?

process! supervision

7. How do I work to increase my knowledge and understanding of individual, institutional, and sociopolitical oppression and discrimination, as well as how these factors influence diverse family systems?

research / prof dev.

8. What social and learning experiences do I actively seek out to increase my awareness, knowledge, and skill in working with a wide range of families?

under a culture

9. How do I work to establish egalitarian personal and client-counselor relationships?

they have power re: self

Worldview Awareness

1. How do I work to understand, assess, and empathically communicate how minority identity development, discrimination, and oppression affect the families with whom I work?

ask! awareness

2. How do I respect indigenous beliefs, practices, and rituals that are important to family functioning?

acknowledge
- dates? Values

3. How effective am I in joining with the family, accepting where they are and understanding life from their perspective?

I try

Culturally Appropriate Intervention Strategies

1. How do I work to send and receive communication effectively in cross-cultural interactions?

joining

2. How do I work to identify external barriers that prevent optimal family functioning?

discussion

3. How do I advocate for the family to reduce or eliminate these barriers and help the family negotiate them?

w/in school
connect to resources

4. How do I interpret and understand cultural bias in assessment data?

manuals

5. What culturally competent interventions am I able to use with families?

6. How do I work with families to help them set goals that are relevant to them? *ask them to ID*

Exercise Six continued

7. How well do I understand and work with the effects of trauma, sex-role stereotyping, victim blame, and power differentials?

8. Do I continue to self-monitor my attitudes and actions for bias and discriminatory practice? When I become aware of problems in these areas how do I seek to change them? Yes.

Conclusion

May (1998) summarizes the professional call in working with culturally diverse families:

> A diversity of challenges confronts us. We must be cultural brokers. We must broaden and deepen our professional roles. We must distinguish between cultural sensitivity, cultural relativism, and the cultural defense. We must facilitate a change for all families from separation, isolation, despair, and emptiness to contact, community, hope, and commitment. (p. 299)

References

Alberti, R., & Emmons, M. (1995). *Your perfect right: A guide to assertive living* (7th ed.). San Luis Obispo, CA: Impact Books.

American Counseling Association. (1992). ACA professional standards. *Journal of Counseling and Development, 20,* 64–88.

Anderson, H., & Sabatelli, R. M. (1999). *Family interaction: A multigenerational developmental perspective* (2nd ed.). Boston: Allyn & Bacon.

Aponte, J. F., & Wohl, J. (2000). *Psychological intervention and cultural diversity* (2nd ed.). Boston: Allyn & Bacon.

Atkinson, D. R., Morten, G., & Sue, D. W. (1989). A minority identity development model. In D. R. Atkinson, G. Morten, & D. W. Sue (Eds.), *Counseling American minorities* (pp. 35–52). Dubuque, IA: W. C. Brown.

Bucher, R. D. (2000). *Diversity consciousness: Opening our minds to people, culture, and opportunities.* Upper Saddle River, NJ: Prentice Hall.

Cheek, D. (1976). *Assertive Black . . . puzzled White.* San Luis Obispo, CA: Impact Books.

Cross, W. E. (1971). The Negro-to-Black conversion experience: Towards a psychology of Black liberation. *Black World, 20,* 13–27.

Dancy, B. L., & Handal, P. J. (1980). Perceived family climate, psychological adjustment, and peer relationships of black adolescents: A function of parental marital status or perceived family conflict? *Journal of Community Psychology, 8,* 208–214.

Duvall, E. M., & Miller, B. (1985). *Marriage and family development.* New York: Harper & Row.

Goldenberg, H., & Goldenberg, I. (1998). *Counseling today's families* (3rd ed.). Pacific Grove, CA: Brooks/Cole.

Gordon, L. (1988). *Heroes in our lives.* New York: Viking.

Hardiman, R. (1982). White identity development: A process oriented model for describing the racial consciousness of White Americans. *Dissertation Abstracts International, 43,* 104A (University Microfilms No. 82–10330).

Harper, F. D. (1988). Alcohol and Black youth: An overview. *Journal of Drug Issues, 18,* 15–20.

Helms, J. E. (1984). Toward a theoretical explanation of the effects of race on counseling: A Black and White model. *The Counseling Psychologist, 12,* 153–165.

Ho, C. K. (1990). An analysis of domestic violence in Asian American communities: A multicultural approach to counseling. *Women & Therapy, 9,* 129–150.

Hughes, M., & Demo, D. H. (1989). Self-perceptions of Black Americans: Self-esteem and personal efficacy. *American Journal of Sociology, 95,* 132–159.

Ibrahim, F. A. (1985). Effective cross-cultural counseling and psychotherapy: A framework. *The Counseling Psychologist, 13,* 625–638.

Ivey, A. E., D'Andrea, M., Ivey, M., & Simek-Morgan, L. (2002). *Theories of counseling and psychotherapy: A multicultural perspective* (5th ed.). Boston: Allyn and Bacon.

Jackson, D. D. (1957). The question of family homeostasis. *The Psychiatric Quarterly Supplement, 31,* 79–90.

Jacobson, N. S., & Gurman, A. S. (1996). *Clinical handbook of couple therapy.* New York: Guilford Press.

Kenney, K. (2001). Multiracial families. Advocacy Paper #6, American Counseling Association. Retrieved October 16, 2001 from http://www.counseling.org/conference/advocacy6.htm

Kids Help Phone website. (2001). Available: http://kidshelp.simpatico.ca.

Kluckhohn, F. R., & Strodtbeck, F. L. (1961). *Variations in value orientations.* Evanston, IL: Row, Patterson, & Co.

Martin, T. C., & Bumpass, L. L. (1989). Recent trends in marital description. *Demography 26*(1), 37–51.

May, K. (1998). Family counseling: Cultural sensitivity, relativism, and the cultural defense. *The Family Journal: Counseling and Therapy for Couples and Families, 4*(6), 296–299.

McGoldrick, M. (1993). Ethnicity, cultural diversity, and normality. In F. Walsh (Ed.), *Normal family processes.* New York: Guilford Press.

McIntosh, J. L. (1984). Suicide among Native Americans: Further tribal data and considerations. *Omega: The Journal of Death and Dying, 14,* 215–229.

McLuhan, M. (1967). *The mechanical bride: Folklore of industrial man.* Boston: Beacon Press.

McNeilly, M. (1996, March 18). Stress of racism may kill, study finds. *Honolulu Advertiser,* p. A7.

Meichenbaum, D. (1994). *A clinical handbook: Practical therapy manual for assessing and treating adults with post-traumatic stress disorder (PTSD).* Waterloo, Ont.: Institute Press.

Morrison, N. C. (1995). Successful single-parent families. *Journal of Divorce and Remarriage, 22,* 205–219.

National Council of La Raza. Making a difference for Hispanic Americans website. Retrieved October 24, 2001 from http://www.nclr.org/policy/census.html.

Offer, D., & Sabshin, M. (1974). *Normality: Theoretical and clinical concepts of mental health* (2nd ed.). New York: Basic Books.

Paniagua, F. (1996). Cross-cultural guidelines in family therapy practice. *The Family Journal: Counseling and Therapy for Couples and Families, 4*(2), 127–138.

Pedersen, P. B. (1988). *Handbook for developing multicultural awareness.* Alexandria, VA: American Association for Counseling and Development.

Pickett, J. P. et al. (Eds.). (2000). *American heritage dictionary of the English language* (4th ed.). Boston: Houghton Mifflin.

Ponterotto, J. G. (1988). Racial consciousness development among White counselor education programs. *Journal of Multicultural Counseling and Developments, 65,* 146–156.

Reiss, I. L., & Lee, G. R. (1988). *Family systems in America* (4th ed.). New York: Holt, Rinehart, & Winston.

Ridley, C. R., (1995). *Overcoming unintentional racism in counseling and theory.* Thousand Oaks, CA: Sage Publications.

Rogers, C. R. (1957). The necessary and sufficient conditions of therapeutic personality change. *Journal of Consulting Psychology, 21,* 95–103.

Rotter, J. (1966). Generalized expectancies for internal versus external control of reinforcement. *Psychological Monographs, 80,* 1–28.

Ruiz, P. (1990). Cultural and historical perspectives in counseling Hispanics. *Journal of Multicultural Counseling and Development, 18,* 29–40.

Saucier, J. F., & Ambert, A. M. (1986). Adolescents' perception of self and of immediate environment by parental marital status: A controlled study. *Canadian Journal of Psychiatry, 31,* 505–512.

Skolnick, A., & Skolnick, J. (1992). *Family in transition* (7th ed.). New York: HarperCollins.

Stacey, J. (1990). *Brave new families: Stories of domestic upheaval in late-twentieth-century America.* New York: Basic Books.

Stinnett, N., & DeFrain, J. (1985). *Secrets of strong families.* Boston: Little, Brown.

Sue, D. W., Arredondo, P., & McDavis, R. J. (1992). Multicultural counseling competencies and standards: A call to the profession. *Journal of Counseling and Development, 70,* 484–486.

Sue, D., Bernier, J., Durran, A., Feinberg, L., Pedersen, P., Smith, E., & Vasquez-Nuttall, E. (1982). Position paper: Cross-cultural counseling competencies. *The Counseling Psychologist, 10,* 45–52.

Sue, D. W., & Sue D. (1999). Counseling the culturally different: Theory and practice (3rd ed.). New York: John Wiley & Sons.

Szapocznik, J., Kurtines, W., Santiesteban, D. A., Pantin, J., Scopetta, M., Mancilla, Y., Aisenberg, S., McIntosh, S., Perez-Vidal, A., & Coatsworth, J. D. (1997). The evolution of a structural ecosystemic theory for working with Latino families. In J. G. Garcia & M. C. Zea (Eds.), *Psychological interventions and research with Latino populations* (pp. 166–190). Boston: Allyn & Bacon.

Thomas, A., & Sillen, S. (1972). *Racism and psychiatry.* New York: Brunner/Mazel.

U.S. Bureau of the Census. 1997. *Statistical abstract of the United States, 1997* (117th ed.). Washington, DC: U.S. Government Printing Office.

Vontress, C. E. (1981). Racial and ethnic barriers in counseling. In P. B. Pedersen, J. G. Draguns, W. J. Lonner, & J. E. Trimble (Eds.), *Counseling across cultures.* (2nd ed., pp. 87–107). Honolulu: University Press of Hawaii.

Walsh, F. (1989). Perceptions of family normality: Refining our lenses. *Journal of Family Psychology, 2,* 303–306.

Walsh, F. (1993). Conceptualization of normal family processes. In F. Walsh (Ed.), *Normal family processes* (2nd ed., pp. 3–69). New York: Guilford Press.

Westley, W. A., & Epstein, N. B. (1969). *The silent majority.* San Francisco: Jossey-Bass.

Whitehead, B. D. (1993, April). Dan Quayle was right. *Atlantic Monthly,* pp. 47–84.

Williams, C. (1999). Ethical considerations in multicultural family counseling. In P. Stevens (Ed.), *Ethical casebook for the practice of marriage and family counseling.* Alexandria, VA: American Counseling Association.

Worell, J., & Remer, P. (1992). *Feminist perspectives in therapy: An empowerment model for women.* New York: Wiley.

Wrenn, C. G. (1962). The culturally encapsulated counselor. *Harvard Educational Review, 32,* 444–449.

Yuen, N. G. (2000). *Politics of liberation* (3rd ed.). Dubuque, IA: Kendall/Hunt.

Chapter Ten

Off the Couch and Online: Technology in Family Counseling

Patricia W. Stevens and Kerrie Shulman

In the month of June 2001, 167.1 million people accessed the Internet. Over the past 12 months 40 million Internet searches were done to access health and medical information, with 40% of these searches seeking mental health information. To date, more than 60,000 mental health sessions have been conducted using telecommunication methods, with the number of e-mail sessions ranging from 5,000 to 25,000 per day (Freeny, 2001). Although reliable statistics about Internet use are difficult to obtain because of the newness of the technology and the intricacies of the cyberworld, the Internet is clearly having an impact on our professional and personal lives.

The use of the Internet to access health information is by no means limited to the young. One survey shows that, in fact, seniors over age 60 "are moving toward the Internet at a faster pace than other age groups" (MCOL, 2001). As the Baby Boomers move into their sixties, the prediction is that Internet usage will increase at an even higher rate. These statistics have vast implications for counselors.

As professionals with a long history of face-to-face counseling sessions conducted behind closed doors, many counselors are having difficulty shifting into this new dimension. Whether you are a reluctant computer user or an excited computer user, our clients are using the Internet. They are seeking information and consultation through the web.

As with any innovation, professionals need to be well trained and knowledgeable before they begin using online technology. This article will provide an overview of different ways to use the Internet in your practice—not necessarily as a replacement for face-to-face counseling, but as a tool with a variety of purposes within the therapeutic process.

Features of Internet Counseling

Traditional counseling occurs in an atmosphere utilizing all five senses of both the counselor and client. Counseling in the cyberworld has a very different dimension. In cybercounseling the sensory exchange between client and counselor is limited. Video technology, which allows clinicians to see the visual cues they frequently use for the purpose of diagnosis and treatment, is not commonly available. This absence of nonverbal behavior may influence (either positively or negatively) the way a client perceives counseling and consequently affect the dynamics of the therapeutic relationship (either positively or negatively). Critics of online counseling cite this loss of visual cues as a pitfall with the potential to hinder counseling and treatment. Proponents, in contrast, consider this a potentially positive feature for both the client and counselor. They sometimes give Freudian counseling as an example of an approach that does not use the client's visual cues in treatment or diagnosis and that, in fact, discourages interaction between the client and counselor. Freeny (2001) states, "Counterintuitively, it appears that the absence of visual cues during e-mail counseling is actually disinhibiting, even if the client is known to the clinician" (p. 34). Moreover, Internet language has begun to develop its own means of affective communication. Suler (1999) gives the following examples of language and symbols used as visual cues to affect: "smileys, spacing, punctuation, ASCII art, special keyboard characters, and font size, color, and style" (p. 5). These symbols are becoming common language for anyone who uses the Internet with any regularity. In fact, Internet language is changing our daily face-to-face interactions as we incorporate these words into our speech (Suler, 2001).

Another dimension that distinguishes cybercounseling from live counseling is the increased level of anonymity. Clients have the option of presenting themselves in any manner they choose. Clients may use this freedom to present themselves as they truly are with no restrictions or to present themselves as someone totally different than who they are. Grohol (cited in Freeny, 2001) notes, "people's sense of anonymity on the web seems to free them and encourage more candid communication. It helps many people overcome the stigma of seeking mental health treatment" (p. 34). Clients further reported that they were able to respond without worrying about how the counselor would react to their comments and that they appreciated not being restricted by time, so they could take time to consider and frame their communications.

Cybercounseling transcends temporal and spatial boundaries. The Internet brings together a diverse group of people from a variety of locations in a way that was not possible before the web was available. "Geographical distance makes little difference in who can communicate with whom . . . the irrelevance of geography has important implications for people with unique interests or needs" (Suler, 1998a, p. 2). This removal of the geographic limitation results in immense availability of resources for both client and counselor. The Internet also opens up an avenue for a varied assortment of relationships. Suler remarks on these relationships, saying, "With relative ease, a person can contact people from all walks of life and communicate with hundreds, even thousands of people" (p. 3).

Participants in online counseling may take a few minutes or a few days to think about their responses. This allows them to articulate their feelings or thoughts on the presented subject with care. Another interesting feature of cybercounseling is that the communication can be permanent and tangible. Both client and clinician may print out or save communications for later reference. Having the client review e-mail correspondence from time to time can be a powerful tool for measuring growth or proximity to completing goals. For the counselor this e-mail record provides an opportunity to regularly analyze the process and effectiveness of the counseling.

The shifts in the constructs of time, geographic location, physical presence, and availability of resources are just a few of the examples of how technology is changing the profession. The rules of the counseling relationship as we currently conceptualize them are no longer applicable as we begin the twenty-first century. We need to familiarize ourselves with the variety of methods for using online technology effectively in our counseling work, our business management, and our professional development.

This chapter provides a plethora of examples to whet your appetite. As with any new technique, it is important to learn to use the technique appropriately rather than letting it use you. With this in mind, you must begin by determining whether the clients or families you choose to work with are appropriate candidates for electronic counseling.

Assessing Appropriateness for Internet Counseling

Because the Internet has created the ability to transcend geographic and personal boundaries, mental health professionals can now serve populations that might otherwise not seek services. Families with individuals who are disabled and unable to leave the house, who do not speak, who have agoraphobia, or who are concerned about the stigma of seeking mental health services may embrace online counseling and psychoeducation. For families living in rural areas, online technology facilitates their access of counseling services (Powell, 1998). Online counseling may be appealing to clients who are frequent business travelers or those whose schedules are so hectic that they find maintaining a consistent office visit schedule difficult. The increasing availability of online counseling through the Internet has triggered a heated and highly polarized debate among professionals concerning the appropriateness of this means of service delivery (Powell, 1998). The American Counseling Association's Ethical Standards for Internet Online Counseling (1995) contains a section devoted to this issue. It states, among other things, that "professional counselors develop an appropriate intake procedure for potential clients to determine whether online counseling is appropriate for the needs of the client" (p. 13).

Further, the International Society for Mental Health Online (ISMHO) has been created to meet the growing needs of online counselors. ISMHO established a list of questions to help assess client appropriateness for online counseling and develop clear and appropriate intake procedures. Here are some of these questions (ISMHO, 2001, pp. 1–5):

- What communication methods are adequate or preferable for assessing the client?
- How might the person's computer skills, knowledge, platform, and Internet access affect the counseling?
- How knowledgeable is the person about online communication and relationships?
- How well suited is the person for the reading and writing involved in text communication (e-mail, chat)?
- How might previous and concurrent mental health treatment affect online counseling?
- How might personality type, presenting complaint, and diagnosis influence the person's suitability for online counseling?
- How might physical and medical factors affect online counseling?
- How might cross-cultural issues affect the counseling?
- What other online resources might be appropriate to incorporate into a treatment package?

The ISMHO (2001) suggests that assessing the clients within the medium in which counseling will be performed (in this case, electronically) is important. You may need to employ other media as well in order to conduct an accurate assessment with a family, including an initial face-to-face or telephone meeting. Another factor of major importance is whether or not a family has access to the resources (e.g., software, Internet access) necessary for counseling. You will also want to verify that family members have sufficient knowledge of the technology to ensure successful interaction. In addition to technical skills, the potential clients need to understand the dynamics of Internet relationships. You will want to examine the family members' abilities to read and write adequately and in a manner suitable for text-based interventions. Another factor to address is the family's expectations for online counseling as opposed to face-to-face counseling, especially if they have received prior counseling. Finally, you will want to evaluate the level of care family members need and be ready to make referrals if necessary.

Another ISMHO criterion for Internet counseling focuses on client characteristics:

> As a rule of thumb, severe pathology and risky behaviors—such as lethally suicidal conditions—may not be appropriate for online work. Tendencies towards poor reality testing and strong transference reactions may become exacerbated in text communication, thereby making them difficult to manage and potentially destructive to treatment. People with borderline personality disorders can often challenge the boundaries of therapy, which can be especially problematic in e-mail communication and when combining different methods of communication. (ISMHO, 2001, p. 5).

Once you have familiarized yourself with the differences between the processes of counseling online and off-line, and have carefully screened the appropriateness of counseling candidates, online counseling can begin. Any numbers of therapies are available through the Internet. Individual, couples, family, and group counseling are all accessible via the Internet, as are psychoeducational and professional development sites. These services are provided through a variety of methods.

Methods of Cybercounseling

According to John Grohol (cited in Freeny, 2001) approximately 90% of online counseling is text based. Text-based communications are written messages typed via a keyboard (or for clients with disabilities possibly other means). Text-based communication encompasses e-mail, chat rooms, bulletin boards, and web pages. Text-only communication obviously provides no visual cues. The use of a web or video camera in conjunction with text or telephone communication is becoming more feasible as the price of the video equipment drops, the quality of the image increases, and the bandwidth available for a computer connection expands. Suler (2001, p. 5) outlines the value of using typed text in cybercounseling:

- The absence of face-to-face interaction encourages some people to be more honest and expressive.
- Some people, due to their cognitive or interpersonal styles, may naturally express themselves better, comprehend others better, or both through writing.
- Some people who balk at seeing a counselor in person (due to factors such as anxiety about self-disclosure or the stigma of being a patient) may be more willing to seek text-based help because of the anonymity it offers.
- The process of writing may tap therapeutic cognitive processes and encourage an observing ego, insight, working through of issues, and the therapeutic construction of a personal narrative, as in journal writing or bibliotherapy. For some people, text communication taps and strengthens cognitive processing, which could be an asset in cognitive therapies.

Types of Text Communication

There are two general types of text communications: synchronous and asynchronous. In synchronous communication, all parties are meeting in real time. Everyone involved in a synchronous chat is sitting at a computer at exactly the same time. No matter where they are geographically located, they are interacting with one another almost instantaneously. Two types of synchronous chats are instant messaging and chat rooms. In rare cases, synchronous communication can be achieved via e-mail, if messages are delivered immediately. Synchronous communication allows counselors to interact instantaneously with all family members, even if they are geographically distant, providing immediate feedback and ongoing conversation. Suler (2001) characterizes synchronous chats as "message by message conversations in which a button is pressed to transmit a message, as well as more synchronous chat conversations where everything that both parties type can be seen as it is being typed, including typos, backspacing, and deletions" (p. 3). A specific example of a synchronous communication is a parenting skills chat room (available through a variety of Internet browsers such as AOL, Yahoo, and Netscape) in which all participants are logged in and responding to one another immediately in writing. Another example is a private chat between a family and counselor in a real-time chat room hosted by an Internet provider. In such a case, the counselor and family make an appointment and agree on how long the chat will last, and only the family and the counselor are involved. As such, this situation mimics an in-office appointment. Suler (2001) summarizes a few of the pros and cons of synchronous text communications as related to the therapeutic relationship. A synchronous chat allows the family and the counselor to make a time-limited appointment during which to meet. The real-time text communication simulates actually being in the counselor's office and invites inspiration by all parties involved. On the other hand, it may also be difficult to schedule synchronous communication around differing time zones and geographical locations.

Asynchronous communication allows for time distance between the participating members because they do not need to be sitting at their computers at the same time. In fact, hours or days may elapse between a communication and the response to it. Suler (2001) characterizes asynchronous communication as "a stretching of the time frame in which the interaction occurs, or no sense of time boundary at all" (p. 4). Examples of asynchronous communication include message boards or listservs, e-mail, and online groups.

Message Boards or Listservs

Message boards are threaded discussions available through a variety of Internet sites such as the Stepfamily Association of America (http://www.saafamilies.org). In a threaded discussion, participants post messages and respond to other people's messages. The message board may be open to anyone or it may be password protected and available only to a certain group of participants. Threaded discussions usually do not happen in real time. One person posts a question, and over a period of time, other people respond to the question, sharing their experiences. Participants may post and respond at their leisure. The structure of the message board creates the thread because the original message can be shown first and responding messages connected to it, usually by indenting the reply under the original message. Examples of message boards are discussion forums on how to handle curfew issues with adolescent children or how to engage in a "fair" fight with your partner.

E-mail

E-mail, another means of asynchronous communication, is "the method most often used by psychotherapists to work with clients, mostly because it is easy to use and rapidly becoming a very popular method of communicating" (Suler, 2001, p. 5). E-mail can be used as the medium for counseling or as a means of communication between sessions. "E-mail is a great way for a therapist to stay in touch with clients between sessions, not only for setting up, changing, and reminding them of appointments, but for providing supportive messages and keeping in touch when either the client or therapist has moved away" (Dickerson, 2001, p. 35). Freeny (2001) describes an instance of using e-mail as a between-session counseling technique. While on vacation, he opted to contact a client in crisis via e-mail in order to provide support. Freeny remarks, "When I got back, we resumed our face-to-face sessions as if they had never been interrupted. In fact they hadn't been interrupted, only altered to accommodate the medium of e-mail" (p. 34). The following lists illustrate the pros and cons of asynchronous communications as related to the therapeutic relationship (adapted from Suler, 2001, p. 3):

Pros

- There are no scheduling problems or other difficulties associated with a specific appointment time. Different time zones are not an obstacle.
- Being able to reply when you're ready and have time is a major convenience.
- There is an "enhanced zone for reflection" that allows both you and the client to think about and compose replies. For the client, this might have important implications for issues concerning impulsivity. You have the advantage of being able to plan replies more carefully and manage countertransference reactions more effectively.

Cons

- The professional boundaries of a specific, time-limited appointment are lost. Because there are not yet any standards for interacting in an asynchronous time frame, you must set boundaries in a way that makes sense to the client and that works for you. Otherwise, you might be overwhelmed with numerous and frequent e-mails from the client or might receive only sporadic and infrequent communications.
- There is a reduced feeling of "presence" because you and the client are not together in the same place and time.
- Some of the spontaneity of interacting in the moment is lost, along with the information about a person that spontaneous actions may reveal.
- Not meeting at a specific place and time may lessen the client's sense of commitment.
- Pauses in the conversation, late arrival at a session, and not

showing up are lost as psychologically significant cues (although pacing and length of replies in asynchronous communication do provide some cues).

Although there is much value in using text communication as a means of counseling or an adjunct to counseling, this mode raises pertinent issues:

1. With increased anonymity comes the risk of not knowing with certainty the identity of the person(s) typing the text.
2. People vary in their skill in using written words, and written communication may become difficult to understand at times.
3. Third, for some individuals, establishing trust may be more difficult with a counselor they have never met.

Online Groups

A popular way of using technology in counseling today is the provision of group services via the Internet. A various assortment of online groups have been created in many genres, including therapeutic groups, support groups, and psychoeducational groups. Some groups are set up by a professional, and others are e-mail groups in which no formal leader is identified. Suler (1998b) says of this type of online counseling, "such groups can exist as mailing lists or newsgroups, in which the meeting is asynchronous, or in conference/chat environments, which involve synchronous communication" (p. 1). Online groups transcend both time and space. They create a sense of universality that eliminates geographical boundaries, and perhaps also gender and culture. Suler (1998b) describes online groups as a true "grass roots phenomenon" in which one of the advantages "as compared to the real world is that people with similar concerns easily find each other and form meetings" (p. 1). "Online support groups are based on the same tenets of traditional support groups. Both types of support groups encourage members to express concerns, emotions, and ideas; offer advice and support; ask questions; and share information in an anonymous setting" (Gary & Remolino, 2000, p. 98).

Computerized Assessment Tools

Another important use of technology in counseling is computerized assessment tools. "Under the right conditions and with proper use, using technology to foster assessment is a great way to go" (Wall, 2000, p. 237). Computerized assessment provides accessibility and immediate feedback, assesses higher-order skills, and assists people with disabilities. Clients can take computerized tests from home or at their leisure. Wall (2000, p. 239) adds, "The potential for immediate test scoring and feedback is a key advantage with technology-delivered assessment that can be a significant motivator for persons taking assessment instruments." Computer-based assessments tap into and utilized a client's cognitive skills in a way that paper-and-pencil assessments do not. For example, people with disabilities may take a test using individualized modifications that suit their particular special needs, such as an enlarged font, a touch screen, or a voice-activated computer. Two examples of assessment web sites are www.powerinside.com, a for-profit site where counselors may purchase services, and http://assessments.ncs.com, which offers free assessments.

Although computerized assessment does have many advantages, Wall (2000) mentions possible pitfalls as well: "Persons with limited resources, and especially those without computers, who may in fact be more in need of assessment services, could be blocked from using essential assessments due to resource restrictions" (p. 240). Another concern is whether or not computerized tests are as secure as paper-and-pencil tests. Confidentiality may be compromised or the identity of the test taker unknown. Wall also points out that "gender and racial and ethnic fairness" may be an issue with regard to differences in access to and degree of comfort with computers and technology (p. 243). Finally, as with all tests and assessments, proper interpretation is critical. Although immediate feedback is a positive, this immediacy should not in any way detract from proper interpretation.

Professional Development Through Technology

Technology has provided new avenues for counselors to enrich the business and clinical aspects of their practice. The Internet offers "an abundance of mental health sites featuring practice management, useful products, professional advice, research articles, clinical advice, and peer networks" (Dickerson, 2001, p. 34). A survey conducted by *Psychotherapy Finances* published in October 2000 ("Fee, Practice, and Managed Care Survey," p. 11) shows that more than 50% of clinicians surveyed in both solo and group practice use computers for Internet access, word processing, billing, and e-mail communication. One in four keeps electronic records and less than one in three files claims or authorizations electronically. It is of interest to note, however, that only 3% of group practitioners and 14% of solo practitioners surveyed did not use the computer for any professional applications.

Table 1. Percentage of Counselors Using the Computer for Various Functions		
Type of Activity	Solo Practice (% of Counselors)	Group Practice (% of Counselors)
Word Processing	76	91
Billing	55	84
E-mail	52	50
Internet	50	53
Patient records	25	28
Electronic claims	11	37
Electronic authorizations	2	8
No computer	14	3

The Internet is a convenient option for professional development activities. Several web sites have been created for the purpose of counselor professional development. Sites such as www.digitalceu.com, www.capellauniversity.edu, and www.planet-therapy.com offer online continuing education units for family counselors and other mental health practitioners. (Note: We offer these sites and others in this chapter as examples only and do not necessarily endorse them over other sites.)

Many state licensure boards require counselors to take courses for licensure or licensure renewal. For example, in Colorado a jurisprudence workshop is mandatory for practicing in the state. This workshop is available either as an all-day traditional workshop or on the Internet (www.digitalceu.com). This gives clinicians an alternative to taking time away from home or work to complete the workshop requirement.

Clinicians' support communities, such as clinical discussion groups, have also proliferated on the web.

> One example,www.shrinksonline.com, describes itself as a format that enables professionals everywhere to communicate with one another, so they can share ideas and experiences in an atmosphere of support from their professional community. ShrinksOnline gives everyone working in behavioral healthcare an opportunity to exchange dialogue, challenge convention, and help shape public policy. We have created areas on the site where serious discussion about current issues is encouraged, as well as areas that make it fun and easy to debrief, share experiences and just blow off steam. (www.shrinksonline.com/about-us.cfm)

The Internet provides a wealth of information right at the fingertips of the discriminate user. Clinicians can access useful information in order to stay current on particular topics of interest. For example, a subscription to www.Medscape.com, yields weekly cyber newsletters giving current psychiatric information, including medication information.

Professional organizations such as the American Counseling Association (www.counseling.org), the International Association of

Marriage and Family Counselors (www.iamfc.org), and the American Association for Marriage and Family Therapy (www.aamft.org) offer a variety of up-to-date articles on a variety of pertinent subjects. Other organizations in many specialty areas offer online educational information (www.aasect.org, www.iapt.org, or www.bgsu.edu/colleges/edhd/programs/AMCD/HomePage.html).

These sites and others can assist you in staying current on information in the field. Because clients also can access much of the same information, they may research information on the Internet before they seek services. As clients become more knowledgeable, family counselors have an ethical responsibility to maintain a high level of expertise. As an example, one way you might gather information would be to visit the same bulletin board on communicating with partners that your clients accessed. This serves two purposes: It gives you a context for understanding some of the couple's behaviors, and the fact that you took the time to visit the web site may strengthen your bond with the couple.

Cyber Ethics

As mentioned earlier, with new concepts introduced into the field come new considerations for ethical practice that professional organizations and individual clinicians need to address. Cybercounseling must uphold the same ethical codes as face-to-face counseling, but additions or modifications to the codes may be necessary to meet the unique challenges of family cybercounseling. Web-based family counseling presents new challenges in the management of ethical dilemmas. Hughes (2000) cites confidentiality, duty to warn, and competence as central ethical issues relevant to using technology within the counseling arena.

Confidentiality

Confidentiality, both online and in person, is an extremely important ethical concern. Online counseling gives rise to unique and novel questions about the limits of confidentiality. In online counseling, you cannot be aware of who is actually in the room with the family or which individuals within the family are participating. In addition, non–family members may have access to the server or e-mail accounts that are being accessed. It is important to be aware that by law messages transmitted to or from a client's place of employment may be accessed and read by a supervisor. As such, the 2001 National Board of Certified Counselors Standards for the Practice of Webcounseling states that "encryption methods should be used whenever possible. If encryption is not made available to the family, families must be informed of the potential hazards of unsecured communication on the Internet. Hazards may include authorized or unauthorized monitoring of transmissions and/or records of webcounseling sessions (p. 2). The American Counseling Association's Ethical Standards for Internet Counseling (1995) contain a similar warning. ACA goes a step further by stating, "Professional counselors provide one-on-one counseling only through 'secure' web sites or e-mail communications applications which use appropriate encryption technology" (p. 12). According to ACA, "professional counselors provide only general information from 'non-secure' web sites or e-mail communication applications" (p. 12).

Duty to Warn

Duty to warn becomes more complicated in the cyberworld. In some cases you may not know the identity of the family members who are clients. You may live in a different state than your clients, which raises concerns about legal jurisdiction regarding licensure and the right to practice as well as how to report abuse or imminent danger to authorities. The physical distance between you and your clients creates another problem. In the event of imminent danger, you must rely on the information the clients give you in order to provide protection. You are also reliant on professionals in the geographic location where the clients live (sometimes across the country) to keep the clients or potential victims from harm. Therefore, there are even fewer viable methods of keeping clients safe than in traditional counseling settings. Although web sites have been established to assist suicidal clients (e.g.,www.samaritans.com) these also create potential hazards for you and your clients.

Competence

King, Engi, and Poulos (1998) discuss the boundaries of competence as one of the central issues surrounding the use of technology in counseling. Section C.2a of the ACA code (1995) reads:

> Counselors practice only within the boundaries of their competence, based on their education, training, supervised experience, state and national professional credentials, and appropriate professional experience. Counselors will demonstrate a commitment to gain knowledge, personal awareness, sensitivity, and skills pertinent to working with a diverse client population. (p. 5)

With the use of the Internet within the family counseling professions being so recent, it is difficult to gauge the appropriate competency level of practitioners. King and colleagues (1998) comment on the newness of the Internet in the profession: "The Internet is a new medium for assisting in the therapeutic process, and to date there is not a body of empirical research to determine the effectiveness of using this method. When acquiring informed consent for any as-yet-untested clinical approach, clients should be informed in writing that the method is new and untrialled [sic]" (p. 47). To ensure that you are competent to practice counseling via technology, you can seek consultation and supervision from other professionals practicing in this realm.

Other Ethical Concerns

Some additional ethical issues are worth mentioning: Review your liability insurance to find out whether it covers electronic transmissions prior to incorporating this tool into your practice. Also research any state-specific regulations regarding the limitations and liabilities of cybercounseling. As in any counseling setting, you have a responsibility to complete a thorough assessment to ensure that clients are appropriate for entry into this type of counseling, and you should provide links to regulatory agencies and directions for reporting ethical violations.

Another important ethical concern in the practice of online counseling is the issue of consent, particularly when dealing with minors. It is important to use due diligence to try and ascertain that the person is legally of age to seek counseling services or, in the case of family therapy, that you have parental consent to work with minor clients.

Additional Online Family Interventions

The types of online counseling methods mentioned in this article lend themselves well to family counseling. King and colleagues (1998) comment on using the asynchronous chat in family counseling: "This ensures that each family member involved will be able to find the most appropriate time to participate according to their own schedule. Also, they can delay responding to their family members until they have considered fully their intended communication" (p. 45). This type of chat allows marriage and family counselors to reach family members in different geographical locations and time zones. The Internet may open communication channels for family members who are emotionally cut off. When participating in this type of asynchronous communication you would monitor the conversation and reply to everyone involved. In your e-mails back to the family, you might offer therapeutic insight and comments on family interactions and patterns.

The Internet and e-mail have become a major method of communication among children and adolescents. This avenue has given youth a new voice and a new way of conversing. It further gives parents and counselors a way to meet children and adolescents at their level. Casey (1992) talks about using home entertainment software to encourage relationship building, commenting that "professionals have infused video games into the relationship-building stage of the counseling process through several strategies" (p. 1). Video games can be used to strengthen the parent-child relationship as well as the therapeutic relationship.

Conclusion

Mental health professionals can no longer ignore the Internet and the variety of methods for engaging families through this medium. As professionals we need to be proactive in integrating technology into our field. Ethical guidelines, training, and supervision and licensure issues continue to be muddled. The challenge for the future is to ensure that Internet use in the field is of high quality, ethical, and legal. These issues, not the use of the Internet itself, are the ones we continue to struggle with.

References

American Counseling Association. (1995). *Ethical standards for internet online counseling.* [Online]. Available: http://www.counseling.org/resources/internet.htm.

Casey, J. (1992). Counseling using technology with at-risk youth. *Eric Digest* [Online]. Available: http://www.ed.gov/databases/ERIC_Digests/ed347480.html.

Dickerson, V. C. (2001, March/April). Five ways to use the Internet in your practice. *Psychotherapy Networker,* 34–36.

Fee, practice, and managed care survey. (2000, October). *Psychotherapy Finances,* 26(10), 1–12.

Freeny, M. (2001, March/April). Better than being there. *Psychotherapy Networker,* 31–39.

Gary, J. H., & Remolino, L. (2000). Coping with loss and grief through on-line support groups. In J. W Bloom & G. R. Walz (Eds.), *Cybercounseling and cyberlearning: Strategies and resources for the millennium* (pp. 95–113). Alexandria, VA: American Counseling Association.

Hughes, R. S. (2000). Cybercounseling and regulations: Quagmire or quest? In J. W Bloom & G. R. Walz (Eds.), *Cybercounseling and cyberlearning: Strategies and resources for the millennium* (pp. 321–338). Alexandria, VA: American Counseling Association.

ISMHO [International Society for Mental Health Online]. (2001). Assessing a person's suitability for online therapy [Online]. Available: http://ismho.org/casestudy/ccsgas.htm.

King, S. A., Engi, S., & Poulos, S. T. (1998). Using the Internet to assist family therapy. *British Journal of Guidance & Counseling, 26*(1), 43–52.

MCOL find seniors' Internet usage outpaces younger users (2001). [Online] Available: http://www.mcol.com/052600.htm.

National Board of Certified Counselors (2000). Standards for the ethical practice of webcounseling [Online]. Available: http://www.nbcc.org/ethics/wcstandards.htm.

Powell, T. (1998). Online counseling: A profile and descriptive analysis [Online]. Available: http://www.netpsych.com/powell.html.

Suler, J. (1998a). The basic psychological features of cyberspace [Online]. Available: http://www.rider.edu/users/suler/psycyber/basicfeat.html.

Suler, J. (1998b). Online therapy and support groups [Online]. Available:http://www.rider.edu/users/suler/psycyber/therapygroup.html.

Suler, J. (1999). Online lingo [Online]. Available: http://

www.rider.edu/users/suler/psycyber/pal_lang.html.

Suler, J. (2001). Psychotherapy in cyberspace: A 5-dimensional model of online and computer-mediated psychotherapy [Online]. Available: http://www.rider.edu/users/suler/psycyber/therapy.html

Wall, J. E. (2000). Technology delivered assessment: Power, problems, and promise. In J.W. Bloom & G.R. Walz (Eds.), *Cybercounseling and cyberlearning: Strategies and resources for the millennium* (pp. 237–251). Alexandria, VA: American Counseling Association.

What is shrinks online? (n.d.). Available:http://www. shrinksonline.com/about-us.cfm

Chapter Eleven

Ethical Issues in Family Work

David M. Kaplan

For more than half a decade, Mary Culkin and I edited a quarterly ethics column focusing on family work, first in the *International Association of Marriage and Family Counselors Newsletter* and later in *The Family Journal: Counseling and Therapy for Couples and Families*. These columns responded to ethical dilemmas in family work submitted by counselors across the spectrum of specialties and modalities. What follows is a selection of the most interesting columns. The compendium starts off with our last column, describing important ethical lessons we have learned over the years. Following that are columns speaking to a variety of ethical dilemmas. Enjoy!

Lessons Learned

We have been editing a quarterly ethics column written by the International Association of Marriage and Family Counselors (IAMFC) Ethics Committee for more than five years, first in the *IAMFC Newsletter,* and then in this journal. Although the ethical dilemmas that have been presented have admittedly not been a scientific sample, we think that we have learned some valuable lessons by trying to solve real world problems. This is our last column, and so we thought we might pass on some of what we have learned.

Obtain Informed Consent From Family Members

This is so important we are going to say it again. Obtain informed consent. It cannot be stated too emphatically that obtaining informed consent from every family member in counseling prevents many misunderstandings and problems down the road. When you have informed consent, you have the client's agreement to the specific rules of your practice. Clients have both a right and a need to know about fees and payment schedules, your theoretical framework and treatment approach, rules about appointments, how and when they are allowed to contact you, rules about confidentiality, and your educational background and training. This information should be given to clients in a packet that includes an acknowledgement sheet that can be signed and returned to you. Obtaining informed consent in writing is important because, contrary to what we often believe, clients do not hang on therapists' every word and can misinterpret or disregard verbal statements we make about our practices. An excellent source for creating an informed consent brochure is *The Paper Office* by Edward L. Zuckerman and Irwin P. R. Guyett, Pittsburgh, PA: Clinician's Toolbox, 1992.

One important aspect of informed consent that came up over the years in the ethics column was determining exactly who the client is. In family counseling, we often work with individuals, families, and institutions (i.e., schools or courts). Every person that you provide counseling to has a right to know who the primary client is. In this way, each individual knows which will come first when there is a conflict between the needs of the individual, family, and institution. One column presented a situation in which a high school counselor smelled alcohol on the breath of a student in counseling. The school policy for students found to be under the influence of alcohol was, among other things, immediate suspension. The counselor wanted to know whether her first priority was to follow school policy and report the intoxication, or to focus on the student and continue the counseling without reporting it. This dilemma can be avoided by letting students know when they first come for counseling the conditions under which the school becomes the primary client and when counselors must follow school policies. If the counselor thinks that the school intoxication policy must be upheld, getting informed consent will assure that clients are aware of what will happen if they walk into the school counselor's office intoxicated.

Know When to Keep Confidentiality and When to Break It

Now we know why confidentiality is often referred to as the cornerstone ethic. Over half of the dilemmas presented in our column had confidentiality as a main theme. It is important for professional counselors to become thoroughly familiar with Section II of the IAMFC ethical code, which states that information shared with a counselor by a client will not be disclosed to others unless the following conditions are present: There is clear and imminent danger to the client or someone else, the client completes a signed waiver form, the law mandates disclosure, the counselor is a defendant in a court case arising from professional activity, or the counselor needs to discuss a case for consultation or educational purposes (in which case facts about the client are disguised to prevent disclosing the exact identity of the client).

Although these statements on confidentiality seem cut-and-dried, things can become less clear when counselors deal with real families and real counseling situations. One column focused on the issue of ensuring confidentiality when providing both family counseling and individual counseling for a family. The ethics committee decided that there were a number of ways to approach this. One was to decide that it was in the best interest of the family not to provide individual counseling. A second approach was to let families know at the beginning of the first session, preferably in writing, what your policy on confidentiality is (we are now back to informed consent). You may decide to tell families that because important information that relates to the family counseling may come out in individual counseling, you cannot promise to keep everything confidential if an individual family member speaks to you. Or you may decide to agree to maintain confidentiality. In either case, letting family members know about this in writing before you begin counseling makes the rules clear. It is also clear that in the absence of any such statement to the family, you are bound to keep an individual family member's statements confidential, even if that puts you in a bind.

A very interesting and complicated family dilemma that involved important confidentiality issues was published in the third year of our column. It focused on a woman who had administered a lethal dose of sleeping pills to her grandmother and withheld cardiac medication from her mother when both had been in advanced stages of Alzheimer's disease. The client had viewed this as a compassionate approach to their suffering, but was now concerned that she was soon to be in the position of taking care of a third relative with Alzheimer's disease, an elderly aunt. This situation presented some very difficult judgment calls for the counselor. First, the question arose as to whether the counselor had an obligation to break confidentiality and report the manner in which the mother and grandmother had died. The answer is no. Clear and imminent danger refers to current clear danger. Situations revolving around alleged crimes or wrongdoings that have occurred in the past are kept confidential because they do not pose any clear danger in the here and now. Nevertheless, the counselor in this situation does have a responsibility to assess whether there is clear danger to the aunt. If the counselor makes a professional judgment that the client is likely to cause her aunt's death, then the counselor would need to break confidentiality to protect a life.

Finally, another confidentiality issue was presented by the director of a graduate program in marriage and family counseling. The director wanted to know how to ethically approach applicants who had previously been in therapy with one of the faculty members. The ethics committee clearly stated that the confidentiality of the applicant should be protected. This meant not disclosing the knowledge that the client received counseling from a professor. An applicant to a graduate program cannot be denied acceptance simply because of a past counseling relationship with one of the faculty. Instead, programs can set up procedures to allow faculty members to abstain from participating in the admissions process without having to give an explanation as to why they are abstaining.

Avoid Dual Relationships Like the Plague

Engaging in dual relationships is probably the most common ethical violation that counselors commit. We have often heard the statement, "I'll be careful," when counselors allow themselves to become a friend, lover, or business partner, or to enter into other types of relationships with a current or former client. Our response to this has been that ethical codes are set up not to prevent what *will* happen, but to prevent what *might* happen. It is selfish for counselors to engage in dual relationships with current or former clients, and doing so may cause great psychological damage to clients. That is why Section I.J of the IAMFC ethical code states that members must not engage in dual relationships or engage in sex with any current or former client or family member to whom they have provided professional services.

An ethical dilemma was sent from Maui by a pair of family counselors. They were concerned that some colleagues went on camping trips with their clients, spent time in hot tubs together with these same clients, and conducted support groups in which they participated both as therapists and as group members at the same time. The responses from the ethics committee members noted a number of pitfalls in this situation. Judy Ritterman pointed out that a therapist who becomes too emotionally attached to a family is rendered useless in the counseling process. The therapist becomes part of a system helping to perpetuate things as they are rather than acting as a change agent. Martin Ritchie pointed out that it would be very difficult in this situation to maintain confidentiality. He wrote, "Even if the therapists felt they could separate counseling and socializing interactions, it is unfair to expect their clients and friends to make that distinction."

Be Knowledgeable About the Legal Aspects of Counseling

It is our responsibility to uphold all legal requirements of the counseling profession. Needless to say, it is difficult to uphold laws if you don't know what they are. Whereas there are many important legal issues to be aware of, such as duty to warn, laws against having sexual contact with clients, and privileged communication, one of the most common legal issues that comes up in marriage and family counseling revolves around state laws focusing on the reporting of child abuse, maltreatment, and neglect of minors. When was the last time you actually looked at your state law that stipulates what a counselor must do when confronted with these issues? If you are unaware of or don't understand the law, how are you going to know what to report?

A counselor wrote to us that she was in a training course at a marriage and family counseling institute. She observed a session in which an eight-year-old child stated that he was whipped with a belt buckle on a regular basis by his stepfather. The mother acknowledged that her son had welts and bruises all over his body and that she could not get the stepfather to stop the beatings. The therapist in charge of the training refused to report the situation, and the frustrated counselor who wrote to us wanted to know what to do. We responded that the duty to report child abuse does not stop if a supervisor or trainer refuses to acknowledge the situation or tells a counselor not to report the incident. If trainers or supervisors will not cooperate, the counselor still has the responsibility to call the state hotline and give as much information as possible.

Take Your Responsibility to Report Ethical Violations of Other Counselors Seriously

Section I.M of the IAMFC ethical code specifically states that members have the responsibility to confront unethical behavior conducted by other counselors. The section says that the first step should be to discuss the violation directly with the counselor. If the problem continues, the member should use institutional procedures to address the issue. If that does not work, they should contact IAMFC and any appropriate licensure or certification board.

Promote the Dignity and Well-Being of Your Clients

Although a major focus of counseling ethics is preventing harm from occurring to clients, ethical codes are also useful for enhancing the integrity of our clients. We encourage counselors to read the preambles of ethical codes. The IAMFC code preamble states that members should commit themselves to protect and advocate for the healthy growth and development of the families that they work with, and that members recognize that the relationship between counselor and client is characterized as egalitarian.

An example of how these statements can be used came up in a column in which a counselor in private practice asked about his responsibility in dealing with individuals who make contact but do not schedule an appointment. The ethics committee pointed out that regardless of whether an appointment is made, the counselor is representing our profession and, in keeping with the IAMFC preamble, has a responsibility to set up an appropriate referral system and assist the individual in finding the help that he or she needs.

The IAMFC Ethics Committee responds to a counselor with a client who reveals that she knowingly caused the death of two elderly family members with Alzheimer's disease. In addition, the client anticipates taking care of a third elderly family member with Alzheimer's in the near future. This question comes from a real counselor and represents an actual client. However, due to the sensitivity of the situation, the counselor has requested a pseudonym and a fictitious city.

I have been counseling an adult woman with a presenting problem of difficulty in coping with the death of her mother. Her mother and grandmother (who is also deceased) suffered from progressive Alzheimer's disease. My client revealed to me that she administered a lethal dose of sleeping pills to her grandmother during the final stages of the Alzheimer's, and that she had also caused the death of her mother by withholding cardiac medication. It was then revealed that it is likely that she will have to take care of a third relative with Alzheimer's disease, an elderly aunt. It is important to understand that my client is not a bad person and did what she did while under tremendous stress and pressure and with feelings of compassion for the deteriorating condition of her mother and grandmother. My question is in two parts. First, what are my ethical obligations upon hearing the manner in which my client's mother and grandmother died? Second, am I responsible to do anything about the upcoming situation with the aunt?

Betsy Culip
Sarington, Missouri

Responses to Ms. Culip's questions come from six IAMFC Ethics Committee members: Ed Beck, director of the Susquehanna Institute in Pennsylvania; Frank Browning, University of North Carolina at Greensboro; Michelle Dennison, a private practitioner in Houston, Texas; Sherry Martinek, Youngstown State University; Patrick McGrath, National-Louis University; and Martin Ritchie, University of Toledo.

It was the committee's opinion that a primary issue in this case centers on confidentiality. Regarding the client's admission of causing two deaths, Martin Ritchie writes:

> Ms. Culip is not under an ethical obligation to report the circumstances surrounding their deaths. Ethical standards do not require counselors to report crimes. In the absence of specific legislation such as statutes mandating the reporting of child abuse, she is under no legal obligation to report knowledge of suspected crimes conveyed to her during counseling. If Betsy were to report these activities

without her client's permission, it would constitute a breach
in confidentiality.

In other words the disclosure of a past crime should be kept confidential since it presents neither clear not imminent present danger.

As to the possibility that the client will become the caretaker for her elderly aunt, it was of concern to the committee that the aunt could be at risk. It should be noted that all the major associations provide for the breaking of confidentiality where there is life-threatening danger involved. Martin Ritchie points out that it is important for Ms. Culip to be clear as to whether the aunt is in clear and imminent danger before breaking confidentiality, as stated in the American Counseling Association (ACA) Ethical Standard B.4 and the International Association of Marriage and Family Counselors (IAMFC) Ethical code II.A. ACA Ethical Standard B.4 states in part, "When the client's condition indicates that there is clear and imminent danger to the client or others, the member must take reasonable personal action or inform reasonable authorities." IAMFC Ethical Code 2.A(2) states that confidentiality should be broken when the client has placed himself or herself or someone else in clear and imminent danger. In addition, the American Psychological Association's (APA) Ethical Principle 5 states, in part, "[Psychologists] reveal [confidential] information to others only with the consent of the person or person's legal representative, except in those unusual circumstances in which not to do so would result in clear danger to the person or others."

Martin Ritchie argues that

there is a clear danger to the aunt, but since the client has not begun caring for her, it is doubtful that the danger is imminent. If the client begins caring for the aunt, and if in Betsy's opinion, the danger is both clear and imminent, how to legally exercise the duty to warn becomes difficult. If the aunt does not have the ability to protect herself, it is doubtful that warning her would be considered sufficient. A court in Vermont ruled, in the case of *Peck v Counseling Services,* 1985, "We hold that a mental health professional should know that his or her patient poses a serious risk of danger to an identifiable victim and has the duty to exercise reasonable care to protect him or her from that danger."

Sherry Martinek also refers to a well-published case that set legal precedent as to counselors' responsibility in reporting potential danger to known persons. She writes:

Corey, Corey, and Callanan (1984) cited the conclusion of the Tarasoff case: "The public policy favoring protection of the confidential character of patient-psychotherapist communications must yield to the extent to which disclosure is essential to avert danger to others. The protective privilege ends where the public peril begins." (p. 176)

Therefore, legally the "would-be-victim" may need to be notified, or in this case, the victim's guardian.

Frank Browning further notes that

Section I.A of the IAMFC Code of Ethics states, "Members demonstrate a caring, empathic, respectful, and active concern for family well-being." Failure of the counselor to warn other family members of the potential harm that her client might cause may be a violation of this section. The code implies that in this case there is a systematic, ethical, and moral obligation to the family."

All of these opinions revolve around a professional judgment as to whether there is clear and imminent danger to the aunt. If Ms. Culip makes that determination then Sherry Martinek suggests that she refer to Roth and Meisel's (1977) guidelines for retaining the therapeutic relationship when breaking confidentiality because of a "duty to warn":

- The therapist might consider asking the clients themselves to warn the person whom they have threatened. If this approach is likely to escalate a dangerous confrontation, the therapist should warn the client of that possibility.
- The therapist should attempt to get the client's consent for the therapist to warn the intended victim.
- The therapist might consider having a joint session with the

client's consent for the therapist to warn the intended victim.

- The therapist could have the client turn in any weapons he or she possesses.
- The therapist might consider medication as an adjunct to the therapy process.
- The therapist might consider voluntary hospitalization.

Frank Browning adds, "The counselor should do these things in an empathic and supportive manner, possibly with other family members in attendance. The client should be encouraged to continue in counseling. It should be her decision if she wants to continue with this counselor or another counselor. A judgmental atmosphere concerning the client should be avoided. The attitude and counseling atmosphere should be one of support and concern." It should also be kept in mind that thorough documentation is essential whenever the "duty to warn" is exercised. Specific notes on the date, person, and content of the contact need to be kept. This documentation is vital to support your approach in case of a lawsuit. In summary, Patrick McGrath writes: "Support, understanding, compassion, and growth and development are our second concern. The correctness and rightness of past behavior are our third concern and must be determined in light of the legal requirements."

References

Corey, G., Corey, M., & Callanan, P. (1984). *Issues and ethics in the helping profession* (2nd ed.). Monterey, CA: Brooks/Cole.

Roth, L. H., & Meisel, A. (1977). Dangerousness, confidentiality and the duty to warn. *American Journal of Psychiatry, 134,* 508–511.

A 16-year-old daughter seeks your consultation independent of the family therapy that she is attending. The girl informs you that she has received a positive pregnancy test and is in need of confidential individual counseling regarding whether to abort the pregnancy. So do you provide her with the session and/or a referral to an appropriate facility? Do you encourage her to tell her family of the pregnancy? What other questions do you need to consider?

Deborah Miora
Adjunct Clinical Professor
California School of Professional Psychology, Los Angeles

This issue's provocative dilemma from Deborah Miora poses a hypothetical situation that marriage and family counselors could easily run across. It is not unusual during marriage and family counseling for a family member to request individual sessions to work on his or her own issues. As a result, marriage and family counselors need to plan ahead. Ed Beck, director of the Susquehanna Institute, points out that "good clinical practice dictates that you establish the ground rules for disclosure of information provided by one family member at the outset of counseling." Michelle S. Dennison, a member of the International Association of Marriage and Family Counselors (IAMFC) Ethics Committee in private practice in Houston, Texas, adds, "I address this issue during the initial family session. I explain to the family that when they are in family sessions, the family as a unit owns the right to confidentiality. I then go on to inform them that should any of the family members decide they would like to pursue individual therapy, those sessions would focus on their individual issues, and they would, therefore, own the right to confidentiality in those sessions. I explain to all family members in the initial session that the exceptions to confidentiality include suicidal or homicidal ideation and child abuse issues."

Dennison's comments are supported by IAMFC Ethical Code Section II.E, which states, "Unless alternate arrangements have been agreed upon by all participants, statements made by a family member to the counselor during an individual counseling or consultation contact are to be treated as confidential and not disclosed to other family members without the individual's permission. If a client's refusal to share information from individual contacts interferes with the agreed upon goals of counseling, the counselor may have to terminate treatment and refer the client to another counselor" (IAMFC, 1993, p. 74).

Judith Ritterman, a committee member and a private practitioner in Holbrook, New York, notes that a counselor could handle this request within the context of family therapy. She writes that one possibility is to "see the girl alone and try to encourage her to tell her parents about the pregnancy. The counselor could offer to help the girl set up a therapy session with her parents to talk about the pregnancy. Another possibility would be to refuse to see the girl alone and instead refer her to an appropriate independent counselor."

R. P. Ascano, an ethics committee member and psychologist in private practice in Minnesota, brings up the potential legal issues of this problem. Based on his interpretation of IAMFC Ethical Code Section II.A.3, which states that information obtained from a client can be disclosed to a third party if the law mandates disclosure, Ascano stresses the importance for all practitioners to be familiar with their state laws concerning counseling minors and mandatory reporting status. He states, "Consult with an attorney to determine if a 16-year-old has statutory rights within their state to privacy and privileged communication even to her own legal guardian."

Joe Hannon, a committee member from Kirksville, Missouri, adds that it is also the counselor's responsibility to "determine whether the girl became pregnant due to rape, sexual abuse, or incest, which may legally mandate a report to appropriate parties."

Ed Beck further notes that "if the law requires you to tell the parents, you may ask her which parent, if not both, she would choose to reveal this information to." He also suggests, "The counselor should ascertain the reason that the girl is disclosing her problem. If it is for informational purposes, no action may be indicated on your part unless there are statutes otherwise."

Reference

International Association of Marriage and Family Counselors. (1993). Ethical code for the International Association of Marriage and Family Counselors. *The Family Journal: Counseling and Therapy for Couples and Families, 1,* 73–77.

This issue's question comes from Dan Longenecker, a marriage and family counselor at the Oak Tree Enrichment Center in Greensboro, North Carolina:

> *How ethical is it to counsel individual family members when you are also providing counseling for the entire family?"*

Responses to this issue come from J. Scott Hinkle, David Steele, and Austin Chandler, counselors in the Greensboro, North Carolina, area. All three respondents agree that there is not one clear-cut answer to this question, but rather the decision to counsel individual family members while providing counseling for the entire family is situational at best.

More specifically, J. Scott Hinkle, IAMFC Board member suggests that if the nature of the individual session is to address personal issues not related to the work of the family, then individual counseling can be very beneficial. He states, "I can envision some circumstances in which this may be appropriate and others in which it would be inappropriate. For instance, an adolescent could be provided with information about how to deal with parents that may be more effectively delivered without the parent attending the session. On the other hand, if this is a family in which coalitions have been extremely threatening, the family may be best served by seeing them all at once and dealing with parents right there in the session."

David Steele, a psychologist with Carolina Psychological Associates, feels that when working with families it is critical to consider the therapeutic contract agreed upon by the therapist and family. He states, "If your initial contract was for family therapy, I would suggest seeking the permission of every family member who has been involved in the family sessions before beginning individual therapy. The limits to the individual therapy and confidentiality should be delineated with each family member to be involved in individual sessions. If the initial contract was for individual therapy and family therapy was begun at the instigation of the therapist, careful explanation of the relative roles of the individual and family work would need to be given to the family. Again your contract has to be negotiated and renegotiated before changing expectations."

David's comments are supported by AACD standard B.2, B.8, and AAMFT Standard 2.1. Standard B.2 states in part, "The counseling relationship and information resulting therefrom must be kept confidential, consistent with the obligations of the member as a professional person. In a group counseling setting, the counselor must set a norm of confidentiality regarding all group participants' disclosures." Standard B.8's first sentence states, "The member must inform the client of the purposes, goals, techniques, rules of procedure, and limitations that may affect the relationship at or before the time that the counseling relationship is entered." AAMFT Standard 2.1 in part states, "In circumstances where more than one person in a family is receiving therapy, each such family member who is legally competent to execute a waiver must agree to the waiver required by sub-paragraph (4). In absence of such a waiver from each family member legally competent to execute a waiver, a marriage and family therapist cannot disclose information received from any family member."

Dr. Steele further points out that an important clinical issue is whether or not individual therapy will disrupt the process necessary for effective family therapy. He writes, "Will the clinician be seen as allied with the person in individual therapy? Will objectivity be lost? Will the therapist be perceived as more distant by other family members? The ethical dimension of this question is the obligation of the therapist to provide effective treatment. At times it will be necessary for a second therapist to do the individual work, so that your role as the family's therapist is not threatened."

Finally, Austin Chandler, a psychologist and director of the Greensboro College Counseling Center states, "My thinking is bound by the question, 'Do the perceived benefits to the client outweigh the perceived risks to the client?' If the answer to this question is yes in my mind, then I feel I am obligated to proceed and offer both services. Conversely, if the answer is no, I do not proceed."

As a high school counselor I have worked hard to provide students with counseling services that meet their individual needs. I have established a reputation as being open-minded, accessible, and respectful of students. As a result, a 17-year-old woman came to me because she had heard I was nice. After discussing the parameters of our counseling relationship to include the terms of confidentiality, the client revealed that she had a drinking problem. She began to cry, at which time I smelled alcohol on her breath. The school policy for students found to be under the influence of alcohol is to notify their parents and place them on immediate suspension.

The question is, do I follow school policy and break confidentiality? If I do, I risk losing a majority of my referrals from students because they may feel a lack of trust in me. If I go against school policy and work with this client, have I set the stage for how I will have to work with future alcohol/chemically dependent students?

The dilemma is a good example of how systems theory comes into play regardless of the number of people in your office. Even when conducting individual counseling, as in the above situation, a counselor must take into account ethical obligations to a variety of different systems such as the family, the school, the legal system, and even the counseling profession.

Responses to this issue from IAMFC Ethics Committee members pointed to various aspects of these systems. In terms of the individual, R. P. Ascano, a forensic psychologist in Breckenridge, Minnesota, points out that an obvious ethics issue is confidentiality. He writes, "the American Counseling Association's ethical standards state in Section B.2 that "the counseling relationship and information resulting therefrom must be kept confidential, consistent with the obligations of the member as a professional person." The American Psychological Association's ethical principles mandate in Principle 5 that "psychologists have a primary obligation to respect the confidentiality of information obtained from persons in the course of their work as a psychologist." The American Health Association's ethics state in Principle 4 that "the members, officers, and employees of ACHA must recognize the importance of confidentiality in personnel and medical information."

Judy Ritterman, from Community Family Growth Services in Holbrook, New York, notes that the revised 1992 American School Counselor Association ethical standards in Section A.9 makes its position clear: Confidentiality must not be abridged except where the law or ethical standards (clear and present danger) mandate such an abridgement. The Ethical Code for the International Association of Marriage and Family Counselors is very specific, stating in Section II.A that information obtained from a client can only be disclosed to a third party under the following conditions: the client signs a waiver and has a full understanding of the nature of the waiver; there is clear and imminent danger to the client or someone else; the law mandates disclosure; or the counselor is a defendant in legal action arising from professional activity.

Dealing with legal aspects in an ethical way presents a challenge because laws are often ambiguous and conflicting. Robert Crawford, from Memphis State University, presents one view of how the legal aspects of confidentiality need to be examined in this situation. He states, "It is a important to note that the description of the client as a 17-year-old 'woman' is a misnomer; the client in this case is a minor. Legally, a 17-year-old person is not an adult except in cases where there has been emancipation due to marriage, etc. Legal and ethical protection of confidentiality between counselors and minor clients is less than that provided for counseling relationships with adult clients. These limits are further restricted in secondary schools where *in loco parentis* rights and responsibilities often create limits on confidentiality between counselors and students. At last report, a bare minority of states in the nation provide legal protection of confidentiality for students and school counselors, and there is no indication that this case took place in a state with such legislation."

R. P. Ascano presents an alternative view. He feels that a 17-year-old can be mature enough to give informed consent, and thus the school policy may violate state statutes pertaining to privileged communication or confidentiality.

Robert Crawford notes that the counselor must also examine his or her responsibility to the family, school, and professional systems. "There is no doubt that the student in this case is the client, but the counselor has responsibilities to other persons as well as a variety of systems. ASCA Ethical Standards Section B.1 requires the school counselor to respect the inherent rights and responsibilities of parents for their children, and ASVCA Standard D.2 requires the counselor to inform school officials of conditions that may be damaging to the school's mission. In addition, ASCA Standard F.1 requires counselors to conduct themselves in such a manner as to bring credit to self and to the profession."

So how do you act in an ethical manner that takes into account your responsibilities to a number of systems including the individual, the family, the school, the law, and the counseling profession? At the beginning of your counseling relationship, determine which system is your primary client (keeping in mind that the American School Counseling Association's Ethical Standards Section A.1 clearly states that a school counselor's primary obligation and loyalty is to the student). If the student who came to you for counseling is not your primary client for some reason, he or she has a right to know that from the beginning.

Robert Crawford points out that counselors should also comply with ASCA Ethical Standard A.3 and ACA Ethical Standard B.8, which state, in part, that clients must be informed about any legal or authoritative restraints on the counseling relationship at or before the time counseling is initiated. In this case, the school counselor's discussion of the terms of confidentiality should have included information about the school's policy about notifying parents of children who are found to be under the influence of alcohol.

Without having informed the student about the alcohol policy before sensitive information was disclosed, confidentiality should be maintained since the client (or the client's legal representative) was not aware of the limitation. The counselor can use various ethical guidelines for support in educating the school administration that information about a client is released only with the consent of the client or client's legal representative (APA and ACA); and that this release should be in writing (AMHCA).

R. P. Ascano notes that if the counselor feels the school policy is not in the best interest of the students and violates ethical guidelines or state confidentiality laws, then he or she has the responsibility to approach the administration about modifying or eliminating it. In situations where there is a conflict between the interest of the client or student and the academic institutions, APA states that psychologists must state the commitment to their association standard and "wherever possible work toward a resolution of the conflict" (Principle 3.d). However, ACA (in Section A.2) indicates that when a person accepts employment in an institution it is implied that he or she accepts the institution's policies and principles. If a conflict arises for which an agreement cannot be reached, the employee should consider terminating affiliation with that institution.

Finally, the counselor must deal with the potential that there is clear danger to the client in this case. Judy Ritterman presents an interesting approach that takes the family system into account. She writes, "The counselor may be making an erroneous assumption that the student came to her thinking that the counselor would keep her alcohol problem a secret. Teenagers who are unable to stop themselves from continuing potentially dangerous behaviors may very well seek out an appropriate adult who can 'put on the brakes for them.' A teenager with a drinking problem who didn't want her problem known by the important adults in her life would not have gone to the counselor, would not have openly admitted a drinking problem, and certainly would have found some way to cover the smell of alcohol on her breath as she most likely does to avoid detection at home."

"If my assumption is correct, that the student wanted her problem revealed, then the counselor now has to work with the student on the most appropriate way to do it. To keep the student's confidence in the counselor (and maintain confidentiality), the counselor can work with the student on ways the student herself (or with the aid of the counselor) can tell the parents about the problem. In this way, the counselor can offer this family options for treatment and hope for recovery. However, if the client continues to drink heavily and refuses to let her parents be contacted, the counselor may well have to determine that there is clear danger and inform the parents and the school."

In summary, R. P. Ascano states, "While these statements may be ideally desirable, it is realistically difficult at best. It is not always possible to resolve conflicts of this nature and uphold the obligation to all parties. In the final analysis, counselors need to make a moral decision as to their loyalty to students versus the school versus the ethical guidelines of professional organizations, taking into consideration their legal responsibility as defined by the state statutes pertaining to privacy and confidentiality."

A couple has come to you for couples therapy. They state that they love each other and intend to stay married. They have two children, a 14-year-old boy and a 17-year-old girl. All four members of this family are extremely bright and quite committed to obtaining therapy. Cost and time are not a consideration.

After a few sessions it becomes obvious that the couple has not been attempting several of your suggestions, although they do proceed with others that you have made. You do notice that they are attempting other activities, the nature of which are clearly the kind of suggestions made by mental health professionals. Further exploration of this leads to the discovery that each family member is in individual counseling as well as participating in group therapy or a self-help group. Essentially, there are 10 different mental health professionals or groups involved with this family, and the clients are spending approximately 10 to 12 hours per week in therapeutic sessions.

With the couple's and children's permission, you contact each individual therapist, the group facilitators, and even talk with the self-help group sponsors. There is little interest from other treating personnel in coordinating an overall approach. You seem to be the only one concerned that so many approaches are theoretically quite different in technique, in choice of issues being addressed, and in activities suggested for the client. In addition, the couple sees no problem and wants to continue to work with all of their therapists and groups because "it is their right."

You are aware that the Ethical Code for the International Association of Marriage and Family Counselors (IAMFC) states in Section I.K, "Members have an obligation to withdraw from a counseling relationship if the continuation of services is not in the best interest of the client. . . ." As such, what are your ethical responsibilities to this family?

Although it may be unusual to encounter a family spending 10 to 12 hours per week in therapy with 10 different therapists, it is not unusual for family members to be working with more than one mental health professional. Martin Ritchie, from the University of Toledo writes, "The American Psychological Association's (APA) recently revised ethical standards state the following in Section 4.04:

> In deciding whether to offer or provide services to those already receiving mental health services elsewhere, psychologists carefully consider the treatment issues and the potential patient's or client's welfare. The psychologist discusses these issues with the patient or client, or another legally authorized person on behalf of the client, in order to minimize the risk of confusion and conflict, consults with the other service providers when appropriate, and proceeds with caution and sensitivity to the therapeutic issues when a client is being seen by another counselor.

"Section B.3 of the Ethical Standards of the American Counseling Association (ACA) provides less flexibility. This section states in part, 'If the member discovers that the client is in another counseling relationship after the counseling relationship begins, the member must gain the consent of the other professionals to terminate the relationship, unless the client elects to terminate the other relationship.' Therefore, the counselor's attempts to contact the other therapists and to ensure coordination of treatment are consistent with APA and ACA standards. Keep in mind, however, that the IAMFC Ethical Code clearly states in Section I.C, 'Members respect the autonomy of the families that they work with. They do not make decisions that rightfully belong to family members.' Therefore, the counselor needs to make a professional judgment as to whether this decision is one that should be made by the family, by the counselor, or should be a shared decision."

Sherry Martinek, from Youngstown State University in Ohio, suggests that counselors in this situation should discuss their professional concerns about the therapeutic problems related to lack of coordinated care with their couple. She writes, "One counselor could provide individual, couple, and/or family counseling, meeting with different subsystems when appropriate. I would not object to members attending their respective self-help recovery groups as long as a 'team approach' was enacted to ensure follow-through on mutual goals. If this conflict could not be resolved, in accordance with the previously mentioned IAMFC Ethical Standard I.K, I would engage in a discussion to help this couple decide on the best alternative treatment services for them."

Ed Beck, the director of the Susquehanna Institute in Pennsylvania, agrees stating, "Surely patients have a right to get as much support as they want or can afford. However every clinician has the right to accept or not accept cases which are incompatible with scope of training and practice. In following the IAMFC Ethical Code Standard I.K as stated previously, in this case, unless the family gave me coordinating and supervisory authority in writing, I would terminate treatment."

As for the ethical judgment of the other therapists, Martin Ritchie suggests that if the counselor suspects that one or more of the other therapists is violating ethical standards, the counselor is obligated to inform the family and confront the therapist. He writes, "IAMFC Ethical Code Section I.M states, 'Members have the responsibility to confront unethical behavior conducted by other counselors. The first step should be to discuss the violation directly with the counselor. If the problem continues, the member should first use procedures established by the employing institution and then those of the IAMFC. . . . Members may contact the IAMFC executive director, president, executive board members, or chair of the ethics committee at any time for consultation on remedying ethical violations.'"

Resources

American Counseling Association (ACA). (1988). *Ethical Standards* (rev. ed.). Alexandria, VA: Author.

American Psychological Association (APA). (1992). Ethical principles of psychologists and code of conduct, *American Psychologist, 47*(12), 1597–1611.

International Association of Marriage and Family Counselors (IAMFC). (1993). Ethical code for the International Association of Marriage and Family Counselors. *The Family Journal: Counseling and Therapy for Couples and Families, 1,* 73–77.

I am the director of a master's program in marriage and family counseling. An integral part of our admissions process is a personal interview. During a recent interview, an applicant revealed that she had been in therapy with one of the faculty a few years ago.

While we rejected the candidate for reasons unrelated to her being a former client, we became uncomfortable with the potential for exploitation and harm to the previous therapist-client relationship and decided that any faculty member could veto an applicant to protect previous counseling relationships and confidentiality. However, some faculty members weren't comfortable with this decision, and recently a potential applicant argued that the decision should be made by the candidate.

What kind of ethical guidelines can help us deal with applicants who have been former clients of faculty?

Faculty admissions committees should make every effort to respect and promote the autonomy and privacy of potential candidates for admissions into their graduate programs. Faculty members who are called on to evaluate candidates and make recommendations for the purposes of admissions have an obligation to make such decisions objectively and impartially. Faculty members should avoid any actions that would diminish or violate a past counseling relationship. The American Mental Health Counselors Association (AMHCA) Principle 1.e states:

> As practitioners, mental health counselors know that they bear a heavy social responsibility because their recommendations and professional actions may alter the lives of others. They, therefore, remain fully cognizant of their impact and are alert to personal, social, organizational,

financial, or political situations or pressures that might lead to misuse of their influence.

In keeping with the preceding statements, the consensus of the International Association of Marriage and Family Counselors (IAMFC) Ethics Committee is that vetoing the acceptance of an applicant into a graduate program simply because the applicant has been a past client is unethical. The preamble of the IAMFC Code of Ethics very quickly directs us to recognize "that the relationship between the provider and consumer of services is characterized as an egalitarian process." The preamble further emphasizes that "co-participation, co-equality, co-authority, and co-responsibility" (i.e., a shared process of decision making) are what characterize an egalitarian relationship.

An alternative is for the program to set up procedures to allow faculty members to abstain from input into the admissions process. To protect the confidentiality of a former client, a faculty member needs to be able to abstain without explanation so that the former counseling relationship is not revealed. Avoiding the disclosure of the previous counseling relationship is in accordance with the guidelines for confidentiality outlined in the American Counseling Association (ACA) Ethical Standard B.2 and the IAMFC Ethical Code II.A. ACA Standard B.2 states in part, "The counseling relationship and information resulting therefrom must be kept confidential, consistent with the obligations of the member as a professional person." IAMFC Ethical Code II.A states in part, "Clients have the right to expect that information shared with the counselor will not be disclosed to others. . . . The fact that a contact was made with a counselor is to be considered just as confidential as the information shared during that contact."

Although protecting the confidentiality of the past counseling relationship is the first priority of the admissions committee, a second major issue is the autonomy and personal-professional growth of the prospective student. Kitchener (1984) enumerated five moral principles that can guide decision-making behavior: (a) autonomy of the client, (b) welfare of the client, (c) nonmalfeasance to the client,

(d) justice or fairness for the client, and (e) loyalty to the client. The faculty admissions committee is obligated to respect the dignity, the worth, and the ability of the applicant to be self-directed. As such, the majority of the IAMFC committee members felt the revelation of a past counseling relationship should not preclude the admission of a client. AMHCA Principle 11.D states, "The mental health counselor relationship must be one in which client adaptability and growth toward self-direction are encouraged and cultivated. The mental health counselor must maintain this role consistently and not become a decision maker or substitute for the client."

It should also be pointed out that rejecting a student based on the fact that they had been in counseling is probably a violation of the Americans With Disabilities Act of 1990, which states that individuals cannot be discriminated against on the basis of a physical or emotional disability. The IAMFC Ethical Code also states in Section I.D that members do not discriminate on the basis of disability.

In addition, once the students are admitted, counselor education programs should encourage and support students' personal and professional growth, which could include seeking therapy in order to develop one's potential. The American College Personnel Association's (ACPA) Ethical Principle "Do no harm," states in part, "Student affairs professionals are especially vigilant to assure that the institutional policies do not (a) hinder students' opportunities to benefit from the learning experiences available in the environment; (b) threaten individuals' self-worth, dignity, or safety; or (c) discriminate unjustly or illegally.

In summary, the IAMFC Ethics Committee supports a professor's abstention rather than veto when a former client has applied to a counseling program. Program policy should allow the abstention in such a way that protects the confidentiality of the former counselor-client relationship. Also, the applicant should not be denied admission based solely on the fact that they were in counseling, because this violates both professional ethics and possible legal statutes.

References

Americans With Disabilities Act of 1990, 42 USCA 12101 *et seq.*

Kitchener, K. S. (1984). Intuition, critical evaluation and ethical principles: The foundation for ethical decisions in counseling psychology. *The Counseling Psychologist, 12,* 43–55.

Resources

American College Personnel Association. (1990). Statement of principles and standards. *Journal of College Student Personnel, 31,* 197–202. American Counseling Association. (1988).

Ethical standards (rev. ed.). Alexandria, VA: Author.

American Mental Health Counselors Association. (1990). *Ethical code.* Alexandria, VA: Author.

International Association of Marriage and Family Counselors. (1993). Ethical code for the International Association of Marriage and Family Counselors. *The Family Journal: Counseling and Therapy for Couples and Families, 1,* 73–77.

I am a school counselor in an urban high school. The mother of a 12-year-old girl attending a local junior high called me to express concern that a 15-year-old boy attending my school was harassing her daughter. (The girl does not want anything to do with him.) After talking to the boy, it became clear that he was obsessing about a relationship with the seventh grader, making such statements as, "She is everything," "In a dark room she is the only light," and "I only derive happiness when with her."

Subsequently, the boy showed up at both the girl's home and school, frightened her, and was charged by police with harassment. His friends then told school officials that statements had been made about wanting to buy a gun to kill both the girl and himself. On the basis of this information, the boy's parents admitted their son to an inpatient psychiatric unit. Unfortunately, this unit has the reputation of not taking patients' threats to themselves or to others seriously and of prematurely releasing them.

As the school counselor in the boy's home school, what ethical obligations do I have to the girl and her parents after the boy is released from the hospital?

As is frequently the case when many people and systems are involved in a case, one of the counselor's primary obligations is to determine who the client is. Principle A.1 of the Ethical Standards for School Counselors promulgated by the American School Counselors Association states that a school counselor's primary obligation and loyalty is to students, and it can be inferred from the preamble that this refers to students in the counselor's school. Therefore, the IAMFC Ethics Committee suggests that the counselor in this situation make the 15-year-old boy her primary concern. In keeping with IAMFC Ethical Code Section I.I, which states in part, "Members have an obligation to determine and inform all persons involved who their primary client is—i.e., is the counselor's primary obligation to the individual, the family, a third party, or an institution?," the identification of the boy as the primary client should be communicated clearly to all parties involved. An important aspect of focusing the counselor's obligation toward the boy is to make it known that all counseling contacts after release from the hospital will be kept confidential. Keep in mind, though, that the boy and his parents have the right to informed consent and to know the limits of confidentiality. An important legal case that has potential impact on informed consent in this case is the well-known court case *Tarasoff v Board of Regents of the University of California*. Decided in 1976, this decision revolved around a psychologist who had been told by a male client that the client was going to kill his former girlfriend, Tatiana Tarasoff. Although the psychologist did notify the police, she did not warn the potential victim. Subsequently, the client did kill his former girlfriend, and her parents sued the psychologist for not breaking confidentiality and issuing a warning to Tatiana. The court ruled in favor of Tatiana's parents, stating that when it seems a client is dangerous, psychologists (and by implication all mental health professionals) have a duty to warn an intended victim and that this duty overrides confidentiality.

Therefore, in the present case, the school counselor has an obligation to immediately warn the girl and her parents (along with other people as necessary, such as police or school officials, depending on the situation), if at any time the boy discloses anything that causes the counselor to make a professional judgment that there is clear danger of harm to the girl. As stated previously, the necessity of breaking confidentiality and warning responsible parties if clear danger of harm is present needs to be explained to the boy and his parents as part of informed consent. It is also suggested that because of the potential legal aspects of this case coming from the *Tarasoff* case and resulting state laws, the counselor should consult with the school district's attorney about that particular state's liability standards and "duty to warn and protect" statutes.

In terms of the psychiatric unit that discharged the boy, the counselor should not get involved in any consideration as to the correctness of their judgment unless the counselor has specific information about unprofessional behavior (which should then be discussed with the clinical director). It is in the best interest of our clients to recognize the competence of other professional groups, cooperate with them, and to make sure we do not interfere in the relationship between them and the client. The National Board for Certified Counselors Code of Ethics Section B.3 supports this, stating in part, "Certified counselors know and take into account the traditions and practices of other professional groups with whom they work and cooperate fully with such groups." Therefore, instead of putting distance between the school and hospital, the counselor should attempt to become an active and cooperative participant in the discharge planning process.

> *I am a family therapist in private practice. I am very busy and find that I am unable to accommodate the needs of all those who call. I find these contacts very time consuming because I must explore the individual's or family's need and then provide appropriate referrals. Do I have any ethical responsibility to people who call or are referred to me whom I cannot take on as clients?*

The therapist in this situation is to be commended for diligence in considering the responsibility to individuals who are not clients. Although the person calling is clearly not yet a client, the counselor does have a professional relationship with the individual requesting services in the sense that this may be the first contact that the person has had with a marriage and family counselor. In this capacity, then, the counselor represents the profession and has an obligation to present it in a responsible manner.

Various counseling ethical codes speak to the obligation of counselors to assist individuals, couples, and families who contact them but whom they choose not to see. For example, section B.12 of the American Counseling Association's (ACA; 1988) *Ethical Standards* states, "If the member determines an inability to be of professional assistance to the client, the member must . . . suggest appropriate alternatives. In the event the client declines the suggested referral, the member is not obligated to continue the relationship."

The code of ethical principles of the American Association of Marriage and Family Therapy (AAMFT; 1988) states in Section 1.6, "Marriage and family therapists assist persons in obtaining other therapeutic services if the therapist is unable or unwilling, for appropriate reasons, to provide professional help."

The ethical code of the American Mental Health Counselors

Association (1990) proposes, in Section 6.K, that "if the mental health counselor is unable to be of professional assistance to the client, the member is obligated to suggest appropriate alternatives."

The *National Board for Certified Counselors' Code of Ethics* (1987) states, in Section B.11, "When certified counselors determine an inability to be of professional assistance to the potential or existing client, they must, respectively, not initiate the counseling relationship or immediately terminate the relationship. In either event, the certified counselor must suggest appropriate alternatives. Certified counselors must be knowledgeable about referral resources so that a satisfactory referral can be imitated."

Therefore, it is clear that marriage and family counselors have an ethical responsibility to help contacts who cannot be accommodated to find alternative resources. The referral process need not be time consuming. The busy therapist can prepare a one-page listing of other local resources, which could be mailed to those who inquire. This directory would include the name, address, and phone number of each resource, with a description of specific areas of competence. By providing several agencies, competent therapists, or both for the potential client to choose from, the counselor not only gives a range of resources but also is protected against a malpractice lawsuit if the potential client is dissatisfied with the services provided by the next therapist or agency.

Counselors can also suggest that the person seeking help look for other private counseling services in the phone book Yellow Pages, call the area community mental health center, or contact the local crisis center. For the busy therapist, information can be provided by an office manager or even by an answering machine.

A final solution, which has been used by one of the column editors, is to form an association of counselors with various areas of expertise who practice in the same office suite. Referrals often become a simple matter of arranging for the client to meet with an in-house counselor who has expertise with the presenting problem and has an open appointment.

The issue of a potential client in crisis deserves special attention. If the person inquiring about services is suicidal or in danger of physical harm to self or others even the busiest of therapists has the responsibility to react immediately to such emergencies to preserve life. This does not necessarily mean taking the individual on as a client, but rather that the counselor should maintain contact with the person until an appropriate resource (e.g., crisis hotline, ambulance, or police) can be notified and placed in charge.

Finally, in any referral situation, it is appropriate (though not mandatory) for the counselor to call back to see whether the person requesting help was able to contact the resources to which they were referred.

References

American Association of Marriage and Family Therapy. (1988). *Code of ethical principles for marriage and family therapists.* Washington DC: Author.

American Counseling Association. (1988). *Ethical standards* (rev. ed.). Alexandria, VA: Author.

American Mental Health Counselors Association. (1990). *Ethical code.* Alexandria, VA: Author.

National Board for Certified Counselors. (1987). *National Board for Certified Counselors code of ethics.* Alexandria, VA: Author.

You have just had a productive session with a family that you were seeing for the first time. As you wrap up the session, the parents state that your fee is too steep for them to pay out of their pocket on a regular basis. They add that their insurance company will not reimburse for family therapy and request that you bill the insurance company for individual therapy (which their insurance will reimburse) so that they can continue their counseling.

How do you handle this situation?

Steven Mullinix
Human Resource Consultants
Chapel Hill, North Carolina

It can certainly be disheartening as a family counselor to find yourself in Dr. Mullinix's dilemma. Judith Ritterman, a member of the International Association of Marriage and Family Counselors (IAMFC) Ethics Committee and a private practitioner in Holbrook, New York, reflects that "it is unfortunate that many insurance companies are slow in acknowledging the need for couples and families to have reimbursable services. They still cling to the medical model of the individual as the appropriate focus of therapeutic intervention even though couple and family therapies are often more cost-effective due to their short-term nature."

This can make it easy to rationalize an inaccurate insurance procedure code, and a number of therapists and counselors probably do this. However, Stuart Bonnington, an ethics committee member from Austin Peay State University, warns, "It may be that billing third parties for individual psychotherapy when marital or family therapy is being performed is 'accepted professional practice,' (i.e., 'everybody does it'), but it is not honest." As such, it is a violation of the IAMFC Ethical Code, which states in Section III.F, "Members do not engage in actions that violate the moral or legal standards of their community."

Joe Hannon, a committee member from Kirksville, Missouri, adds, "Too many of us play little games just for money."

Ritterman points out that agreeing to inaccurate billing is also clearly a violation of Section 7.4 of the American Association of Marriage and Family Therapists (AAMFT) Code of Ethical Principles, which states, "Marriage and family therapists represent facts truthfully to clients, third party payers and supervisees regarding services rendered." (Editor's Note: Interested counselors can obtain this code of ethics by writing to: AAMFT, 1717 K Street, NW, Suite 407, Washington, DC 20006.) Judy Ritterman also poses the following questions: "When we make the decision to enter into collusion with clients in order to deceive an insurance company, what are we telling our clients about honesty and integrity? Will our clients trust us to be honest with them as well as encouraging them to be honest with themselves?"

Ed Beck from the Susquehanna Institute, Harrisburg, Pennsylvania, brings up some legal issues surrounding this problem. He states, "Dr. Mullinix's dilemma is not just an ethical problem, it is also a legal one. Most states with licensing codes and insurance codes have regulations dealing with diagnostic procedures for insurance processes. What the family is proposing and what the therapist is considering may be insurance fraud—a serious crime."

So what are your alternatives to agreeing to misrepresent billing codes to an insurance company for your clients to be able to afford counseling? The ethics committee came up with a few suggestions, as follows:

- Use a sliding scale.
- Refer the family to a not-for-profit counseling agency.
- Arrange for extended payments.
- See one or more family members individually if you have a sound theoretical rationale for doing so.

Note: Reprinted by permission of the IAMFC

Chapter Twelve

Pulling It All Together:
The Vorset Family

David M. Kaplan

Now we have reached the end of our journey. In the preceding chapters, we have looked at how to conceptualize family work, presented a process for conducting family counseling, and examined ways to fit this process into the counseling skills you have already developed in working with individual clients. We have discussed approaches and techniques for establishing a relationship with families, assessing family issues related to the presenting problem, selecting family interventions, assessing family interventions, and reaching closure with families. We have devoted chapters to the important issues of diversity and technology in family work, and have presented resources that will catalyze your continuing growth and development in family work.

To pull together all the information you have read in this book, I now present a brief glimpse of the Vorset family. With a nod to Gus Napier and Carl Whitaker, authors of *The Family Crucible,* I invented the Vorset family from a composite of many families I have worked with over the years. The remainder of this chapter provides a snapshot of the course of therapy with this family.

The Beginning

My contact with the Vorsets began, as much of my family work does, with an individual session. Megan Vorset, a thirty-two-year-old graduate student in history, made an appointment because she was depressed and, as she stated, "feeling lousy." When I asked her to tell me more, she said, "I love history and majored in it as an undergraduate. I graduated from college ten years ago and was hired by a title insurance company because of my training in searching out historical documents. While I made good money, I hated the job because it ended up being more routine clerical work than anything else. I had always wanted to further my education in history and finally got up the nerve to apply to graduate school eight months ago. "I started graduate school last semester and really love the program. The professors are terrific and really know their stuff. But the farther I get into my history classes, the worse I feel. Help me!"

Establishing a Relationship

As with all clients, it was important to establish trust with Megan. I wanted her to know that I saw her as a person rather than a problem. So I said, "We clearly have very important issues to talk about and I am really glad you came in. Would it be okay if we take a step back so I can get to know you?"

Megan began to tell me about her family: "I am the youngest of four daughters. My sisters are Rose, Janet, and Amber. My parents have been divorced since I was three and mom died when I was five. My father has remarried twice, the first time to Babs and the second time to Jane. Dad and Babs have two children, Michael and Karen. Karen is married to Jim and they just had a son named David. I have been married to my husband, Kiel, for seven years. We have a five-year-old son, Elton. For some reason Elton doesn't like David, but other than that we all get along pretty well."

With all these names and relationships being thrown at me, I was becoming a little confused, so I asked Megan if we could construct a genogram (as discussed by Dennis Pelsma in chapter 5). I explained to her that a genogram is a way to make a visual road map of her family to help me understand who she is talking about when she names a particular person. I tacked a large piece of newsprint to the corkboard I had mounted on the back of my office door for just such purposes, and we spent the rest of the session talking about her family and developing the genogram shown in Figure 1.

Figure1. Vorset Family Genogram

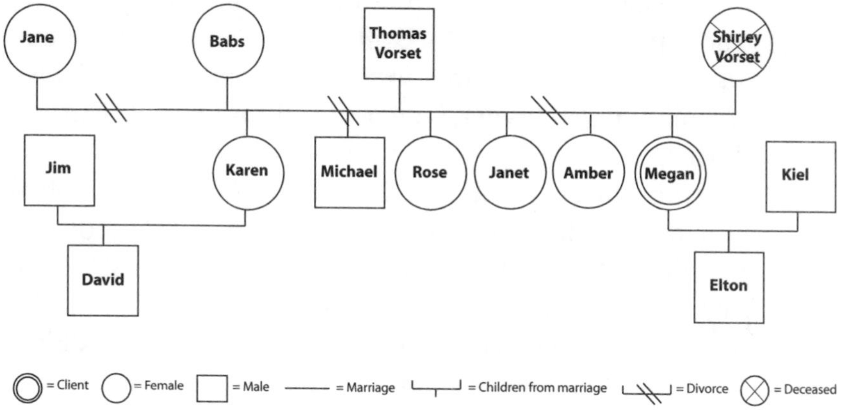

As we completed the genogram and talked about her family, Megan became more comfortable with me. She saw that I was taking the time to get to know her world. What she didn't know was that she was also giving me useful assessment information.

Assessing the Problem

In constructing her genogram, Megan spent much time talking about her immediate family. She told me that her husband, Kiel, was an electrical engineer who worked at a local hydroelectric plant. Megan was very much in love with Kiel and felt that they had a terrific marriage. There were some stresses, however. One was that Kiel was objecting to Megan's evening classes. He felt that the family should be together at night. He also had been objecting more and more to the hours that Megan spent in the library on the weekends. And recently he had been getting really angry that Megan was spending a lot of time at the homes of fellow students working on group projects.

Megan enjoyed telling me about her son, Elton. He was a typical five-year-old, loving and inquisitive and getting into anything and everything. Elton's favorite color was purple and his favorite TV show was "Tele-Tubbies." Megan stated that although he could be a handful, she could not imagine life without Elton. Recently, however, Elton had become less loving and more irritable. He had begun hitting Megan and refusing to kiss her goodnight. In the past, Elton would always run to Megan for comfort when he hurt himself. Now, when her son fell and started crying, he would call for his dad. This was breaking Megan's heart.

As we continued through the genogram, Megan told me about her nuclear family. Her father, Thomas Vorset, was an accountant with a local firm. Megan told me, "Dad is a pretty traditional guy. He even wears bow ties. He is much quicker to criticize than to hug, but I know that he loves me and that his bark is worse than his bite." Megan then told me about her mom. Shirley Vorset had been a secretary before she was diagnosed with ovarian cancer and died when Megan had just turned five. Megan described the relationship with her mother as very close and stated that she was devastated when Mom died. She didn't remember much about her parents' divorce because it happened when she was three.

Megan stated that she got along quite well with both Babs and Jane, her dad's second and third wives. Megan also told me about her sisters Rose, Janet, and Amber. All three had gone straight into the workforce after high school and had become secretaries like their mother. Rose, Janet, and Amber all lived (as did Megan) in the same city they grew up in. Megan stated that all four sisters got along well and saw each other frequently. However, tension had been developing over the fact that Megan was missing the family's traditional weekend get-togethers due to her school responsibilities.

Continuing with my assessment, I went through the BASIC ID (as discussed in chapter 3) with Megan. I noted with interest that in each area she kept returning to family issues. When I asked her what behaviors were associated with her depression, Megan stated that she withdrew from her husband and child and spent more time with her fellow graduate students. Her affect revolved around alternating feelings of resentment and loneliness toward Kiel, Elton, her sisters, and her dad. Sensations focused on a knot in the pit of her stomach. When I asked her to describe the images or pictures she saw in her head when the lousy feelings were at their worst, she stated that she very clearly saw a scene where her husband took her son and abandoned her. Megan's cognitions also focused on her family. When asked, "Word for word, what are the thoughts that go through your head when you are most depressed?" She replied, "My family is abandoning me at a time when I really need their support. Why don't they understand that graduate school is important to me? This could be the happiest time of my life, but my family is making it the most miserable. I feel like I have to choose between my happiness and their happiness."

Megan and I spent a lot of time focusing on the interpersonal relationship component of the BASIC ID. Ironically, she told me that she was spending less and less time with her father and sisters because every time she did make an effort to be with them, they complained that she didn't spend enough time with them. Her husband, Kiel, complained that she had changed and that he wanted the old Megan back. Elton didn't seem to want or need her any more and was now looking to Dad for the things Megan used to do for him.

Megan told me that as the interpersonal relationships with her family weakened, she had begun to seek out her fellow graduate students for support. She felt that her peers were empathetic and understood what she was going through in a way that her family did not. In addition, the students all had a common interest, history, which they loved to talk about. Megan stated that her family never asked about her classes, and that really hurt. One other issue worried Megan about her interpersonal relationships. Eric, a fellow student, was taking a great interest in Megan and she was enjoying the attention. Nothing improper had happened yet, but Megan was afraid that she might have an affair with Eric if she continued to spend time with him.

The final area of the BASIC ID to assess was drugs/biology. Megan told me that she got headaches when she was feeling down. She had seen her physician, who had found nothing physically wrong and had concluded that the headaches were stress related. Other than that, Megan had no medical problems and took no medicines. She did not smoke or take any illegal drugs. In reviewing her history of alcohol use, Megan said that in the past she had drunk little alcohol, but was now getting used to it in social situations with her fellow students, as they always seemed to have a bottle of wine around. She did not see her drinking as a problem other than being concerned that it might lower her inhibitions around Eric.

Setting Goals

Megan had come to my office with the goal of feeling less depressed and "lousy." I pointed out that most of our discussion about her emotional pain kept coming back to family issues: a lack of empathy, the need for support, feelings of disengagement and resentment, and the fear that her husband would take her son and leave.

Because Megan's depression had its roots in family issues, I proposed that we set an additional goal: to figure out a way for Megan not to be caught in the middle between her family and her schooling. Our discussion had helped Megan to see the connection between her depression and family issues, and she readily agreed to add family work to the list of goals.

Selecting a Theoretical Framework

Because family dynamics were the cause of Megan's depression, I selected family systems theory (discussed in chapter 2) as my theoretical framework. As such, it was time to make another suggestion to Megan. I stated, "In my experience, it is much more efficient and effective to deal with family issues by working with the entire family. What do you think of the idea of bringing your loved ones into my office so we can all talk directly about your depression and feelings of being caught in the middle? We can ask them for help and support."

Megan said that the thought of bringing her family into my office was scary and she wanted to think about it. When she came back for the next session she said, "I have been thinking a lot about how my family stresses are making me feel. So while I am nervous about it, I think bringing in my husband, child, dad, and sisters makes sense."

Megan and I spent the rest of the session brainstorming how best to approach each person to get his or her participation. Megan decided that she would simply talk to her family members and ask them to come to my office. I suggested that she focus on the positive: on how they would be able to help Megan because they might have good ideas for helping her be less depressed. We also revisited informed consent and confidentiality. I told her that because she had originally come in for individual counseling, I was bound to keep anything she had told me confidential in front of her family unless she gave me permission to disclose the information. I then asked Megan if there was anything we had talked about that she was not comfortable with me bringing up in front of her family. After thinking about it for a minute Megan said, "You can talk about anything you want except for Eric, the student I am attracted to. If Eric comes up, I want it to come from me." Given that Megan's feelings for Eric were a symptom of her disengagement from her family and not a primary cause of the family problems, I agreed to this stipulation.

We arranged a convenient time for the family to come in and ended the session. Two days later I received a phone call from Megan. "Everyone has said they will be there except for Dad. He refuses to come." I asked Megan if she wished me to call her father. She was grateful that I made the offer, and we brainstormed what I would say to him. When I called Mr. Vorset (Megan had kept her maiden name), he was surprised to hear from me. I explained that Megan needed her family to help her through this difficult period. Mr. Vorset told me that he did not like the idea of going to a "shrink's" office and was uncomfortable talking about himself and his feelings. I replied, "I tell you what, I'll make you a deal. If you are willing to show your love for your daughter by coming to my office, you don't have to say anything. You are welcome to come and show support by your presence and can be as quiet as you wish." With the visit framed in such a manner and with permission not to talk if he didn't want to, Mr. Vorset agreed to attend the family session.

Establishing a Relationship with the Family

Even though I had established a relationship with Megan, I had to start all over again when her loved ones came for the family session— *especially because* her loved ones were there. Not only had her family members never met me, but I suspected that they believed I was on Megan's side because I had talked with her individually for a few sessions. This was evident from the way family members chose to seat themselves when they came into my office. Megan took the seat next to my chair. The rest of the family (including Megan's husband) took chairs on the other side of the office and clustered around each other. Visually, it looked like there were two teams: Megan and myself on one side of the room against Megan's family on the opposite side of the room. Interestingly, Megan's father placed his chair between the family cluster and my chair, almost as if he were protecting the family. I thought, "He looks like a potential gatekeeper to me!" It was clear that I would have to work especially hard at utilizing the ideas in chapter 4 to establish a relationship of trust with Megan's son, husband, father, and sisters.

I began by reviewing informed consent. As part of the discussion, I talked about the rules I like to set when working with families. I said, "One rule is that we are here to focus on strengths and how to help each other. We are not here to blame anyone for any problem or to beat up on anyone. Is that okay with everyone?" All heads nodded yes. I continued, "I would also like to set the rule that all family members are free to talk when they choose and free to be quiet when they choose. No one has to talk if he or she would prefer not to. Is that also okay with everyone?" Again, everyone nodded in agreement, with Mr. Vorset making the most enthusiastic gesture. Finally, I asked for one more rule: "Because we are meeting as a family, I would like to speak to what might happen if you choose to talk to me alone after a family session, whether in person, on the telephone, by e-mail, or by letter. The information you give me might be crucial to discuss with the family. Therefore, I cannot promise you I will keep it confidential. So if you have information or thoughts that you do not want me to share in a family session, please do not tell them to me. Is that okay with everyone?" The family also agreed to this final rule.

I then followed the protocol for a first family session, as discussed in chapter 4. It soon became evident that Megan's dad was indeed the gatekeeper. His nonverbal gestures determined the order in which family members spoke about themselves. Even Kiel, Megan's husband, deferred to the patriarchy of Mr. Vorset. Violating his own edict not to speak, Mr. Vorset expressed concern that Elton should not be hearing this "adult conversation." I replied that children are smart and know a lot of things. Therefore, it was unlikely that we would be discussing anything that Elton was not already aware of on some level. I then said to Mr. Vorset, "If the family feels that we have begun to talk about a topic that Elton should not be listening to, we can ask him to draw in some coloring books in our play room under the watchful eye of my office manager. Will this work for you?" Mr. Vorset thought about it for a moment and agreed.

Since Mr. Vorset was the gatekeeper, I decided to make him my co-therapist. I asked Mr. Vorset if it would be okay for me to get to know the family, and he nodded yes. I then took the time to learn about each family member, making sure to include Megan's five-year-old son, Elton (who confirmed that his favorite color was purple).

At this point, I felt that it would be useful to talk about goals. I stated, "We have all come together to help Megan, but everyone in this room is important. As such, it is valuable for me to hear each family member's goals for our work. What would all of you like to get out of our time together?" Megan's husband, Kiel, spoke first.

He said that it was difficult for him to see Megan depressed and that he wanted to see Megan being her old self again. Rose, Megan's eldest sister, stated, "I miss Megan. I never get to see her anymore, and I want that to change." Janet, the middle sister chimed in, "I agree. Our family get-togethers are not the same without her." There was anger in Amber's voice as she said, "As the two youngest girls, Megan and I always did everything together. We don't anymore."

Mr. Vorset had been silently watching his family, so I asked him if he wanted to add anything. His reply was, "Not really. Everything that has been said is correct. We need the old Megan back." At that point I realized that everyone except Elton had spoken about goals. So I looked at him and asked, "Elton, what would you like?" He replied, "I want Mommy and Daddy to stop fighting and to stay married!"

We were getting close to the end of our first family session. I asked the Vorsets one last question: "If we could wave a magic wand and everything was the way it used to be, would everything be okay or would there still be issues for the family to work on?" Janet spoke up. "We have a very loving and good family. But sometimes I wish that Dad weren't so sexist and old-fashioned." Rose glared at Janet, and I made a mental note to watch for an alliance between Mr. Vorset and his eldest daughter. I asked Rose if she would like to add working on gender issues to our goals. Ignoring her sister's glare, Janet shook her head yes.

Suddenly, Amber began to cry. I handed her a tissue but otherwise remained silent as everyone's attention was drawn to this unexpected display of emotion. Amber lightly sobbed for a minute and said almost in a whisper, "We have never dealt with Mom's death. We never talk about her. Dad won't let us." All three sisters reached for the tissues, and Elton went over to his aunt, crawled on her lap, and gave her a big hug. Mr. Vorset, clearly uncomfortable with this topic, announced that it was time to go.

I ended the session with a summary that focused on the goals presented by all family members. I thanked everyone and stated that we were meeting to help both Megan and the family feel more comfortable and less angry with each other. I then invited them to set a five-session contract. I must have done something right, because they all agreed to continue our work together as a family.

Assessing Family Issues

I took the time over the next few sessions to conduct a developmental differential diagnosis as discussed by Dennis Pelsma in chapter 5. I assessed the four areas that have an effect on healthy family balance: communication, problem solving, roles, and boundaries. Each area presented useful information:

Communication

For the most part, the Vorset family exhibited healthy communication patterns. They spoke directly to each other and expressed both positive and negative emotions to each other. There was some triangulation among the sisters: Rose, Janet, and Amber complained to each other about Megan's school commitments. Also there was clearly a family rule set by Dad that the family was not to talk about Mom, her illness, or her death.

Problem Solving

I asked the family how they dealt with conflict. Kiel, Megan's husband, said that he and Megan rarely had fights and that when there was an occasional disagreement, they just ignored it and waited for it to pass.

Megan spoke up for her sisters and said that her family of origin dealt with problems by doing what Dad wanted. All three sisters nodded in agreement as their father smiled slightly. I then asked Megan why that did not work now. She replied, "Going to graduate school is too important to me. I am not going to quit and be the good housewife Dad thinks I should be. For the first time in my life, I am going to do what I want to do."

Elton had not said anything, so I asked him what he liked to do when there was fighting. He replied, "I give Mommy and Daddy a kiss, and that makes them feel better." I then asked him why he had been hitting Mom recently instead of kissing her. He exclaimed, "Because the kissing doesn't work anymore!"

Roles

I spent quite a bit of time discussing family roles with the Vorsets. It became clear that Mr. Vorset had fairly rigid gender stereotypes. He stated that women do best when they stay home and raise the kids and that men do best when they go out and make money for the family. I then asked him if his irritation at Megan had to do with the fact that she was in graduate school. He replied, "Of course. It was bad enough when she worked for the title insurance company, but at least she was able to come home and take care of her family at five o'clock. Now she is always gone. While Kiel does his best, her house is a mess and Elton never gets to see her." Kiel, Megan's husband, was much more flexible about gender roles. He told me that he did not mind doing extra cooking, cleaning, and housework because of Megan's academic requirements. He was upset only that he and Elton had so little time to spend with Megan. Interestingly, Megan had more gender issues than her husband. She stated that she was greatly appreciative of the extra work Kiel did around the house. Then she said, "I feel terribly guilty that, as a mother, I am putting my graduate studies before my son." I made a mental note to address gender issues (as discussed by Fran Steigerwald in chapter 9) with Megan and her family.

Boundaries

In statement after statement, Kiel, Elton, Rose, Janet, Amber, and Mr. Vorset, told me that they felt disengaged from Megan. They spoke of the graduate history program as if it were a thief that had been robbing them of time with Megan. Clearly, helping Megan and her family increase intimacy and move from disengagement to interdependence (while still allowing Megan to enjoy and finish graduate school) was going to be a major part of our work.

Selecting an Intervention

Based upon the goals and assessment information provided by Megan and her family, I decided to take a solution-focused approach (as discussed by Richard Watts in chapter 6). Why? Because, in my view, the Vorsets were basically a loving, healthy, functional family that simply had come up against a problem they couldn't solve. In the past, Megan had resolved conflicts by either doing what her father wanted (in her family of origin) or agreeing to ignore the problem until it went away (in her marriage). However, this issue was different. Going to graduate school was so important to Megan that she felt she had to break the family rule and stand up for her needs against her father's wishes. Megan also found that the stresses created by her decision to go to graduate school were too great to ignore with her husband and son.

Getting into my solution-focused framework, I asked the family to come to a consensus about the first goal that needed to be addressed. Universally, the answer came back, "We need to have the old Megan back." I then turned to Megan and asked her to tell us what would have to happen in order for this to happen. Megan replied, "Well, the first thing that needs to happen is that I need to stop feeling torn between my family and school." I then turned to the entire family and asked, "What specific things can each of you do to help alleviate Megan's feelings of being caught between her family and her studies?"

Janet spoke up first, "We could ask Megan to tell us more about her program." "In fact," Rose chimed in, "we could have Megan give us a tour of the campus." I asked Megan if these things would help. She smiled, "No one asks me about my classes. I would love to talk about them and to show my family where I go to school." I then asked the family if they would be willing to set two family gatherings, one to talk about Megan's program and the other to go on a tour of the university. Amber offered to cook dinner the following Friday for the "program discussion" task. Kiel then stated that he and Megan had a big SUV that everyone could pile into to go to the campus together. All agreed to have Megan give them a tour the following Sunday.

I then turned to Megan's father. "Mr. Vorset, what do you think needs to happen in order to get the old Megan back?" I knew that he wanted to say that Megan should drop out of school and focus on her family. But he didn't, in large part because he had now directly seen the pain that Megan's dilemma was causing her. So instead he replied, "She needs to spend more time with her family." All the family shook their heads affirmatively upon hearing this, with Megan's husband and son showing the most vigor. "This seems to be a particularly important issue," I stated. "Let's begin to problem solve how Megan can spend more time with her husband, son, father, and sisters while at the same time still being able to devote the time she needs to her schoolwork. Megan, what ideas do you have?"

Megan frowned as she thought "I could set aside some specific down time." I encouraged her to continue. "I don't have classes on Tuesday or Thursday evenings. I could read Elton a story on those two evenings." I asked Elton if he would like that and he smiled broadly. The family continued to problem solve and came up with two additional decisions. Megan, Kiel, and Elton would set aside every Saturday afternoon from noon to three o'clock and do something fun together, such as watching a movie or visiting the zoo. Additionally, Megan's sisters would rotate hosting a family get-together every second Sunday afternoon.

This initial discussion was the beginning of a focus on giving both Megan and her entire family support in the face of a system that had changed homeostasis. In future sessions we continued to brainstorm ideas for supporting all family members. In order to help Megan, all three of her sisters agreed to baby-sit Elton once a week. This would give Megan some guilt-free study time and allow Elton to spend more time with his aunts. In keeping with the suggestions Stevens and Shulman offer in chapter 10, I asked if it would be helpful to set up a listserv for family members of the other students in Megan's history program. Kiel got quite excited about this idea and volunteered to contact all the students in Megan's program and ask for e-mail addresses of family members who might be interested in setting up an electronic support network.

During the third family session, after basic problem solving had been discussed in the solution-focused paradigm, I decided it was time to address two other issues. I asked the family if they would be interested in dealing with a couple of emotional family issues: gender roles and coming to closure about Shirley Vorset's death. It was clear that the decision as to whether these topics were going to be approached lay with Mr. Vorset, and everyone in the room could not help but look at him expectantly. I think he surprised us all when he said, "I know I come from the old school, and I know that my feelings about my daughters' mom have hurt us all. But I can't talk about it in front of my girls." He then looked at me, saying, "Can I set up a time to talk to you about it alone, man to man?" And that was the beginning of going in and out of individual counseling with Thomas Vorset, where I found the concepts discussed in the chapter on diversity issues and the scenarios focusing on balancing family work against simultaneous individual counseling (chapter 11) to be of great help.

Assessing the Interventions

In order to monitor the impact of my work with the Vorset family, I decided to utilize the circumplex model discussed by Steven Benish in chapter 7. As we went along, I regularly assessed the cohesion, flexibility, and communication patterns of the Vorset family. I observed that as the family focused on supporting Megan instead of giving her a hard time, there were increasing amounts of laughter, joke telling, and smiling. Little Elton stopped hitting his mom and started giving her goodnight kisses again. Megan came in beaming one day saying, "Elton fell off the swing last night and came running to me for a hug. That is the first time in months he has chosen me instead of his dad!"

The family seating pattern even changed. At the beginning of our work together, the Vorset family had physically distanced themselves from Megan—visually isolating her and nonverbally labeling her as the identified patient. Now the family sat close together, and there were frequent gestures of physical affection such as hand holding and light touches. The Vorsets also spent more time talking directly to each other about disagreements instead of triangulating. The family was clearly moving away from disengagement and toward greater intimacy.

Megan began to let go of her resentment at the family for keeping her from her studies, and Kiel and Megan's sisters started to let go of their anger over the time Megan was spending on class projects and at the library. Everyone was adjusting to the change in family homeostasis in a healthy and flexible way.

Somewhere around the eighth family session, I received an e-mail from Megan about Eric, her fellow graduate student. She wrote, "I wanted you to know that I no longer am concerned about having an affair with Eric. I still think he is a neat guy, but I now realize that my feelings were a result of being emotionally separated from my husband. Now that Kiel and I don't fight about school and are back on track, I would never jeopardize my marriage by doing something stupid with Eric."

Chapter 7 points out that the circumplex model encourages us to assess the family's flexibility around roles, leadership, and family rules. I kept this in mind as I worked with Mr. Vorset on gender issues and his rule about avoiding any mention of his daughters' mother. A positive step occurred when, after a few individual sessions, Mr. Vorset said to me, "You know, we really should be having this conversation with my kids. Let's continue this discussion at the next family session."

What followed were some very painful but important family sessions. Megan, Rose, Janet, and Amber got a chance to talk to their father about his views on women, and Mr. Vorset was able to deal with a family secret he had been keeping for decades. It turned out that he had initiated the divorce with Shirley. Mr. Vorset felt that it was the man's role to earn the family wages and the woman's role to stay home with the kids. His wife, however, had insisted on working after she had children, which both enraged and emasculated Mr. Vorset. He gave Shirley an ultimatum to either quit her job or get a divorce. When she refused to quit, Mr. Vorset filed divorce papers, even though he very much loved his wife. Within a few years after the divorce, Shirley developed ovarian cancer and died. Mr. Vorset was convinced that there was link between the stress of the divorce and the development of the cancer. He felt that somehow his actions had killed the mother of his children. That was why he had forbidden the children to mention her name in his presence. He could not stand the guilt.

As Mr. Vorset finally shared his secret after all these years, his children saw him cry for the first time. As he wept, his daughters went over, one by one, to hug him. I have a lasting memory of four daughters and a father holding each other and having the cry of their lives. This benchmark moment marked the beginning of dealing with a ghost that had been haunting the family for many years.

Reaching Closure

After working with Megan and her family for about four months, it became clear that our work was nearing completion. The family had achieved a new homeostasis that allowed Megan to incorporate both school and family into her life. It was time to plan for closure.

I suggested to the family that we change from our weekly meeting schedule to sessions every other week. Things had been getting better, so the family readily agreed to this change. After another month, we decided to continue to spread out sessions and meet once a month, in order to make sure that the family did not backslide into old patterns.

As I got closer to ending my relationship with the Vorset family, I was mindful of Steven Craig and Gary Bischof's point in chapter 8 that it is important to plan a way to say goodbye. We set a specific date for the last session, and I asked each family member to think about how he or she would like to end our counseling relationship. I also told them that I would think about how I wanted to say goodbye.

When the last session arrived, family members had thought up different approaches. Megan's sisters had baked a cake with "Thank

You" written in blue icing across the top. We polished off the entire cake during the session. Megan's dad said that he wanted to shake my hand. He told me that he hadn't thought much of "shrinks" in the past, but that I had changed his opinion.

Elton couldn't wait to give me a gift-wrapped present. When I opened it, I saw two crayon drawings. Both depicted the family. In the first drawing, everyone was frowning or crying and the colors were somber shades of black, brown, and dark red. In the second picture, everyone was smiling. There were birds and the sun, and the colors were bright and cheerful. I asked Elton about the difference between the pictures. He said, "The first one was before. The second one is now."

Kiel stated that he wanted to say goodbye by thanking his extended family. He said, "I know this has not been easy for anyone. We have all had to look at issues and make compromises. But now Megan is happy again, and that is all that counts. I salute all of you!"

Megan was the last family member to take a turn. She said that she, too, wanted to thank her family for their support. She no longer had to choose between her family and her graduate studies. Megan said she wanted to say goodbye by giving each of us a hug. She went around and embraced her husband, son, father, sisters, and me, one by one.

Finally, it was my turn to say goodbye. I had decided to borrow the idea in Steven Craig's and Gary Bischof's closure chapter of using certificates to say goodbye. Using my computer, I created the following document:

This certificate is hereby given to the Vorset family in honor of the healthy balance they have achieved.

Signed,
David M. Kaplan, Ph.D.

I told them that I was proud of the way that they had effectively dealt with their family issues and handed a certificate to each family member. With some final words, handshakes, and hugs, my work with the Vorset family had come to an end.

Conclusion

Megan Vorset had come to my office stating that she was depressed and "feeling lousy." Given her particular situation, I cannot imagine how I could have helped her in individual counseling alone. Megan needed to deal with issues that were affecting her entire family. Therefore, systems theory was the theoretical framework of choice and family counseling was the primary modality of choice.

In conducting counseling with the Vorset family, I was able to reach beyond Megan to help her loved ones. I assisted the family to resolve issues that had been festering for decades due to a family secret. This would not have been possible if I had taken a linear approach and selected individual counseling as my modality with Megan. All in all, the Vorsets were a good example of why it is useful for counselors to work with families across counseling specialties.

Ethical Code for the International Association of Marriage and Family Counselors

Preamble

The IAMFC (The International Association of Marriage and Family Counselors) is an organization dedicated to advancing the practice, training, and research of marriage and family counselors. Members may specialize in areas such as: premarital counseling, intergenerational counseling, separation and divorce counseling, relocation counseling, custody assessment and implementation, single parenting, stepfamilies, nontraditional family and marriage lifestyles, healthy and dysfunctional family systems, multicultural marriage and family concerns, displaced and homeless families, interfaith and interracial families, and dual career couples. In conducting their professional activities, members commit themselves to protect and advocate for the healthy growth and development of the family as a whole, even as they conscientiously recognize the integrity and diversity of each family and family member's unique needs, situations, status, and condition. The IAMFC member recognizes that the relationship between the provider and consumer of services is characterized as an egalitarian process emphasizing co-participation, co-equality, co-authority, co-responsibility, and client empowerment.

This code of ethics promulgates a framework for ethical practice by IAMFC members and is divided into eight sections: client well-being, confidentiality, competence, assessment, private practice, research and publications, supervision, and media and public statements. The ideas presented within these eight areas are meant to supplement the ethical standards of the American Counseling Association (ACA), formerly the American Association for Counseling and Development (AACD), and all members should know and keep to the standards of our parent organization. Although an ethical code cannot anticipate every possible situation or dilemma, the IAMFC ethical guidelines can aid members in ensuring the welfare and dignity of the couples and families they have contact with, as well as assisting in the implementation of the Hippocratic mandate for healers: Do no harm.

Section I: Client Well-Being

A. Members demonstrate a caring, empathic, respectful, fair, and active concern for family well-being. They promote client safety, security, and place-of-belonging in family, community, and society. Due to the risk involved, members should not use intrusive interventions without a sound theoretical rationale and having thoroughly thought through the potential ramifications to the family and its members.
B. Members recognize that each family is unique. They respect the diversity of personal attributes and do not stereotype or force families into prescribed attitudes, roles, or behaviors.
C. Members respect the autonomy of the families that they work with. They do not make decisions that rightfully belong to family members.
D. Members respect cultural diversity. They do not discriminate on the basis of race, sex, disability, religion, age, sexual orientation, cultural background, national origin, marital status,

or political affiliation.

E. Members strive for an egalitarian relationship with clients by openly and conscientiously sharing information, opinions, perceptions, process of decision making, strategies of problem solving, and understanding of human behavior.

F. Members pursue a just relationship that acknowledges, respects, and informs clients of their rights, obligations, and expectations as a consumer of services, as well as the rights, obligations, and expectations of the provider(s) of service. Members inform clients (in writing if feasible) about goals and purpose of the counseling, the qualifications of the counselor(s), the scope and limits of confidentiality, potential risks and benefits associated with the counseling process and with specific counseling techniques, reasonable expectations for the outcomes and duration of counseling, costs of services, and appropriate alternatives to counseling.

G. Members strive for a humanistic relationship that assists clients to develop a philosophy of meaning, purpose, and direction of life and living that promotes a positive regard of self, of family, of different and diverse others, and of the importance of humane concern for the community, nation, and the world at large.

H. Members promote primary prevention. They pursue the development of clients' cognitive, moral, social, emotional, spiritual, physical, educational, and career needs, as well as parenting, marriage, and family living skills, in order to prevent future problems.

I. Members have an obligation to determine and inform all persons involved who their primary client is—i.e., is the counselor's primary obligation to the individual, the family, a third party, or an institution? When there is a conflict of interest between the needs of the client and the counselor's employing institution, the member works to clarify his or her commitment to all parties. Members recognize that the acceptance of employment implies that they are in agreement with the agency's policies and practices, and so monitor their place of employment to make sure that the environment is conducive to the positive growth and development of clients. If, after utilizing appropriate institutional channels for change, the member finds that the agency is not working toward the well-being of clients, the member has an obligation to terminate his or her institutional affiliation.

J. Members do not harass, exploit, coerce, engage in dual relationships, or have sexual contact with any current or former client or family member to whom they have provided professional services.

K. Members have an obligation to withdraw from a counseling relationship if the continuation of services is not in the best interest of the client or would result in a violation of ethical standards. If a client feels that the counseling relationship is no longer productive, the member has an obligation to assist in finding alternative services.

L. Members maintain accurate and up-to-date records. They make all file information available to clients unless the sharing of such information would be damaging to the status, goals, growth, or development of the client.

M. Members have the responsibility to confront unethical behavior conducted by other counselors. The first step should be to discuss the violation directly with the counselor. If the problem continues, the member should first use procedures established by the employing institution and then those of the IAMFC. Members may wish to also contact any appropriate licensure or certification board. Members may contact the IAMFC executive director, president, executive board members, or chair of the ethics committee at any time for consultation on remedying ethical violations.

Section II: Confidentiality

A. Clients have the right to expect that information shared with the counselor will not be disclosed to others and, in the absence of any law to the contrary, the communications between clients and marriage and family counselors should be viewed as privileged. The fact that a contact was made with a counselor is to be considered just as confidential as the information shared during that contact. Information obtained from a client can only be disclosed to a third party under the following conditions.

1. The client consents to disclosure by a signed waiver. The client must fully understand the nature of the disclosure (i.e., give informed consent), and only information described in the waiver may be disclosed. If more than one person is receiving counseling, each individual who is legally competent to execute a waiver must sign.

2. The client has placed him- or herself or someone else in clear and imminent danger.

3. The law mandates disclosure.

4. The counselor is a defendant in a civil, criminal, or disciplinary action arising from professional activity.

5. The counselor needs to discuss a case for consultation or education purposes. These discussions should not reveal the identity of the client or any other unnecessary aspects of the case and should only be done with fellow counseling professionals who subscribe to the IAMFC ethical code. The consulting professional counselor has an obligation to keep all shared information confidential.

B. All clients must be informed of the nature and limitations of confidentiality. They must also be informed of who may have access to their counseling records, as well as any information that may be released to other agencies or professionals for insurance reimbursement. These disclosures should be made both orally and in writing, whenever feasible.

C. All client records should be stored in a way that ensures confidentiality. Written records should be kept in a locked drawer or cabinet and computerized record systems should use appropriate passwords and safeguards to prevent unauthorized entry.

D. Clients must be informed if sessions are to be recorded on audio- or videotape and sign a consent form for doing so. When more than one person is receiving counseling, all persons who are legally competent must give informed consent in writing for the recording.

E. Unless alternate arrangements have been agreed upon by all participants, statements made by a family member to the counselor during an individual counseling or consultation contact are to be treated as confidential and are not disclosed to other family members without the individual's permission. If a client's refusal to share information from individual contacts interferes with the agreed upon goals of counseling, the counselor may have to terminate treatment and refer the clients to another counselor.

Section III: Competence

A. Members have the responsibility to develop and maintain basic skills in marriage and family counseling through graduate work, supervision, and peer review. An outline of these skills is provided by the Council for Accreditation of Counseling and Related Educational Programs (CACREP) *Environmental and Specialty Standards for Marriage and Family Counseling/ Therapy.* The minimal level of training shall be considered a master's degree in a helping profession.

B. Members recognize the need for keeping current with new developments in the field of marriage and family counseling. They pursue continuing education in forms such as books, journals, classes, workshops, conferences, and conventions.

C. Members accurately represent their education, areas of expertise, training, and experience.

D. Members do not attempt to diagnose or treat problems beyond the scope of their abilities and training.

E. Members do not undertake any professional activity in which their personal problems might adversely affect their performance. Instead, they focus their energies on obtaining appropriate professional assistance to help them resolve the problem.

F. Members do not engage in actions that violate the moral or legal standards of their community.

Section IV: Assessment

A. Members utilize assessment procedures to promote the best interests and well-being of the client in clarifying concerns, establishing treatment goals, evaluating therapeutic progress, and promoting objective decision making.

B. Clients have the right to know the results, interpretation, and conclusions drawn from assessment interviews and instruments, as well as how this information will be used.

C. Members utilize assessment methods that are reliable, valid, and germane to the goals of the client. When using computer-assisted scoring, members obtain empirical evidence for the reliability and validity of the methods and procedures used.

D. Members do not use inventories and tests that have outdated test items or normative data.

E. Members do not use assessment methods that are outside the scope of their qualifications, training, or statutory limitations. Members using tests or inventories have a thorough understand of measurement concepts.

F. Members read the manual before using a published instrument. They become knowledgeable about the purpose of the instrument and relevant psychometric and normative data.

G. Members conducting custody evaluations recognize the potential impact that their reports can have on family members. As such, they are committed to a thorough assessment of both parents. Therefore, custody recommendations should not be made on the basis of information from only one parent. Members only use instruments that have demonstrated validity in custody evaluations and do not make recommendations based solely on test and inventory scores.

H. Members strive to maintain the guidelines in the *Standards for Educational and Psychological Testing,* written in collaboration by the American Educational Research Association, American Psychological Association, and National Council on Measurement in Evaluation, as well as the *Code of Fair Testing Practices,* published by the Joint Committee on Testing Practices.

Section V: Private Practice

A. Members assist the profession and community by facilitating, whenever feasible, the availability of counseling services in private settings.

B. Due to the independent nature of their work, members in private practice recognize that they have a special obligation to act ethically and responsibly, keep up to date through continuing education, arrange consultation and supervision, and practice within the scope of their training and applicable laws.

C. Members in private practice provide a portion of their services at little or no cost as a service to the community. They also provide referral services for clients who will not be seen pro bono and who are unable to afford private services.

D. Members only enter into partnerships in which each member adheres to the ethical standards of their profession.

E. Members should not charge a fee for offering or accepting referrals.

Section VI: Research and Publications

A. Members shall be fully responsible for their choice of research topics and the methods used for investigation, analysis, and reporting. They must be particularly careful that findings do not appear misleading, that the research is planned to allow for the inclusion of alternative hypotheses, and that provision is made for discussion of the limitations of the study.

B. Members safeguard the privacy of their research participants. Data about an individual participant are not released unless the individual is informed about the exact nature of the information to be released and gives written permission for doing so.

C. Members safeguard the safety of their research participants. Members receive approval from, and follow guidelines of, any institutional research committee. Prospective participants are informed, in writing, about any potential danger associated with a study and are notified that they can withdraw at any time.

D. Members make their original data available to other researchers.

E. Members only take credit for research in which they made a substantial contribution, and give credit to all such contributors. Authors are listed from greatest to least amount of contribution.

F. Members do not plagiarize. Ideas or data that did not originate with the author(s) and are not common knowledge are clearly credited to the original source.

G. Members are aware of their obligation to be a role model for graduate students and other future researchers and so act in accordance with the highest standards possible while engaged in research.

Section VII: Supervision

A. Members who provide supervision acquire and maintain skills pertaining to the supervision process. They are able to demonstrate for supervisees the application of counseling theory and process to client issues. Supervisors are knowledgeable about different methods and conceptual approaches to supervision.

B. Members who provide supervision respect the inherent imbalance of power in the supervisory relationship. They do not use their potentially influential positions to exploit students, supervisees, or employees. Supervisors do not ask supervisees to engage in behaviors not directly related to the supervision process, and they clearly separate supervision and evaluation. Supervisors also avoid dual relationships that might impair their professional judgment or increase the possibility of exploitation. Sexual intimacy with students or supervisees is prohibited.

C. Members who provide supervision are responsible for both the promotion of supervisee learning and development and the advancement of marriage and family counseling. Supervisors recruit students into professional organizations, educate students about professional ethics and standards, provide service to professional organizations, strive to educate new professionals, and work to improve professional practices.

D. Members who provide supervision have the responsibility to inform students of the specific expectations surrounding skill building, knowledge acquisition, and the development of competencies. Members also provide ongoing and timely feedback to their supervisees.

E. Members who provide supervision are responsible for protecting the rights and well-being of their supervisees' clients. They monitor their supervisees' counseling on an ongoing basis, and create procedures to protect the confidentiality of clients whose sessions have been electronically recorded.

F. Members who provide supervision strive to reach and maintain the guidelines provided in the *Standards for Counseling Supervisors* published by the ACA Governing Council (cf. *Journal of Counseling & Development*, 1990, Vol. 69, pp. 30–32).

G. Members who are counselor educators encourage their programs to reach and maintain the guidelines provided in the CACREP *Environmental and Specialty Standards for Marriage and Family Counseling/Therapy.*

Section VIII: Media and Public Statements

A. Members accurately and objectively represent their professional qualifications, skills, and functions to the public. Membership in a professional organization is not to be used to suggest competency.

B. Members have the responsibility to provide information to the public that enhances marriage and family life. Such statements should be based on sound, scientifically acceptable theories, techniques, and approaches. Due to the inability to complete a comprehensive assessment and provide follow-up, members should not give specific advice to an individual through the media.

C. The announcement or advertisement of professional services should focus on objective information that allows the client to make an informed decision. Providing information such as highest relevant academic degree earned, licenses or certifications, office hours, types of services offered, fee structure, and languages spoken can help clients decide whether the advertised services are appropriate for their needs. Members advertising a specialty within marriage and family counseling should provide evidence of training, education, and/or supervision in the area of specialization. Advertisements about workshops or seminars should contain a description of the audience for which the program is intended. Due to their subjective nature, statements either from clients or from the counselor about the uniqueness, effectiveness, or efficiency of services should be avoided. Announcements and advertisements should never contain false, misleading, or fraudulent statements.

D. Members promoting psychology tapes, books, or other products for commercial sale make every effort to ensure that announcements and advertisements are presented in a professional and factual manner.

Note: Mary Allison, R. P. Ascano, Edward Beck, Stuart Bonnington, Joseph Hannon, David Kaplan (chair), Patrick McGrath, Judith Palais, Martin Ritchie, and Judy Ritterman are members of the IAMFC ethics committee who formulated the IAMFC code of ethics. Reprinted by permission of the IAMFC.

About the Contributors

David M. Kaplan, Ph.D., is professor and chair of the Department of Counselor and Rehabilitation Programs at Emporia State University. He is the 2002–2003 president of the American Counseling Association and a past president of the International Association of Marriage and Family Counselors. David is a certified family therapist (CFT), and a national certified counselor (NCC). The International Association of Marriage and Family Counselors and the New York Counseling Association have both honored him with service awards. With more than a dozen years of experience working with families and couples in private practice, David has published extensively on the process and ethics of couples and family counseling.

Steven Benish, MSE, LPC, has counseled in private practice, schools, and agencies in Texas and Wisconsin. He has served as a psychotherapist, school counselor, workplace violence prevention consultant, and business personnel consultant. Having completed coursework for his master's degree at the University of Minnesota–Twin Cities and University of Wisconsin–Platteville, Steven received a master's degree in counselor education in 1997. He has helped to develop both psychotherapy process measures and psychotherapy outcome measures for counseling organizations. Currently, Steven is a psychotherapist in private practice near Madison, Wisconsin.

Gary H. Bischof, Ph.D., LMFT, is an assistant professor and clinical director of the Marriage and Family Therapy master's program in the Department of Counselor Education and Counseling Psychology at Western Michigan University in Kalamazoo. He obtained his master's degree from Virginia Tech and his doctorate from Purdue University, both in the specialty of marriage and family therapy. Gary is a clinical member and approved supervisor with AAMFT. He has nearly ten years of clinical experience in a variety of private and public mental health and medical settings. He has been actively involved with the Collaborative Family Healthcare Association, a multidisciplinary group of professionals committed to family-oriented, collaborative approaches to healthcare. His research and professional interests include medical family therapy, couples therapy, brief solution-oriented therapy, and families of adolescent sex offenders. He has published several articles in professional journals and book chapters on these and other topics.

Steven Craig, Ph.D., is an assistant professor in the Department of Counselor Education and Counseling Psychology at Western Michigan University. He obtained his doctorate at the University of North Texas and is a licensed professional counselor (LPC) and psychologist, limited license–doctoral (LLP) in the state of Michigan. His professional and research interests lie in counseling children and adolescents, counselor supervision, and Adlerian psychological theory. Steven is co-president of the Michigan Association for Counselor Education and Supervision (MACES) and member at large for the North Central Association for Counselor Education and Supervision (NCACES). He is an active member in the American Counseling Association (ACA); NCACES; Michigan Counseling Association (MCA); MACES; and the Kalamazoo Counseling Association (KCA). He is also a bargaining unit member of the American Association of University Professors (AAUP).

Dennis M. Pelsma, Ph.D., received his doctorate in counseling psychology from the University of Missouri–Columbia in 1983. Prior to this time, he worked in the public schools as a secondary-level math teacher and school counselor (K–12). After completing his degree, he served as director of career planning and placement at Columbia College and as an assistant professor of counseling psychology at the University of Kansas. In 1989 he returned to the public schools as an elementary school counselor in Lawrence, Kansas. Since 1998, he has been an associate professor and coordinator of school counseling at Emporia State University. His scholarly work includes professional publications in *Professional School Counseling, Measurement and Evaluation in Counseling*, and *Journal of Counseling and Development*. He has also presented numerous papers at state, regional, and national conferences. Dennis is currently a member of the American Counseling Association, the American School Counselor Association, and the Kansas Counseling Association.

Kerrie Shulman recently completed her master's degree at the University of Colorado at Denver, graduating in May 2002. As part of a progressive graduate assistantship, she assisted in the implementation and design of online master's-level education courses at the university. Kerrie currently works as a family clinician at a community mental health agency in the Denver area.

Fran Steigerwald, Ph.D., is an assistant professor in the Department of Counselor Education at Radford University in Virginia. In 2000, she received her doctorate in counselor education from Ohio University, where she also taught in the counseling and family studies program. Prior to that, she was clinic director and taught counselor education at Emporia State University in Kansas for two years. An active member of the American Counseling Association and the International Association of Marriage and Family Counselors, Fran was chairwoman of the IAMFC Ethics Task Force. Having successfully raised four children as a single parent, Fran is now enjoying being a grandmother to three.

Patricia Stevens, Ph.D., is the chair of the Counseling and Education Leadership Department at Eastern Kentucky University. She is the past president of the International Association of Marriage and Family Counselors, and a clinical member and approved supervisor with the American Association for Marriage and Family Therapy. Patricia is a licensed professional counselor and supervisor, a licensed marriage and family therapist and supervisor, and a national certified counselor. A Fulbright Scholar, she has received awards for teaching, research, and service as well as the IAMFC Mentoring Award. Patricia has written and presented extensively at the local, regional, national, and international levels in the areas of marriage and family training, substance abuse, gender issues, and ethical and legal issues in marriage and family therapy. She is an approved online presenter with the State of Colorado Jurisprudence Workshops, which are required for licensure. Additionally, she provides online continuing education for counselors on her web site at www.digitalceu.com.

Richard E. Watts, Ph.D., is director of the Counseling Program in the Department of Educational Psychology at Baylor University in Waco, Texas. He received his doctorate in Counseling from the University of North Texas. Prior to joining the Baylor faculty in 2000, he held faculty positions at Texas A&M University–Commerce and Kent State University. The author of more than 50 published journal articles and book chapters as well as three books, Richard currently serves on the editorial boards of several professional journals. His interests include Adlerian, cognitive, and constructivist/constructionist approaches to individual and couples/family counseling; counselor supervision and counselor efficacy; ethical and legal issues; play therapy; and religious and spiritual issues in counseling. Richard has received several research and writing awards and, in 2000, received the Outstanding Alumnus Award from the Counselor Education Program at the University of North Texas.

ERIC/CASS Virtual Libraries

The difference between a person persisting in pursuing an important initiative and someone who has a brief spurt of activity only to quickly abandon the idea is the availability of new and compelling information. Nothing serves this need for the invigorating new ideas as well as a *virtual library* where a person can quickly search and download in full text ideas that are both highly current and evaluated for quality and utility. ERIC/CASS currently maintains over a dozen virtual libraries encompassing such diverse areas as cybercounseling, career development, learning and achievement testing and assessment, and substance abuse. We strongly encourage you to visit the ERIC/CASS exemplary websites which can be reached by visiting the basic ERIC/CASS website at http://ericcass.uncg.edu And remember, you can be both a user and, importantly, a contributor to our virtual libraries.